Introducing Language in the Workplace

Assuming no prior linguistics background, this introductory textbook summarises key topics and issues from workplace discourse research in a clear and accessible manner. The topics covered include how people issue directives, use humour and social talk, and how they manage conflict and disagreement. The role of language in the enactment of identity is also explored, in particular leadership, gender and cultural identity, along with the implications and applications of workplace research for training and communication skills development. Over 160 international examples are provided as illustration, which come from a wide range of workplace settings, countries and languages. The examples focus on authentic spoken discourse, to demonstrate how theory captures the patterns found in everyday interaction. *Introducing Language in the Workplace* provides an excellent up-to-date resource for linguistics courses as well as other courses that cover workplace discourse, such as business communication or management studies.

BERNADETTE VINE is a researcher on the Wellington Language in the Workplace Project, based at the School of Linguistics and Applied Language Studies, Victoria University of Wellington, New Zealand. Bernadette has been part of the core project team since it began in 1996. Bernadette's research interests include workplace communication, leadership and New Zealand English. She is the author of *Getting Things Done at Work: The Discourse of Power in Workplace Interaction* and is co-author of *Leadership, Discourse and Ethnicity* (with Janet Holmes and Meredith Marra). She is editor of *The Routledge Handbook of Language in the Workplace.*

Introducing Language in the Workplace

BERNADETTE VINE

Victoria University of Wellington

CAMBRIDGE
UNIVERSITY PRESS

CAMBRIDGE
UNIVERSITY PRESS

University Printing House, Cambridge CB2 8BS, United Kingdom

One Liberty Plaza, 20th Floor, New York, NY 10006, USA

477 Williamstown Road, Port Melbourne, VIC 3207, Australia

314–321, 3rd Floor, Plot 3, Splendor Forum, Jasola District Centre, New Delhi – 110025, India

79 Anson Road, #06-04/06, Singapore 079906

Cambridge University Press is part of the University of Cambridge.

It furthers the University's mission by disseminating knowledge in the pursuit of
education, learning, and research at the highest international levels of excellence.

www.cambridge.org
Information on this title: www.cambridge.org/9781108498944
DOI: 10.1017/9781108689984

© Bernadette Vine 2020

First published 2020

Printed in the United Kingdom by TJ International Ltd, Padstow Cornwall

A catalogue record for this publication is available from the British Library.

Library of Congress Cataloging-in-Publication Data
NAMES: Vine, Bernadette, author.
TITLE: Introducing language in the workplace / Bernadette Vine.
DESCRIPTION: Cambridge, United Kingdom ; New York, NY : Cambridge
   University Press, 2020. | Includes bibliographical references and index.
IDENTIFIERS: LCCN 2019049507 (print) | LCCN 2019049508 (ebook) | ISBN
   9781108498944 (hardback) | ISBN 9781108689984 (ebook)
SUBJECTS: LCSH: Communication in organizations. | Communication in
   management. | Business communication. | Organizational sociology.
CLASSIFICATION: LCC HD30.3 .V564 2020 (print) | LCC HD30.3 (ebook) | DDC
   650.01/4–dc23
LC record available at https://lccn.loc.gov/2019049507
LC ebook record available at https://lccn.loc.gov/2019049508

ISBN 978-1-108-49894-4 Hardback
ISBN 978-1-108-71287-3 Paperback

To my family

Contents

List of Tables and Figures

Tables

Figures

Author Biographies

Bernadette Vine is a Researcher on the Language in the Workplace Project, based at the School of Linguistics and Applied Language Studies, Victoria University of Wellington, New Zealand. Bernadette's research interests include workplace communication, leadership and New Zealand English. She is the author of *Getting Things Done at Work: The Discourse of Power in Workplace Interaction* and is co-author of *Leadership, Discourse and Ethnicity* (with Janet Holmes and Meredith Marra). She is editor of *The Routledge Handbook of Language in the Workplace*.

Other Contributors

Jonathan Clifton has a PhD in Applied Linguistics from the University of Antwerp and is currently an Associate Professor at the Université Polytechnique Hauts-de-France, in Valenciennes, France. His research focuses on identities-in-talk and discursive leadership. He has published extensively in both 'management' and 'linguistic' journals.

Janet Holmes is Emeritus Professor of Linguistics and Associate Director of the Wellington Language in the Workplace Project at Victoria University of Wellington, New Zealand (www.victoria.ac.nz/lwp/). She has published on many aspects of sociolinguistics, including workplace discourse, New Zealand English, and language and gender.

Veronika Koller is Reader in Discourse Studies at Lancaster University, UK. Her research focuses on corporate and political discourse as well as healthcare communication. She is co-author of *Language in Business, Language at Work* (with Erika Darics, 2018).

Helen Spencer-Oatey is Professor in the Centre for Applied Linguistics at the University of Warwick, UK. One of her main research interests is interpersonal relations, especially in intercultural contexts, and she has published widely on this, including the books *Culturally Speaking* and *Intercultural Interaction*. She is currently working on a book entitled *Intercultural Politeness*.

Acknowledgements

Many people provided me with advice and support throughout the process of writing this book. First, I would like to express my appreciation to the other core team members of the Wellington Language in the Workplace Project, both present and past: Janet Holmes, Meredith Marra and Maria Stubbe. A special thank you to Janet Holmes who read the full manuscript and patiently answered my many questions about writing a textbook.

Thanks also to the team at Cambridge University Press, who recruited and supported me throughout the process. And thank you to Helen Spencer-Oatey, Janet Holmes, Jonathan Clifton, and Veronika Koller for their enthusiasm and willingness to be part of this project in providing their expert analyses in Chapter 2. My thanks also to Jacynta Scurfield who drew the illustrations. I am very grateful that you found the time to do these round the many other things that I know you are constantly juggling.

A number of people gave me valuable feedback on parts of this book, including Gina Verhaart, Honiara Salanoa, Mark Chadwick, Mary Boyce, May Chadwick, Reuben Sanderson, Shelley Dawson and the staff and students who attend the Discourse Analysis Group at Victoria University of Wellington. Thank you all for your time, advice, and support.

Also to the many people in the workplaces who recorded and were recorded for the Wellington Language in the Workplace Project research – we can never thank you enough for your generosity and the many and varied ways you have contributed to our understanding of talk at work in New Zealand workplaces.

Many examples in this book also come from published research from around the world and I wish to express my appreciation to all the people who undertook and shared their research, and again to those who allowed their words to be the focus of analysis. I am very grateful to the publishers and authors who gave me permission to use all the data samples.

Last, but of course not least, I thank my neglected family and friends, and I dedicate this book to my family.

Foreword

Workplace discourse research has burgeoned over the past two decades and many tertiary institutions now offer courses in this area. Bernadette Vine's excellent and very readable introduction will be a welcome resource for teachers and students interested in this fascinating and complex area.

Bernadette is a core member of the Wellington Language in the Workplace Project team, and she has contributed to the team's research in many different ways since its inception. Her PhD was in the area of workplace directives and her book *Getting Things Done at Work* is a widely cited research resource on this topic; she draws on her in-depth analysis in the chapter on directives and requests in this book. Bernadette and I (with Meredith Marra, the third core team member) have co-authored a book on the role of discourse in doing leadership in ethnically different workplaces, as well as many research articles on a range of topics, including those covered in this book. Bernadette has trained many cohorts of research assistants, teaching them to transcribe accurately and advising them on how to collect good quality data. Her special responsibility has been the organisation of our large and complex corpus of material which she has managed efficiently and helpfully, and which has proved an invaluable source of examples to illustrate the concepts covered in this *Introduction*. Her excellent analytical skills are evident in the perceptive analyses and stimulating discussions presented in different chapters.

Assuming no prior knowledge of Linguistics, Bernadette introduces readers to a range of different theoretical approaches and core concepts in workplace discourse research in an accessible style and using authentic data from a variety of diverse cultural and social contexts to vividly illustrate her points. Key topics and issues are also covered and the book provides interesting and thought-provoking exercises to assist students in coming to grips with the concepts and issues described. Most impressive is the very wide variety of illustrative excerpts from workplace discourse recorded all over the world, ranging from New Zealand to Finland, from Canada to Zanzibar. No previous book on workplace discourse encompasses such an extensive array of illuminating materials.

This *Introducing Language in the Workplace* discourse research thus provides an invaluable research, teaching and learning resource. Students will find the different chapters offer a very helpful guide to a range of topics, concepts and issues within the field of language in the workplace research. I am confident you will find it both stimulating and enjoyable.

Janet Holmes
Emeritus Professor of Linguistics,
Victoria University of Wellington,
New Zealand
April 2019

Preface

People spend a large proportion of their lives at work, and in the course of their work may interact with a wide range of people. Exploring spoken workplace interaction is therefore a crucial area of discourse research, and in the past twenty years an increasing number of researchers have investigated talk within workplace settings. This textbook provides an introduction to the main approaches, topics and issues from this research. This includes theoretical perspectives and analytical frameworks, such as social constructionism and interactional sociolinguistics. Key topics covered are how people issue directives, use humour and social talk, and how they manage conflict and disagreement. The role of language in the enactment of identity is also explored, in particular leadership, gender, and cultural identity, along with the implications and applications of workplace research for training and communication skills development.

Workplace discourse research has involved different settings, including diverse contexts such as white collar meetings, healthcare consultations and interactions recorded on the factory floor. Interaction in each setting has its own characteristics, while workplace research around the world raises interesting cultural considerations, both within and between countries. This research is drawn on throughout to illustrate the issues discussed in this textbook, with over 160 examples of authentic workplace interaction from a wide range of workplace settings, countries and languages. Many examples are drawn from research on authentic workplace talk by leading researchers in each area, although some transcript excerpts have not previously been published.

Introducing Language in the Workplace does not assume a background in linguistics so can provide input not only for linguistics courses but also other programmes that cover workplace discourse, such as those that take a business communication or management studies approach. The number of university courses dedicated to workplace talk is steadily growing and this introductory textbook acknowledges this and provides students and lecturers with a valuable resource.

Requirements and Expectations for Students

This book is intended for undergraduate and postgraduate students studying workplace communication, both within and outside the field of linguistics. Since the textbook covers topics of universal interest and because it draws on international data it is appropriate for use around the world. A key challenge as a student is to understand what authentic data looks like and how to analyse it and this textbook directly addresses this need. Important features of the many examples included in the book are highlighted, and exercises are also provided for students to practise identifying aspects for themselves. Summaries of topics and patterns that are emerging from research are also presented so that common themes are identified and clarified.

Structure of this Book

There are nine chapters in the book organised into four parts. Part I includes two chapters which introduce language in the workplace research and give useful background for students in understanding the field, as well as the data and information provided throughout the rest of the book. Chapter 1 is an introductory chapter which explores what language in the workplace research is, as well as outlining what the book will cover. Chapter 2 introduces the main approaches, methods and concepts drawn on in language in the workplace research. As part of this, it highlights some different approaches to discourse analysis and provides students with illustration of each approach when applied to the same data sample, with each analysis conducted by an expert.

Part II is dedicated to some key topics that have been explored in language in the workplace research. In Chapter 3 primarily transactional (or practical) aspects of workplace discourse are considered with a focus on directives and requests. Chapter 4 considers primarily relational (or interpersonal) aspects of workplace discourse, with social talk and humour as two types of talk that can play this role. Narrative has a role more explicitly at the cross-over between transactional and relational talk and so the functions that narrative can play are also considered. Chapter 5 explores some potentially problematic aspects of workplace communication, in particular complaints and disagreement. Complaints and disagreement can lead to conflict talk, as can impoliteness, so features of conflict talk are also explored in this chapter.

Identity has become a major focus of workplace research more recently and Part III covers three important areas in relation to identity. Chapter 6 begins this section, providing a brief overview of leadership discourse research, with examples illustrating the complexities of leadership. Chapter 7 examines research on gender and gender-related issues in workplace contexts. The intersection of gender and leadership identity is also briefly explored. Chapter 8 reviews topics related to cultural identity. This chapter also briefly considers the intersection of cultural, gender and leadership identity.

In the final section of the book, Chapter 9 explores some implications and applications of workplace research. This provides information on ways workplace research can be and is used to provide practical outcomes for workplace participants and organisations.

This textbook does not assume any previous background knowledge or experience in the field. Each chapter begins with a brief list of what is covered and includes brief summaries throughout. At the end of each chapter, a list of key readings related to the topic is provided, along with exercises for students. The exercises typically present short transcripts of authentic data for students to analyse while considering the points raised in each chapter. There are also notes on answering the exercises at the end of the book, as well as a glossary of key terms. Simplified transcription conventions are used throughout the book to make examples accessible.

Using this Book in Teaching

This textbook is an up-to-date introductory textbook on research on workplace discourse. As such, it covers the main topics and issues from the field. The chapters are designed to be worked through in order, with the first two chapters providing useful background to help students understand the material that follows. This includes introducing core theories and approaches to analysing workplace data.

The chapters in Part II could be taught in any order, although the focus first on transactional talk in Chapter 3, followed by relational aspects in Chapter 4, is a useful way to introduce these topics for students, before exploring problematic talk in Chapter 5. If you teach a course focusing on identity issues, then Part II and Part III could be taught in a different order, or just the chapters in Part III could be used. Identity issues are briefly highlighted in each chapter in Part II, but are more fully explored in Part III.

In Part III, the later chapters build on Chapter 6, since they consider the intersection of different aspects of identity. If, however, you teach a course that only covers one of the topics in this part of the book, e.g., leadership or gender in the workplace, then the chapters can stand alone. Reference is made to particular examples in other chapters that may also illustrate points or concepts that may be helpful so you can easily find relevant sections from other chapters.

The last part of the book, Part IV, reflects on the topics and themes that have been examined in earlier chapters while exploring the implications and applications of workplace discourse research. This may be an aspect you want to explore as a stand alone topic, or integrate into a course while you are teaching each topic.

Some key features and benefits of the textbook include the way it aims to address a number of teaching and learning needs. Firstly, students often struggle to understand how abstract concepts and theory are evident in day-to-day interaction. In order to address this issue, this textbook provides examples of authentic spoken discourse from research to demonstrate theory and concepts. The aim is to enhance students' understanding because they can see how theory captures the patterns found in everyday interaction and they can engage with authentic data.

Secondly, this book is aimed at an international audience and therefore does not focus on data from only one country or from only English. It also draws on research from many different types of workplace settings. Students may therefore come across examples from a language, culture or workplace setting they are familiar with, as well as being able to explore data from contexts they will never personally encounter.

A third feature of this book is that transcription conventions have been simplified and the examples use standard orthography. In some linguistic research complex conventions are used, making it difficult for non-experts to read transcripts. Examples in this textbook are also described in accessible language. Students can easily read and understand data examples and therefore see how speakers achieve goals through their discourse choices. This also means that the book is accessible to students without a background in linguistics or who are unfamiliar with discourse analysis.

A fourth and related issue for students is that it can be a challenge to identify features in real data. As well as drawing attention to features in examples throughout each chapter, exercises are provided for students to apply what they have learned, with notes on the exercises at the back of the book for feedback and guidance. Students can then learn to identify patterns and issues for themselves in authentic data.

Finally, students may not always understand how research can have real world applications. A chapter is provided which focuses on applications and implications of research, demonstrating how research can be applied to real world issues.

The unique features of the book are that it is introductory, theoretically accessible, and international in scope. There are many textbooks on professional communication, but these are seldom written from a linguistics and discourse perspective. *Introducing Language in the Workplace* covers a broader range of topics and includes more explicit consideration of data analysis than these textbooks. Not only does this help students develop useful skills, but it also draws attention to the importance of everyday language and interaction in achieving workplace goals.

Transcription Conventions

Most transcripts in this book use simple orthographic transcription conventions. Speech often has false starts, repetition and speech errors. These are a normal feature of speech and have not been edited out.

   All names are pseudonyms

[laughs]	paralinguistic features such as laughter and replaced words
[laughs]: yes:	colons show scope of the feature marked
[voc]	vocalisation
[tut]	bilabial/alveolar/dental clicks
(yeah)	unclear word, transcriber's best guess
( )	unclear speech
{you}	word added in English translation to clarify meaning
//okay\	simultaneous speech – first speaker's utterance
/okay\\	simultaneous speech – second speaker's utterance
	[overlap marking has been shifted to word boundaries]
=	latching, i.e., no discernible pause between utterances
ke-	incomplete word
#	showing utterance boundaries when ambiguous
…	section of transcript omitted
+	pause of up to one second
(4)	pauses of four seconds or more noted in brackets
<u>yes</u>	<u>underlining</u> indicates stress, emphasis
yes	**bold** highlights important features
yes	*italics* denote English translations from another language. If only the English translation was provided in the source text, then the example will be in italics (with the original language noted)

Sources of examples are noted below each transcript. (Source: LWP) denotes data drawn from the Wellington Language in the Workplace Project database. There are many examples drawn from this database. There are also many examples drawn from published research from around the world and in these cases the transcript conventions have been changed to the ones outlined here. My apologies for any misinterpretation/misrepresentation in adapting the transcripts.

Introducing Language in the Workplace

1 Introducing Language in the Workplace

CHAPTER PREVIEW

This chapter provides an overview of the field of language in the workplace research and an outline of the contents of this book. The chapter demonstrates the appeal and significance of studying workplace discourse. The chapter addresses the following questions:

- what is language in the workplace research?;
- why is it important to research language in the workplace?;
- what are some of the key settings where work talk has been explored?;
- what activity types or genres of talk can be found in different settings?; and
- what is covered in the rest of the book?

What Is Language in the Workplace?

Language in the workplace is a field of research which examines speech and written texts collected from workplace settings.

Consider the following example:

Example 1.1 (Source: LWP)

RUTH: hello
CAROLE: hello missus- Ms Tape [laughs]
RUTH: huh?
CAROLE: I said hello Ms Tape
RUTH: who's Ms Tate?
CAROLE: <u>tape</u>
RUTH: <u>tape</u> oh yeah yeah I'll drive everyone up the wall
           [pointing to the typing Carole has done for her]
           is that a space or not + it is a space?
CAROLE: [quietly]: no it's not a space it's not a space:
RUTH: do you think it should have a space?
CAROLE: yes I do
RUTH: oh //okay\
CAROLE: /(I'll fix that)\\ will bring to you again
RUTH: do you want to just put [slowly]: um:
           leave that leave out the surname
CAROLE: oh sure //yeah yeah you know him\\ okay looks friendlier
RUTH: /cos I actually know him\\
RUTH: [quietly]: yeah: //okay that'd be great\
CAROLE: /okay I'll just\\ do that and I'll bring it to you in a second
RUTH: yep and I'll +++ sign it out
           [interaction ends]

This short forty-two second interaction was collected in a corporate workplace. Even in such a short example there are many interesting points to note. We can see that the main goal of the interaction is to get something done; Ruth wants to check something in a letter that Carole has typed for her and to get Carole to change something. These are what are referred to as the **transactional goals** of the interaction.

The interaction also has some aspects which orient to **relational goals**, i.e., some features which show how the two women relate to each other on a personal level. Carole jokes with Ruth as she greets her, calling her 'Ms Tape'. This refers to the fact that Ruth has been recording all their interactions. Ruth then jokes that she'll be driving 'everyone up the wall' with her recording, before turning to the task at hand.

It is also clear just from this short interaction, which woman has the higher status role. Carole does Ruth's typing so from this we know she is providing administrative support to someone of higher status. We can see the way that Ruth, in the higher status position, both expresses and mitigates power. She directly asks Carole about whether there is a space or not and then asks her to leave out her surname when she fixes the letter. Her first directive is implicit (to add a space once Carole has clarified that there is no space and that there should be one). Her second directive is explicit and expressed directly through the use of imperatives 'leave that leave out the surname'. This is also softened (mitigated) by the false start 'do you want to just put [slowly]: um:' and her explanation 'cos I actually know him'.

Workplace discourse research typically takes interactions such as these and explores a diverse range of issues. These include investigating how directives are issued, how people manage relationships at work, how people enact aspects of their social and professional identities, and the implications of the findings of workplace research using authentic data for developing teaching and training materials.

> Throughout the book you will see examples like Example 1.1. All examples involve authentic spoken workplace data. Many examples come from the Wellington Language in the Workplace Project database, which includes data from a diverse range of New Zealand workplaces (www.victoria.ac.nz/lwp). Other examples come from research conducted around the world in different work and cultural contexts.

Why Study Language in the Workplace?

People spend a considerable portion of their lives at work and they may interact with a range of people during a typical work day. Exploring workplace language is therefore 'an important part of understanding the human experience' (Marra and Angouri 2018: xix).

Business scholars have been exploring workplace communication for several decades. However, this research has typically relied on self-report data and it has been shown that there is a big difference between what people *do* and what they *say* they do. Linguistic and discursive approaches to researching language in the workplace therefore offer insights on what people *actually* do. Only by examining authentic workplace discourse can we understand how people interact at work, and the relevance of a range of factors that might influence how they interact.

There are many applications for language in the workplace research. Knowing how professionals in a particular setting interact, for example, can inform training materials for people interested in working in this area. An important part of any job is not only knowing how to do the required tasks, but also being able to communicate in ways appropriate to a role. This is important for all newcomers and can reduce the chances of miscommunication occurring, increase the chances of transactional goals being achieved, and can help people fit into a new workplace.

What Counts as a Workplace?

Corporate workplaces are what normally come to mind when people talk about 'business' talk, but there are many other settings where people interact 'at work'. In basic terms a **workplace** is anywhere where one or more people are working.

We can identify different types of workplaces. Terms that are used to refer to different types of workplaces include:

- White collar workplaces: office or other administrative settings;
- Blue collar workplaces: settings where the work involves manual labour.

© Jacynta Scurfield 2019

There are many other types of workplaces, for example, settings where the work is related to customer interaction, or other service-oriented work, as well as educational, legal and medical settings.

Another distinction that has been made between types of settings is whether they are **frontstage** or **backstage**. Drawing on the metaphor of the world being a stage, Goffman (1959) used these terms to differentiate between **frontstage** areas of people's lives where they know others are watching and they have an **audience**, like being on stage in a theatre, and **backstage** areas where they do not.

When applied to workplaces, **frontstage** settings are ones where workers interact with the public. Examples of frontstage interactions would be:

- a doctor-patient consultation;
- a nurse taking a patient's blood pressure on a hospital ward;
- someone buying a cup of coffee in a café;

- a journalist interviewing an Olympic athlete;
- a flight attendant interacting with passengers;
- a passenger asking the bus driver which stop they should get off at;
- a meeting between an advertising company and a client;
- a phone call to an emergency help line;
- a lawyer summing up a defendant's case in a courtroom.

In contrast, **backstage** settings involve colleagues working together. Examples of backstage interactions would be:

- staff meetings at a hospital;
- a pilot and co-pilot talking as they prepare for take-off;
- two factory workers dealing with a problem on the packing line;
- two policeman debriefing after making an arrest;
- a shop manager asking a worker to unpack more stock;
- two office colleagues discussing a document;
- teachers in the staff room discussing a difficult student;
- builders working out the best way to install a new type of cladding;
- a lawyer on the way to court ringing the office to clarify some information.

These examples suggest a range of places where workplace interaction can occur, from offices to shops, to vehicles, courtrooms and other official buildings. Sometimes one or more of the people involved in the interaction may be in their own homes. Some workplace settings only involve backstage interactions, in others the primary interaction is frontstage, while other work settings may typically involve both types of interactions.

As can be seen just from the small number of examples given in this section, language in the workplace is a field which can encompass a diverse range of settings and an even more diverse range of occupations. Even when not working, we frequently engage in frontstage workplace interactions with people who are.

Another consideration has been whether the setting involves **high-stakes** talk. This refers to talk where the outcomes of the interaction have the potential for significant loss or gain. High-stakes settings include health care, aviation or emergency management. Employment interviews are also high-stakes.

What Types of Talk Are Found in Workplaces?

In each workplace setting there is a range of types of talk that people engage in. This may include both frontstage and backstage talk. For example, when we look at the lists of examples of frontstage and backstage talk above, we can see that a doctor may interact with a patient in a consultation, or they may attend a staff meeting; a lawyer may be talking in court or consulting another colleague about a case.

Different types of talk that people engage in have been referred to as **genres**. A **genre** is situation-specific talk which involves recurrent and recognisable patterns. Typical workplace genres include interviews, negotiations, meetings, training sessions, business letters, and annual reports. Genres may also be divided up into different activity types. For example, there are many different types of meetings that may constitute the **meeting** genre, for instance company board meetings, teaching staff meetings, factory team briefing meetings, problem-solving meetings or hospital ward handover meetings. Each of these types of meetings has distinct culturally understood purposes, expectations and interactional norms.

Consider the following examples:

Example 1.2

Context: Police interview recorded in the UK.

POLICE OFFICER: for the benefit of the tape can you please [slowly]: um: say your full name and date of birth for me please
SUSPECT: Wayne Tom Barker twenty first of the first eighty

Reprinted from *Journal of Pragmatics 117*, Antaki, Charles and Stokoe, Elizabeth, When police treat straightforward answers as uncooperative, p. 2, © 2012, with permission from Elsevier.

Example 1.3

Context: Job interview recorded in the USA.

INTERVIEWER: … what would you say your strengths are?
INTERVIEWEE: um well I'm very work oriented #
                if I'm appreciated I tend to give more than a hundred percent

Reprinted from *Journal of Pragmatics 39*, Kerekes, Julie, The co-construction of a gatekeeping encounter: An inventory of verbal action, p. 1953, © 2007, with permission from Elsevier.

Both of these excerpts come from interviews. They are very different types of interviews, however; Example 1.2 is a police interview while Example 1.3 is a job interview. Question/answer sequences are typical of the interview genre, with the particular questions from the interviewer in each situation conforming to what we would expect to find in each case. The police interviewer asks the suspect to provide his name 'for the benefit of the tape', while the job interviewer asks the interviewee about his strengths.

Across a range of settings and in different activity types, we can identify more specific types of talk that people engage in. For example, a problem-solving meeting may involve decision-making, disagreement, directives, refusals and advice-giving. Often these are an expected and essential part of an activity, and in this book we will see how people manage these types of talk in different contexts.

What Is Covered in this Book?

This book provides an introduction to the field of language in the workplace research with a focus on spoken interaction. Four main questions are examined.

1. How do people study authentic workplace language?

In the rest of Part I, issues are examined that relate to researching and analysing workplace data. Just as the types of potential workplace settings that can be examined are diverse, so are the approaches to studying language in the workplace.

Much of the research on language in the workplace is qualitative and draws on micro-analytic techniques. In Chapter 2, a brief survey of the main approaches and concepts is provided. This includes:

- Social Constructionism;
- Communities of Practice;
- Conversation Analysis;
- Interactional Sociolinguistics;
- Critical Discourse Studies;
- Theories of (Im)politeness;
- Rapport Management Theory.

Consideration of these theories and approaches provides a solid background for understanding the material covered in the rest of this book.

2. What are some key topics in workplace research?

A wide range of topics has been explored in language in the workplace research. In Part II of this book, three key topic areas will be explored:

i.　The first key topic focuses on transactional aspects of talk at work. As noted above, transactional aspects are those that relate to practical goals, for example, how do people use language to get things done or to reach decisions?

Directives and requests are two explicit discourse types that illustrate how people achieve transactional goals and Chapter 3 explores these two types of talk. Directives and requests have been studied across a range of workplace settings, countries and languages, with research in this area showing how individuals in workplaces achieve practical objectives. Chapter 3 also illustrates how modification strategies are typically utilised when expressing and responding to directives and requests in order to manage relationships, although the cultural context is also important. Both these aspects of directive giving and request making, i.e., achieving practical and interpersonal goals, tell us how a person wants to be perceived, i.e., how they enact identity.

ii.　The second key area is how people use specific strategies to achieve relational goals. Relational goals relate to interpersonal relationships, i.e., how do people use language to get along with the people they interact with?

Building and maintaining good relationships is important across workplace contexts. Social talk and humour are two explicit types of talk that can play this role. In order to achieve this overall goal, they may have a range of more local functions, e.g., to fill time or relieve tension. The functions they have contribute to achieving transactional goals, and Chapter 4 explores how the use of social talk and humour can achieve relational and transactional goals. Narrative can also have the same roles, but may also more directly address transactional goals. People use stories to recount and reflect on their lives, to connect with other people, and also to achieve a range of workplace goals.

iii. The third key area is how people deal with difficult and problematic talk in order to achieve both their transactional and relational goals. How do people use language to get along with the people they interact with when they need to complain or disagree? Sometimes disagreement escalates into conflict. What does this type of talk look like?

The maintenance of good relationships raises issues in terms of how problematic talk is managed in workplace interaction. Activities such as problem-solving and negotiating, for example, may involve the expression of differing views or the pursuit of opposing goals, and depending on the context can be key aspects of workplace communication. They may give rise, however, to disagreement or even conflict. Chapter 5 explores problematic talk at work. This includes complaints, disagreement and conflict talk.

3. What about identity and the way this is enacted in the workplace?

The way people manage transactional and relational goals, as well as how they express and respond to disagreement and conflict, can show us how they present themselves at work. Do they come across as reasonable individuals who skilfully manage sometimes conflicting goals? How do they achieve these goals while presenting key aspects of their professional identity? How do they enact leadership, their gender identity, or cultural identity?

An influential theory in examining identity in the workplace has been social constructionism (see Chapter 2). In this approach the vital role of language in the construction and negotiation of identity is highlighted, rather than treating aspects of identity such as gender as pre-defined and static categories. Adopting this approach, identity is enacted through interaction and people may orient to different aspects of their identity at different times. Chapter 6 explores a topic that has received a great deal of attention in the field, particularly in corporate settings: leadership. Individuals have different styles of leadership and different companies and cultures adopt different organisational models. These factors, along with the demands of a particular situation, all have an impact on how leadership is enacted.

In Chapter 7, gender and language at work is explored. This includes exploring language features that have been linked to gender, along with the way gender has been viewed in research on gender and language. The importance of context in exploring issues related to gender and language is highlighted, with a range of factors potentially influencing how women and men interact in different settings. The intersection of gender and leadership and the ways that women and men lead is also explored.

The last chapter in this section explores cultural identity. Cultural norms influence interaction in any setting. Workplaces in many countries are also increasingly culturally diverse and in these contexts the challenges and affordances of intercultural communication are not always acknowledged. In situations where there is the possibility to use different languages, language choices may be related to the exercise of power, but also to the construction and negotiation of personal and organisational identities. The intersection of culture, gender and leadership identities is also briefly explored.

4. So what?

A question that arises when we study workplace communication is 'so what?' In Part IV of this book, this question will be examined. In what ways can and is workplace research being used to provide practical outcomes for workers and organisations? The obvious ones are the ways it can inform teaching and professional training. A brief survey of applications is provided, including preparing migrants to work in other cultures and helping people develop their workplace communication skills. As part of this we will see how research findings can highlight power imbalances and may then help redress them. The development of the field of workplace discourse research has created possibilities for using our knowledge to improve workplace communication and apply our research findings to real world issues.

Chapter Summary

This chapter has briefly introduced the field of language in the workplace research as well as providing an outline of the book. Two main types of goals have been highlighted: transactional and relational. We have considered why it is important to study language in the workplace, and what counts as a workplace. Two important types of work settings have been introduced:

- frontstage; and
- backstage.

The different types of talk that can be found in different workplace settings have also been highlighted. Considering genres or activity types can provide an understanding of norms and expectations, and how interaction often unfolds in expected ways in different contexts.

Exercises

Exercise 1.1

What do you think is the main goal or function of each of the utterances listed below? Is it transactional or relational? If transactional, does it also show orientation to interpersonal aspects? Can you think of contexts where the utterances might have different functions?

A. how is the baby?
B. can you please make sure the room is booked for the whole day?
C. um I've had a few discussions with people in the corridor which [quietly]: is where I do my best work:
D. so you might get them to score their own work as to the extent to which it satisfies the criteria

Exercise 1.2

Do the workplaces listed below involve frontstage interaction? What types of frontstage interactions can you think of that might occur in each? What backstage interactions may workers in each setting also have?

A. a hospital;
B. a school;
C. a printing company;
D. a café;
E. a tour bus.

Exercise 1.3

Read the excerpts below and then answer the questions following.

Excerpt 1.A (Source: LWP)

GINETTE: let's have a um + a quick review of yesterday +
           we packed fifty six actual tons ++
           fifty six that was ninety seven standard tons (5)
           that wasn't too bad considering the um we were out of powder
           for about four hours three to four hours ++
           and line two ran really well

Excerpt 1.B (Source: LWP)

KIM: hi just this one please
LYDIA: sure (just a second) [says price]
KIM: cool thanks awesome thank you

[KIM LEAVES]

Excerpt 1.C (Source: LWP)

SHANE: what are your basic reasons for leaving? …
LIA: going overseas
SHANE: okay why take
LIA: leave now?
SHANE: yeah well why resign rather than take twelve months leave
         without pay or something?

LIA: yeah I guess just so that I ensured that I had open opportunities
while I'm overseas otherwise I was going to feel some sort of
er I was a bit worried that I'd get lazy and just come back here
and I wanted to ensure
//that I had some incentive [laughs]: not\ to do that:
SHANE: /oh right [laughs]\\
SHANE: so it was a personal challenge?
LIA: [laughs]: yeah: [laughs] personal reasons

1. What workplace settings do you think the excerpts above come from?
2. What types of activities do you think the participants were engaged in?
    What makes you say this?

2 Approaches to Exploring Language in the Workplace

CHAPTER PREVIEW

This chapter provides a brief introduction to some important theories and approaches to exploring language in the workplace. These are:

- Social Constructionism;
- Communities of Practice;
- Conversation Analysis;
- Interactional Sociolinguistics;
- Critical Discourse Studies;
- Theories of (Im)Politeness;
- Rapport Management Theory.

Exploring Language in the Workplace: Introduction

In this chapter, background theory and approaches to analysis are explored. To begin, social constructionism is introduced. This theory has been very influential in a range of fields of social science over the last few decades, including the field of language in the workplace. This is an important social theory underlying approaches to communication in this area.

Next, a concept is presented that is compatible with social constructionism and which has provided useful insights when considering interaction in work teams in backstage settings: communities of practice.

Also compatible with social constructionism are three approaches to data analysis that are briefly introduced in this chapter: conversation analysis, interactional sociolinguistics, and critical discourse studies. The main concepts that are considered important in each approach are outlined, along with some of the insights that research using each approach has afforded when examining workplace discourse.

One aspect of interaction that has received special attention is the interpersonal or relational side. In English the term 'politeness' has been used to refer to this dimension of interaction, and a brief outline is given of theoretical approaches to politeness and impoliteness. A detailed discussion of one such theory is provided as an example, i.e., rapport management theory.

Conversation analysis, interactional sociolinguistics, critical discourse studies and rapport management theory are all qualitative approaches, with analysis focusing on naturally occurring authentic workplace discourse that is audio (and sometimes also video) recorded and then transcribed. They all aim to explore how people *actually* interact and how communication at work is jointly constructed.

In the last section of this chapter, the same transcript is analysed by expert researchers skilled in using the approaches outlined earlier. The same excerpt is used in each case so that the different perspectives and understandings that arise from using the different approaches can be highlighted.

What about data collection?

A challenge when wanting to study workplace discourse is to collect data to analyse. Some approaches to this problem include using data that is in the public domain, for instance, from television documentaries and reality shows, and there are some examples in this book that have come from studies that draw on this type of data.

Other approaches involve eliciting data through role plays or examining people's responses to surveys and in interviews about their workplace language use. Although some important insights have been garnered through this type of research, the focus of this book is authentic workplace discourse. If we want to know how people truly interact in the workplace, we need to observe them at work and not just ask them what they do or get them to act out scenarios. Research has shown that what people say they do and what they *actually* do can be very different.

Social Constructionism

What is social constructionism?

Social constructionism is a theory which highlights the way social knowledge and understandings about the world are created and reinforced. One of its basic principles is that people (as social actors) construct the social world through language. This means that social realities are constructed when people interact with each other. Social constructionism therefore challenges notions of objective realities, rejecting explanations about social phenomena as inevitable, uncontested and never-changing. Language is considered a fundamental tool for people to both represent and construct the social world.

How is social constructionism relevant to workplace discourse?

If language is a fundamental tool for people to represent and construct the social world, then this has important implications when examining language in the workplace. People may have assigned roles in workplace contexts, but these are only realised through interaction and taking on a certain role requires talking and interacting in a certain way. Consider Example 2.1:

Example 2.1

Context: Eve, the manager of a hospital ward, asks a group of registered nurses to provide feedback regarding the way shift handovers are handled. Tina replies. Recorded in New Zealand.

TINA: half the time they're going <u>off</u> the topic …
        people seem to give handovers of patients that aren't there on the floor
        so it's a waste of my time when I just wanna get on the floor …
        it's going back to basic nursing

Republished with permission of Taylor and Francis Group LLC Books, from Lazzaro-Salazar, Mariana, Social constructionism, p. 92. In *The Routledge handbook of language in the workplace*, © 2018; permission conveyed through Copyright Clearance Center, Inc.

In responding to Eve's question, Tina positions herself in relation to expectations of the role of nurses in ward handovers. In doing this, Tina constructs herself as a leader among the group of nurses by constructing the other nurses as an out-group, referring to them as 'they' and 'people' who do not understand appropriate professional practice. This helps her enact her professional identity as someone who is competent and professional and who stands apart from this out-group. Eve's question has given Tina an opportunity to convey her understanding of the social expectations and norms for effective ward handovers and her place in this.

There is more than one way to collect authentic data. Some researchers are present as participants or observers when they record data, others set up recording equipment and leave, while others give control of data collection to members of the workplace. The examples shown throughout this book are drawn from studies of authentic workplace interaction and have been collected using different methodologies, and analysed using different approaches to **discourse analysis**.

© Jacynta Scurfield 2019

The way that people construct the social world draws on social expectations and norms. Tina's enactment of her identity in Example 2.1 draws on her expectations and beliefs about what it means to be a competent and professional nurse, and what behaviours are normal and appropriate within the context of ward handover meetings.

Beliefs, expectations, group knowledge and common knowledge are important concepts when considering social norms. Training in a field or area creates expectations and introduces norms for behaviour in any type of role, from nurses to lawyers to retail workers. Social expectations and social norms also exist when, as a member of the public, someone needs to access services or interact with one of these people. We expect professionals to behave and communicate in ways that are consistent with their roles.

A social constructionist perspective has not always dominated understandings of communication. Until the 1970s, essentialist and realist orientations were prevalent. By the 1980s, however, communication was widely acknowledged as a form of action through which individuals together 'create and manage their social realities', emphasising the idea that meaning must be coordinated and negotiated (Foster and Bochner 2008: 89). An important aspect of this is that meaning is jointly produced when people interact. It is important for instance, that Tina makes her comments about ward handovers in response to Eve's question and also that she does this in front of a group of fellow nurses.

What insights has social constructionism provided when examining workplace communication?

The interactional and relational understandings of communication underlying social constructionism have appealed to workplace researchers. Using this approach, researchers can explore how language creates knowledge, and how people assert, negotiate, reject and align with social stances through social interaction in the workplace.

Workplace research has investigated the social construction of (among other things):

- leadership (see Chapter 6);
- gender (see Chapter 7);
- cultural identity (see Chapter 8).

Social constructionism informs and enhances our understanding of how people communicate at work.

Communities of Practice

The idea that it is through language that group membership is constructed is also at the heart of the communities of practice concept.

What is a community of practice?

A community of practice is a group which has developed established ways of doing things.

The three features required to form a community of practice are:

- mutual engagement;
- creating a joint negotiated enterprise; and
- the utilisation of a shared repertoire of resources (Wenger 1998).

Workplaces consist of groups of people who work together, who share a work purpose and a common goal based on work related knowledge. Workplace groups or teams can therefore generally be understood as communities of practice, each with their own linguistic repertoire used to negotiate meaning, and to develop and display belonging.

Another important aspect of this is that just putting a group of people together does not make a community of practice. The people in the group need to work together over time to develop their own ways of doing things.

The communities of practice framework is compatible with social constructionism. If groups develop ways of doing things through interaction and members of a group negotiate their membership rather than these things just existing and being stable, then ideas of communication as dynamic and involving joint construction are key.

Where did the communities of practice concept come from?

The concept of **communities of practice** was first generated by Lave and Wenger (1991) and Wenger (1998). They wanted to better theorise the social nature of learning. Becoming a member of a new workplace or a new team requires learning the ways of doing things with language that typify the new group. Each community has its own expectations of how members need to engage in its practices (Wenger 1998) and the learning period is crucial, as members learn to perform in an expected and appropriate way. A newcomer begins on the boundaries, at the periphery, but as they learn and integrate into their team they typically move to being a core member of the **community of practice**.

One aspect of this is knowing the jargon and vocabulary, items and tools associated with a particular field or area. In Example 2.2, the importance of shared reference is illustrated with data involving an electrical apprentice and his supervisor.

Example 2.2

Context: An apprentice, Rodney, has constructed an electric board and asks his supervisor, Fernando, to check it. Fernando immediately notices that Rodney forgot to install an earth terminal. It quickly becomes clear to Fernando that Rodney does not even know what this is. Recorded in Switzerland.

RODNEY:	je vais chercher un comme ça?	*should I go and fetch one of these?*
	un millimètre?	*one millimetre?*
	[points to a terminal in one of the units]	
FERNANDO:	quoi? de quoi?	*what? what?*
RODNEY:	une borne pour la terre	*an earth terminal*

FERNANDO:	non mais attends tu rigoles	*wait a minute are you kidding!*
	[looks at the installation plan]	
	tu vois ici	*you see here*
	[reads the installation plan]:	*[reads]:*
	quatre barrettes en laiton	*four brass clips*
	pour raccordement sept pôles:	*for seven-pole connection:*
	ça c'est la terre	*this is the earth*
RODNEY:	quatre barrettes?	*four clips?*
FERNANDO:	ouais +	*yep*
	t'as pas vu dans le tableau hier	*didn't you see in the board*
	que je t'ai fait démonter?	*I asked you to dismantle yesterday*
	là-bas? la démo?	*over there at the demo*
	la terre comment c'était fait?	*the earth connection*
		how it was installed?
	[points with his pen in the direction of the hall]	
RODNEY:	ça j'ai pas remarqué la terre	*I didn't notice the earth*
	[starts to move away]	
FERNANDO:	va voir	*go and have a look*
RODNEY:	okay	*okay*
	[goes to look at the demo board in the hall]	

Reprinted with permission from the *Journal of Applied Linguistics and Professional Practice 7*, Filliettaz, Laurent, Interactions and miscommunication in the Swiss vocational education context: Researching vocational learning from a linguistic perspective, p. 35 © Equinox Publishing Ltd 2010.

Rodney was a new apprentice at the time this interaction was recorded. He did not even know the basic jargon that is used in the industry, being oblivious to what 'earth terminal' is referring to. He does not have a shared reference for this term and initially Fernando does not understand that Rodney does not know what this means. Fernando then

© Jacynta Scurfield 2019

moves to explain what is needed and sends Rodney to look at a board he was working on the previous day so that he can work out what is required. Rodney has not yet acquired the shared resources he needs to work effectively and to become a skilled electrician, and is still on the periphery of the community of practice in his workplace.

Why are shared repertoires important to communities of practice and what can they look like?

Members' joint engagement in the same enterprise over time creates a repertoire of shared practices. It is through shared practices and repertoires that participants construct and jointly negotiate their identity within the context of the community.

Speakers have access to a wide range of verbal repertoires, and certain linguistic strategies may not be specific to a certain community of practice, but may be more standard features commonly used in a variety of communities of practice. Linguistic patterns and accepted ways of doing things that have become normal for a particular group, however, become part of a member's communicative style.

Throughout this book there are many examples where the patterns observed reflect the norms of the community of practice from which the data comes. For instance in Chapter 5, Example 5.14, there is an example of a community of practice where it is acceptable and normal for disagreement to be expressed directly.

Shared practices may also include aspects such as:

- obligatory pre-meeting small talk;
- topics of small talk;
- in-group humour;
- shared stories;
- jargon;
- shortcuts to communication;
- styles that are recognised as displaying membership of the group;
- shared discourse that reflects a certain perspective or view of others outside the community of practice.

What insights can 'communities of practice' provide when exploring language in the workplace?

The communities of practice framework is now widely employed within sociolinguistic workplace research and has proved to be a very fruitful model for exploring workplace communication in teams in backstage settings in a diverse range of workplace environments. It can explain why data from one group may vary greatly from that of a similar group in another workplace, or from another workgroup in the same workplace. It can also explain why communication seems to be proceeding smoothly, or participants comment it went smoothly, when an analyst finds an interaction confusing or potentially problematic.

Throughout this book, the potential importance of the community of practice is considered when thinking about communication in established backstage work teams.

Some Approaches to Analysing Discourse at Work

Organisational scholars from different fields and traditions have increasingly recognised the importance of discourse in the workplace. The assumptions of social constructionism underlie many approaches to analysing workplace discourse, although this is not always acknowledged or explicitly presented from this perspective. These approaches include:

- conversation analysis;
- interactional sociolinguistics;
- critical discourse studies.

Conversation Analysis

by Bernadette Vine with Jonathan Clifton

What is conversation analysis?

Conversation analysis (CA) is a discourse analysis approach which views talk as organised and orderly. CA provides systematic ways of identifying and explaining the patterns and structures that 'make coherent, mutually comprehensible communication and action possible in interaction' (Drew 2005: 79). CA analyses therefore focus not only on sequences of talk, but also what these turns at talk *do*. The key research question driving any analyses therefore is: why this now?

Reflecting its ethnomethodological roots, CA argues that the social order, rather than pre-existing social action, is talked into being by social actors as they orient to a social context which is reflexively (re)constructed in talk. In other words: social order is both a result of and resource for action/talk, or as Heritage (1984) famously put it, talk is context sensitive and context renewing. Consequently, interaction is not about people saying something and others passively receiving the message: meaning, and social order, are co-constructed. Sequences of utterances are therefore an important focus in CA, so analysts using a CA approach want to answer questions such as:

- how does interaction unfold across a sequence of talk as different participants contribute?
- what evidence is there in the interaction of how the hearer has interpreted an utterance and how does the first speaker respond to this?
- what action does this turn-at-talk, partial turn-at-talk, or sequence of talk *do*? (That is, why this now?)

The significance of the placement of an utterance within a sequence is also important in this approach.

What are some key concepts in CA?

One of the concepts central to CA is that talk and people's orientation to who has what rights and obligations to say what, to whom and when, talks into being the social order. Orientation to, and thus reflexively construction of, the social order is thus related to **turn-taking** and the related structure of the **adjacency pair**. This is an ordered pair of utterances spoken by two different participants in an interaction. Once the first has been spoken, the second is required. For instance, when someone asks a question, it is expected that their addressee will answer the question and thus provide a conditionally relevant response (i.e., a reply that is considered to answer the question).

In Example 2.3, Dan asks a question, Roger answers and then asks a question of his own.

Example 2.3

Context: Group therapy session with teenagers. Dan is the therapist.

ROGER: it's always this um image I have of who I am
            and what I want people to think I am
DAN: and somehow it's unrelated to what's going on at the moment?
ROGER: yeah but tell me is everybody like that or am I just out of //it?\
KEN: /I-\\
            not to change the subject but-
ROGER: well don't change //the subject answer me\
KEN: /no I mea- I'm on the\\ subject …

Reprinted from *American Journal of Sociology 97*, Schegloff, Emanuel A., Repair after next turn: The last structurally provided defense of intersubjectivity in conversation, p. 1310, © University of Chicago Press 1992.

In line 4, Roger asks the question, 'is everybody like that or am I just out of it?'. This question, as the first part of a question and answer adjacency pair, therefore requires a conditionally relevant response. In this case, Ken's next utterance does not directly address Roger's question as he begins a turn that projects that he will change the subject, 'yeah but'. However, in line 7, Roger orients to this projected change of subject as a turn that is not allowable and so orients to Roger's moral obligation to provide an answer to the question. In response to this, Ken argues that he is in fact 'on the subject' and so, having accounted for his turn, continues it. Taking turns at talk thus becomes a moral issue, breaches of which become accountable. Ken's response to Roger's question here is what is referred to as a **dispreferred** response. The **preferred** response to a question is to directly answer the question, as Roger did when Dan asked him a question.

Ken also goes on in Example 2.3 to do what is referred to in CA as a **repair**. Having been challenged on his earlier response, he rewords his response, indicating that although his initial response did not appear to answer Roger's question, what he is saying is not completely off topic and is in fact relevant. **Repairs** may be made for a range of reasons and can be made by the person whose interaction produced the problem or by others present.

Roger's question and the related utterances that precede and follow are all part of a longer **sequence** within the interaction. Exploration of **sequence organisation** focuses on how actions are ordered in talk, with adjacency pairs being basic units of sequence construction but with complexity added by speakers as they interact. Roger's question had been preceded by him talking about how he feels. **Sequence organisation** captures the fact that when people communicate they produce a series of coherent, orderly and meaningful utterances.

What insights has CA research provided about workplace communication?

CA research has generated numerous insights into the organisation of language, action, and interaction in workplace contexts. It has led to the identification and description of a multitude of fundamental phenomena from a diverse range of settings. Some of the key settings explored include:

- medical contexts; and
- courtroom discourse.

Some of the key findings of this type of research relate to the way language is used in different settings. For instance, questions from doctors to patients in consultations tend to be worded differently and have different goals when compared to those that lawyers use when questioning defendants and witnesses in court. In both situations, however, questions play a crucial role in the achievement of the transactional goals of the workplace.

A difference between CA and many other discourse analysis approaches is that CA only sees contextual factors as relevant if they are oriented to by the participants in an interaction. External contextual factors are not considered unless they are foregrounded in some way in interaction.

Interactional Sociolinguistics

What is interactional sociolinguistics?

Interactional sociolinguistics is a discourse analysis approach which not only looks closely at authentic interactional data, but also considers wider contextual factors in interpreting what is going on. Its broader aims are to investigate linguistic and cultural diversity. First developed by John Gumperz, interactional sociolinguistics has been applied and further developed by a number of scholars around the world, providing important insights into workplace communication.

What are some of the key concepts in interactional sociolinguistics?

The key concepts of an interactional sociolinguistic approach include:

- contextualisation cues;
- conversational inference.

Contextualisation cues are features which indicate how speakers intend their utterances to be interpreted and which listeners use to interpret meaning.

Consider Example 2.4:

Example 2.4

Context: Selection interview recorded in the mid-1970s in the British Midlands. The applicant has applied for a paid traineeship at a publicly funded institution.

INTERVIEWER:	and you've put here
	that you want to apply for that course
	because there are more jobs in the <u>trade</u>
APPLICANT:	[quietly]: yeah:
INTERVIEWER:	so perhaps you could explain to Mr. C.
	<u>apart</u> from <u>that</u> reason
	<u>why</u> else you want to apply for <u>electrical</u> work
APPLICANT:	I think I like + this job in my-
	as a profession
INSTRUCTOR:	and <u>why</u> do you think you'll <u>like</u> it?
APPLICANT:	why?
INSTRUCTOR:	could you explain to me why?
APPLICANT:	why do I like it? I think it is more job <u>prospect</u>

Reprinted from Gumperz, John J., Interactional sociolinguistics: A personal perspective, p. 318. In *The handbook of discourse analysis* 2nd ed., © 2015 John Wiley & Sons Inc., with permission of the publisher.

The interviewer stresses certain words (underlined above), bringing attention to key aspects where she thinks the applicant needs to elaborate more. The applicant does not pick up on these cues and becomes more and more uncertain. He does not understand and just restates what he had put in his application, that the traineeship will give him good job prospects. This is not the response the interviewer wanted and does not directly answer the interviewer's questions to provide other reasons. Ultimately the applicant was unsuccessful in securing a traineeship.

Speakers can choose features at a number of levels as contextualisation cues, including:

- dialect and style;
- lexis and syntax;
- prosody and non-verbal behaviours (Gumperz 1982: 131).

Conversational inference is the context-bound process of interpretation that listeners use to assess what speakers mean by what they say. Each participant draws upon a set of culturally shaped **contextualisation conventions** to signal and interpret meanings. The applicant in Example 2.4 was from South Asia and Gumperz (2015) points out that the South Asians in his interview dataset often failed to recognise that accenting is used in English to convey key information. Like the applicant in Example 2.4, they did not recognise the significance of the interviewer's contextualisation cues.

An important factor here is that people are members of social and cultural groups. The way they use language therefore reflects the groups they identity with. Again, we see an approach where culture and social norms are constructed through interaction. And if the people interacting do not share or recognise the contextualisation cues of the groups their interlocutor draws on, this can lead to misunderstandings. Misunderstandings can then have damaging social consequences for those from minority groups, restricting their access to resources and services.

How do differing norms affect interaction?

The interviewer and instructor in Example 2.4 had differing expectations and ways of interacting than the applicant. This meant that the applicant, in not sharing or recognising these norms, did not interact in a way the others expected him to. In the next two brief examples we see the contrast between the applicant from Example 2.4 who does not share the norms, seen here in Example 2.5, and one who does, Example 2.6.

Example 2.5

Context: Selection interview recorded in the mid-1970s in the British Midlands. The applicant has applied for a paid traineeship at a publicly funded institution.

INTERVIEWER:	have you visited the skills centre?
APPLICANT:	yes I did
INTERVIEWER:	so you've had a look at the workshops?
APPLICANT:	yes
INTERVIEWER:	you know what the training allowance is? do you?
APPLICANT:	yeah
INTERVIEWER:	do you know how much you've got to live on for the period of time?

Reprinted from Gumperz, John J., Interactional sociolinguistics: A personal perspective, p. 314. In *The handbook of discourse analysis* 2nd ed., © 2015 John Wiley & Sons Inc., with permission of the publisher.

Example 2.6

Context: As for Example 2.5.

INTERVIEWER:	have you visited the skills centre?
APPLICANT:	yep I've been there yeah
INTERVIEWER:	so you've had a chance to look around? and did you look in at the brick shop?
APPLICANT:	er yeah we had a look around the brickshop and um it look okay I mean it's [pause]
INTERVIEWER:	all right
APPLICANT:	pretty good yeah

Reprinted from Gumperz, John J., Interactional sociolinguistics: A personal perspective, p. 314. In *The handbook of discourse analysis* 2nd ed., © 2015 John Wiley & Sons Inc., with permission of the publisher.

The interviewer in both cases asks the same initial question. The applicant in Example 2.5 provides a brief response to this question and the ones that follow and does not expand on any of his answers. The applicant in Example 2.6, however, expands his answers and manages to engage the interviewer. When he pauses to find the right word to describe the brickshop, the interviewer suggests a word and the applicant then agrees with this. This applicant is a native of the local area and responded to the interviewer in a way the interviewer expected. This applicant had a successful interview and secured a traineeship position.

What insights has interactional sociolinguistics research provided about workplace communication?

Workplace discourse has been a focus of interactional sociolinguistics since the beginning, with an early focus on gatekeeping encounters, such as interviews, where speakers from ethnic and linguistic minority groups may face difficulties and experience restricted access to services and resources. Gumperz established interactional sociolinguistics as an approach to intercultural communication that exposes how social injustices are exacerbated when participants have different contextualisation conventions and cultural assumptions.

Insights from interactional sociolinguistic research from around the world include:

- how culture affects workplace discourse;
- how gender and language shape workplaces;
- how professional identities and relationships are discursively created;
- how leadership is enacted and power is negotiated;
- how routine encounters such as meetings (and those that are especially high-stakes, such as interviews) are constructed; and
- how various discourse strategies (including humour and narrative) are used at work.

Critical Discourse Studies

What are critical discourse studies?

Taking a **critical discourse studies** (CDS) approach can look very much like an interactional sociolinguistics approach in terms of analysis. A close analysis of authentic discourse is informed by looking at wider contextual factors. CDS adds another layer however as the beginning point is actually 'a social problem that needs to be described, explained and solved' (Koller 2018: 27). Researchers taking a CDS approach want to not only analyse authentic data therefore, but also to help bring about change where language use reflects inequality and discrimination (Fairclough 2015), or where a lack of knowledge about language use in a particular context may mean people have prejudices or biases against a group.

> In interactional sociolinguistics, ethnographic observations are also used to provide contextual information, and analysis is also informed by interviews. These may involve playing the recording for one or more of the participants to gain their insights on the interaction which can uncover different perspectives that enrich the analysis.

What are some of the key concepts in CDS?

Power is a central concept in CDS approaches. Close linguistic analysis is considered in the light of who holds power in an interaction, how this is evident in talk or written texts, and what this says about a society.

The person in a position of power can control and constrain the contributions of less powerful participants. Fairclough identifies three types of constraints:

- contents, i.e., what is said and done;
- relations, i.e., the social relations people enter into in discourse; and
- subjects, i.e., the **subject positions** people can occupy (Fairclough 2015: 76).

The following example illustrates these three constraints.

Example 2.7

Context: A doctor and a group of medical students are visiting a premature baby unit at a hospital.

DOCTOR: now what I want you to do is to make a basic neonatal examination …
           all right so you are actually going to get your hands on the infant
           and look at the key points and demonstrate them to the group
           as you're doing it will you do that for me please? off you go
STUDENT: well first of all I'm going to //(   )\
DOCTOR: /first\\ before you do that is
           do you wash your hands isn't it? I
           cos you've just been examining another baby [long pause]
           are you still in a are you in a position to start examining yet (   )
STUDENT: just going to remove this
DOCTOR: very good

Reproduced from Fairclough, Norman, *Language and power* 3rd ed., published by Routledge, p. 74, © Norman Fairclough 2015. Reproduced with permission from Taylor & Francis Books UK.

Even in this short extract we can see the three constraints. The **contents** of the student's actions here are constrained by the doctor who directs the student, requiring him to conduct an examination according to a learned routine. The way the student does this is constrained by his **subordinate relationship** with the doctor and his **social relationship** to his audience (his fellow students). And in doing the examination the student occupies the **subject position** of aspiring doctor as well as student.

Fairclough (2015) also discusses the way the doctor exercises control over the student's contributions by telling him when to start, interrupting, explicitly telling him how to sequence his actions, and in the way the doctor evaluates the student's actions (*very good*).

Power, dominance and inequality in the workplace can be evident in discourse due to institutional power and roles, but also because of a whole range of other social factors, for instance, class, gender, ethnicity, race, language, or age. Often more than one factor will be relevant. Resistance or challenges to power may also be observed.

What about the Critical **aspect of CDS?**

The **critical** aspect of this approach is of course of prime importance. It is not enough to highlight and describe discourse practices which construct and reinforce power differences, they must also be critiqued and feedback should be given. This is particularly important when there is an abuse of power or when there may be ignorance about an issue.

Example 2.8 comes from a study by Ruth Wodak which took the problem of a lack of public awareness about how politicians interact in backstage contexts. Wodak (2009) provides an account of the challenges facing members of the European Parliament in terms of how the parliament runs and the demands of their jobs, as well as specifically examining a day in the life of a politician, Hans. Hans works very hard and even lunch is a chance for another meeting and for Hans to present his arguments on an issue in a more informal setting: see Example 2.8.

Example 2.8

Context: Lunch meeting with Slovenian delegates. They are conversing while eating.

HANS:	aber wie sehen Sie ihre Grenzfragen	but how do you see your border issues
	mit Italien und diese	with Italy and these
	da gibt es ja auch Probleme	aren't there also problems there?
S2:	ja mit Italien also Grenzfragen	yes with Italy well border issues
	also mit Kroatien schon	well with Croatia there are
HANS:	Kroatien	Croatia
S1:	ja er	yes er
HANS:	da ist eigentlich die empfindlichste	that is actually the most sensitive
	und schwerigste Frage is die ( )	and most difficult question

Reprinted from Wodak (2009: 143)

Hans has been discussing the political situation while the group wait for the food to arrive and even here when they are eating he is still focused on work. He asks his Slovenian colleagues a question about border issues with neighbouring countries, showing his understanding of the political context and that there are potential problems around this issue when considering Slovenia joining the EU. This type of backstage work is a salient feature of this politician's (and other politicians') interaction with colleagues and others that they come into contact with. Wodak (2009) argues that the invisibility of politicians' backstage work leads to widespread politicisation and misunderstanding.

What insights has CDS research provided about workplace communication?

Research using a CDS approach on spoken interaction is not common due to the critical nature of the approach. Gaining access can be difficult when people know their interaction may be examined for problems. Data that are in the public domain, for instance, the media, or written data, are therefore more commonly the focus of research.

A CDS approach on spoken discourse can, however, highlight:

- the way language reinforces and maintains power differences;
- how close examination of interaction in less understood contexts can demystify language practices and break down prejudice.

Examining Interpersonal Aspects of Interaction

The approaches above have been used to explore relational as well as transactional aspects of workplace interaction. There are some theories and approaches which explicitly focus on the relational or interpersonal side of interaction.

Theories of Politeness and Impoliteness

What is (im)politeness theory?

Approaches to analysing politeness and impoliteness endeavour to account for the ways people accommodate the relational or interpersonal side of interaction. How do people maintain good relations and avoid conflict? And alternatively, how do they cause offence, whether intentionally or not?

Politeness started to become an important area of study in the mid-1980s, following the publication of two important books – Geoffrey Leech's *Principles of Pragmatics* (1983) and Penelope Brown and Stephen Levinson's *Politeness: Some Universals in Language Usage* (1987). Brown and Levinson's approach then dominated the field until the late 1990s. However, there are now a wide range of different theoretical accounts of (im)politeness.

What are some of the key concepts in Brown and Levinson's politeness theory?

One of the key concepts in Brown and Levinson's approach to politeness is face. They define face by drawing on the work of Erving Goffman and identify a model person who has 'two particular wants ... the want to be unimpeded and the want to be approved of in certain respects' (Brown and Levinson 1987: 58). They refer to these two wants as **negative face** and **positive face** respectively. Politeness is then seen as a strategy resulting from a speaker's attempts to avoid or minimise damage either to their own face or to the face of whoever they are interacting with, and to provide approval to others in order to attend to their face needs.

Face is a concept that attracts attention in other theories of politeness too, although it is not always defined in quite this way.

Brown and Levinson's approach to politeness has been criticised for a number of reasons. An early criticism of their theory was that their conceptualisation of face has an underlying bias towards Western values. This is seen to reflect their assumption that individuals have 'individualistic and egalitarian motivations, as opposed to the more group-centred hierarchy-based ethos of Eastern societies' (Leech 2007: 167).

Another problem is that having identified a strategy that a speaker uses, Brown and Levinson (1987) then specify a meaning for this strategy. This does not take into account different values or norms in different cultures, or groups, which affect the intended and/or perceived meaning of a strategy. This aspect of their theory is incompatible with ideas of social constructionism where meaning is negotiated and not fixed.

Another criticism is that the theory examines utterances in isolation. More recent discursive approaches which have underlying social constructionist principles view meaning as being jointly constructed, so they explore politeness phenomena by examining sequences of talk.

What about impoliteness?

Since the early 2000s there has been a move to study impoliteness along with politeness. Impolite behaviour is defined as inappropriate, non-politic and negatively marked behaviour. This is evaluated negatively by interactants and may lead to conflict.

Interpretations of impoliteness depend on the intentions and perceptions of the participants in an interaction. Determining someone's intentions is difficult, therefore many researchers define acts of politeness and impoliteness on the basis of how the addressee reacts to something that has been said.

Research on impoliteness in backstage workplace settings has also considered the role of the community of practice (see above). What counts as polite or impolite is dependent on shared practices. The norms of a particular group or team can affect the way that disagreement is expressed, for instance, and the way it should be interpreted. The same talk may be acceptable and not considered conflictual in one group, while in another it is problematic.

What insights has (im)politeness theory research provided about workplace communication?

Taking an (im)politeness approach to workplace data helps us understand the relational side of interaction in a range of workplace settings.

One discursive approach to interpersonal communication will now be examined in more detail.

Rapport Management Theory

What is rapport management theory?

The term rapport refers to people's perceptions of (dis)harmony or smoothness-turbulence in interpersonal relations and rapport management theory focuses on the management of interpersonal relations.

Rapport management theory was developed by Helen Spencer-Oatey to address some problems that had been identified with Brown and Levinson's politeness theory. In particular she aimed to provide an alternative approach to the interpersonal side of communication that did not have a Western bias, and that did not just focus on the individual with attention concentrated on single utterances.

What are some of the key concepts in rapport management theory?
Spencer-Oatey (2008b: 3) identifies four orientations to rapport:

- enhancement;
- maintenance;
- neglect;
- challenge.

A **rapport enhancement** orientation shows a desire to strengthen or enhance harmonious relations. **Rapport maintenance** involves the interactional work people do to protect already established relationships. When people overlook, ignore or are unconcerned about the quality of relations this is **rapport neglect** and it can and often does threaten rapport. When people actively seek to challenge or impair harmonious relations they **challenge rapport**. Although people commonly orient their interactions towards building rapport, this is not always the case.

Underlying assumptions of rapport management theory are that all language use influences interpersonal rapport, that people try to manage their relations with others, and that what constitutes appropriate behaviour is governed by cultural conventions as well as contextual and individual preferences (Spencer-Oatey 2008b: 8).

Spencer-Oatey identifies three key factors that influence rapport:

- face sensitivities;
- interactional goals; and
- sociality rights and obligations.

Face sensitivities relate to a person's desire to be evaluated positively by others and to not have negative qualities acknowledged. Face sensitivities can apply to any or all of the various aspects of a person's sense of identity: the self as an individual (individual identity); the self as a member of a group (collective identity); and the self in relation to others (social identity).

Interactional goals can be either transactional, relational or both, and the different ways in which these are approached are subject to cultural, individual and contextual factors. Influences include the type of activity and the social/interactional roles and relations of participants. When these differences go unrecognised or are poorly managed they can threaten rapport.

Sociality rights and obligations refers to 'the fundamental social *entitlements*' (Spencer-Oatey 2008a: 13) that each person claims for themselves, i.e., concerns relating to fair treatment, social inclusion,

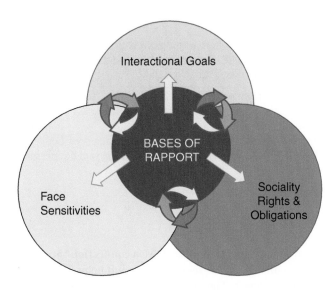

Figure 2.1
The bases of rapport
© Spencer-Oatey, Helen,
2008, Face,
(im)politeness and
rapport, p. 14. In
*Culturally speaking:
Culture, communication
and politeness theory*,
2nd ed., Continuum,
reproduced with
permission of
Bloomsbury Publishing.

and respect, which vary between different socio-cultural contexts. When perceptions and expectations regarding what counts as normal behaviour are not met people may feel annoyed or offended.

As well as differing between cultures, many behavioural norms and conventions reflect deeply held beliefs and values. Termed 'socio-pragmatic interactional principles (SIPs)' (Spencer-Oatey and Jiang 2003), they determine the appropriateness of behaviour in a given context. Awareness and effective management of such conventions has a significant impact on successful intercultural communication.

SIPs may for instance reflect conventions relating to appropriate behaviours for a particular role, or conventions regarding turn-taking. Spencer-Oatey (2008a: 16) identifies two SIPs in particular as being of fundamental importance:

- equity;
- association.

Equity is concerned with consideration and fairness: the belief that we are entitled to personal consideration from others, that we are treated fairly and not unduly imposed upon.

Association is about social involvement with others: the belief that we are entitled to association with others.

How is rapport managed?

People are generally aware of a need to build and maintain rapport. A couple of examples illustrate how people do this in different workplace settings. Example 2.9 comes from an employment interview and involves two native speakers of English.

Example 2.9

Context: Small talk from an employment interview. The interviewer, Amy, and the candidate, Cindy, discover that the candidate's former boss is the father of a friend of Amy's. Recorded in the USA.

CINDY: and I think he's retired ...
AMY: yeah definitely I'm friends with his daughter
CINDY: oh okay
AMY: we used to be friends um in Minneapolis we both lived there
CINDY: is his daughter um is she going to Harvard business school?
AMY: Stanford ...

Reprinted from *Journal of Pragmatics 39*, Kerekes, Julie, The co-construction of a gatekeeping encounter: An inventory of verbal action, p. 1962, © 2007, with permission from Elsevier.

Amy and Cindy realise they have a connection through Cindy's old boss. The small talk that develops at this point helps Cindy develop rapport with the interviewer. The employment interview is characterised by a range of social obligations and expectations on the part of both the candidate and the interviewer, and as a gatekeeping encounter is high-stakes. A key aspect of positive self-presentation by candidates is their competence in developing rapport with interviewers. Successful candidates are able to do this, while those who cannot tend to be unsuccessful.

An important focus of research using a rapport management approach has been interaction between people from different cultures. Consider Example 2.10:

Example 2.10

Context: A Korean migrant shopkeeper is interacting with two African American customers. They joke about the cost of getting keys made. Recorded in the USA.

CUSTOMER 1:   can I get two sets of these keys?
               how much does it cost each key made?
SHOPKEEPER: key made?
CUSTOMER 1:   yeah
SHOPKEEPER: hundred dollar
CUSTOMER 1:   a hundred
SHOPKEEPER: uhuh
CUSTOMER 1:   (that ain't that bad?)
SHOPKEEPER: //yeah I can-\
CUSTOMER 2:   /a hundred\\ dollars for key make
SHOPKEEPER: fourteen karat gold
CUSTOMER 1:   key? ...
SHOPKEEPER: [looks at customer and smiles]
               one dollar
CUSTOMER 1:   er er //give [laughs]\ me
SHOPKEEPER: /[laughs]\\
CUSTOMER 1:   give me [laughs] two sets of each

Reprinted under STM guidelines from *Discourse & Society 16*, Ryoo, Hye-Kyung, 2005. Achieving friendly interactions: A study of service encounters between Korean shopkeepers and African-American customers, pp. 85–6.

In Example 2.10, the Korean migrant shopkeeper uses humour with African American customers to develop rapport. Achieving friendly relations can be especially challenging in intercultural interactions like this and Ryoo (2005) notes that this context is typically known for its tense relations. The Korean shopkeepers in Ryoo's research, however, were able to establish effective rapport through focusing on relational aspects (especially small talk and humour) rather than the transactional aspects of the interaction.

There are many potential problems in intercultural workplace communication and Spencer-Oatey argues that it is especially important to take account of SIPs in such contexts. The potential for misunderstanding is increased when people move between countries and social groups.

What insights has rapport management theory research provided about workplace communication?

Rapport management research has highlighted the importance of relational talk in achieving transactional goals in situations where speakers with similar backgrounds converse, as well as when people with different first languages and different cultural backgrounds interact. Intercultural contexts have been an important focus of rapport management research, where misunderstandings may arise because of different cultural expectations and norms. Research has also shown that communication between people belonging to different workplace groups may also be problematic when expectations and norms do not align.

Another important insight from rapport management studies is the way close analysis of linguistic features and strategies can be combined with consideration of broader level concepts – in particular the three key factors that influence rapport ('face sensitivities', 'interactional goals' and 'social rights and obligations').

Sample Data Analyses

In this section, the same excerpt from a market research interview is analysed using the approaches outlined above: CA, interactional sociolinguistics, CDS and rapport management theory. The simplified version of the transcript analysed is presented at the beginning of the interactional sociolinguistics analysis. The CA analysis uses a more detailed version of the transcript which is presented at the beginning of the CA analysis section.

CA Analysis

by Jonathan Clifton

The transcript presented here is a simplified CA. Nonetheless, this is more detailed than the other transcripts in this book. The different conventions used here are:

(0.5)	pauses timed in tenths of seconds
(.)	micro-pause
°word°	talk or laughter softer than surrounding talk

A note on CA transcription

One difference between CA and other approaches to discourse analysis is the high level of detail recorded in transcripts to facilitate analysis. These follow a set of conventions which capture not only 'what' is said, but also 'how' (see Jefferson 2004). Transcription conventions for the non-vocal features of interaction have also been developed (e.g., Mondada 2014).

word	talk or laughter louder than surrounding talk
[	onset of overlapping talk
< word >	spoken more slowly than surrounding talk
wor(h)d	laughter embedded within a word
heh heh/heuh/	laughter which is transcribed according to its length
khn/ hah	and which tries to catch the actual sound
	of the laughter and its delivery

Data Excerpt 2.A – Detailed CA Transcript (Source: LWP)

```
 1 ANGELA:   now I <under(.)stand> um (0.5) that you would be in the public sector
 2 NAHUM:    that's right government sector
 3 ANGELA:   alright and do you know whether or not you're a custom bill customer or not?
 4           (0.5)
 5 NAHUM:    um now I've heard that word so I (0.5) is that relat-
 6           (0.3)
 7 ANGELA:   [basically
 8 NAHUM:    [is this a trick question?
 9 ANGELA:   not a trick [question at all heh heh we don't have
10 NAHUM:                [no no okay
11 ANGELA:   [any trick questions
12 NAHUM:    [is that re-related to the the um the billing?
13 ANGELA:   yes it is
14 NAHUM:    it is yeah then I think [we are yes
15 ANGELA:                           [°you think you are° okay good
16           (0.5)
17 ANGELA:   and we're in the North Island today (.) the company that I'm speaking to
18           is Kamapene Māori I never get the [pronunciation right but I'm working
19 NAHUM:                                       [actually you said that quite well
20 ANGELA:   on it [heuh
21 NAHUM:          [you said that quite well
22 ANGELA:   if I keep on coming year after year I might get it right [°khn°
23 NAHUM:                                                             [oh ok(h)ay
```

Introduction

This analysis is divided into two parts. The first part, covering lines 1–16, focuses on question and answer adjacency pairs as sequences of talk that drive the interaction and through which the action of *doing* a research interview is achieved and states of knowledge are accounted for. The second part of this analysis (lines 16–24) concentrates on the actions that laughter performs.

Part One: Question and Answer Adjacency Pairs and States of Knowledge

From lines 1–16, the most prominent sequential feature of talk is the question and answer adjacency pair. This is to say that Angela, the interviewer, orients to her right to asks questions, and Nahum orients to his obligation to provide a conditionally relevant response as a second part of the adjacency pair. It is through these sequences of talk that the work of the researcher is accomplished and a research interview, as a social activity, is achieved. In this case, a conditionally relevant response is a response that displays a state of knowledge that is expected of an employee being interviewed by a market researcher. Failure to provide such a response could become a morally accountable issue for which some kind of account (e.g., being new to the job, working in a different department, and so on) would be required.

In line 1, Angela asks a question and in line 2 Nahum provides a conditionally relevant response to this. In the next turn, Angela acknowledges this (line 3: 'alright') and then self-selects to ask a second question. However, on this occasion, there is a problem and delivery of the second part of the adjacency pair (i.e., the answer) is delayed until line 14. Between lines 3 and 14, the trouble source is dealt with in an insertion sequence (i.e., a sequence of talk that is inserted within, thus delaying completion of, another sequence of talk). In this case, after the question, there is a slight pause (line 4) which indicates that there is some kind of interactional problem. The pause is followed by Nahum's turn which, prefaced by a hesitation marker ('um'), also signals the problematic nature of the question. Nahum then displays that he has knowledge of the word (line 5: 'um now I've heard that word'), and in the continuation of his turn ('so I') he projects an answer to the question. However, this projected turn is unfinished and it is followed by a brief pause which again indicates some kind of interactional trouble before Nahum changes trajectory and asks: 'is that relat-'. The word in progress 'relat-' is abruptly cut off, but projects the utterance 'related to'. Since the turn is unfinished, it only projects, rather than actually asks, a question which seeks to repair the trouble source (i.e., the original question that he cannot answer) by asking for clarification (i.e., 'is that related to …').

There is then another slight pause, after which Angela and Nahum both self-select to take a turn and overlap each other. Nahum, however, does not continue the repair that has been projected. Rather, line 8, he asks 'is this a trick question?'. He thus accounts for his lack of knowledge and inability to answer the question by suggesting that the question is a trick question for which he cannot thus be held morally accountable for not answering. This question sets up a question and answer adjacency pair to which Angela, the researcher, is now constrained to reply. She replies that it is 'not a trick question at all'. A slight laugh is inserted into the turn, after which Angela asserts that 'we don't have any trick questions' thus rendering her questioning accountable – market researchers do not ask 'trick questions'.

While this turn is in progress, Nahum overlaps to ask a question (line 12: 'is that re-related to the the um the billing') which, since it asks Angela to clarify the initial question, functions as an attempt to repair a trouble source and retrospectively provides the completion of the turn started in line 5. As before, this sets up a question and answer adjacency pair. Angela is constrained to answer, and she does (line 13: 'yes it is').

Following this repair, Nahum is now able to answer the initial question (i.e., line 3: 'do you know whether or not you're a custom bill customer or not?') and so, finally, he provides the second part of the question-answer adjacency pair. The answer comes with an epistemic downgrade ('I think') which, while providing a conditionally relevant answer, displays a lack of certitude. In line 15, Angela acknowledges the answer and assesses the reply (line 15: 'you think you are good').

Through the work of the repair, together the interviewer and interviewee negotiate a response to the question which displays that Nahum does have knowledge of the organisation for which he could be held morally accountable. Significantly, this knowledge is co-constructed and so hints at the fact that interviewees in research interviews are not simple receptacles of knowledge and that it is not sufficient just to ask questions to get *data*. Rather, data obtained from research interviews is always co-constructed and the interviewer plays an active role in co-constructing such knowledge. It is beyond the scope of this short analysis to go into this point in greater depth, but see for example Silverman (2017) for further discussion. The analysis also points to the accountability of knowledge as a moral issue. An employee of a company is expected to have knowledge of that company and when doubt, through the inability to answer a question, is cast on his knowledge, delicate interactional work has to be carried out by both interviewee and interviewer so that this lack of knowledge is either accounted for ('it's a trick question') or repaired so that he can answer the question.

Part Two: Laughter as an Interactional Resource

Laughter is often assumed to be connected to humour and joking. However, while acknowledging that this may be the case, CA focuses on the actions that laughter achieves and proposes that laughter does much more than 'just' responding to humour.

In line 18, as Angela pronounces the name of the company, she accounts for her poor pronunciation by saying that she is 'working on it'. At the end of this turn, she laughs ('heuh'). This laughter displays orientation to her turn as laughable and through orienting to herself as the butt of the joke, she does laughing at herself and self-depreciation. Nahum also orients to Angela's turn as doing self-depreciation. This is because both, as the turn is in progress and after the turn, overlapping with the laughter, he does disagreement. He thus orients to a preference for disagreement after a turn which does self-depreciation (Pomerantz 1984: 83). In line 22, Angela continues her turn which continues the self-depreciation. At the end of her turn there is a slight guttural laugh ("°khn°") which does laughing at herself. Nahum overlaps this laughter (line 23: 'oh ok(h)ay'). The word 'okay' has a laughter token within it, so he reciprocates Angela's laughter and does laughing *with* Angela. Participants who laugh at the same jokes have something in common and so this does affiliation and builds a bond with her. Thus, as Glenn (1991/1992: 151) notes, 'teasing oneself and inviting other to laugh at self represents one way to bring about shared laughter and this can be useful for achieving affiliative displays'. Moreover, the joint laughter, which has no new propositional content, also displays joint orientation to the end of a self-deprecating sequence of talk and sets up a slot for topic transition which is signalled by the utterance *okay* in which the laughter is embedded.

Thus while some of the laughter does relate to humour in which Angela laughs at her own failings, laughing at oneself, in this case, does self-deprecation. Laughing with another, on the other hand, can build affiliation, and it can also be used to signal a space for topic transition.

Interactional Sociolinguistics Analysis

by Janet Holmes

Data Excerpt 2.A – Simplified Transcript (Source: LWP)

Context: A female market researcher, Angela, employed by a telecommunications company is interviewing a male government employee, Nahum, about services provided by the telecommunications company. Both the researcher and the employee are recording the interaction. Recorded in New Zealand in the 1990s.

```
 1 ANGELA:   now I [slowly]: understand: um + that you would be in the public sector
 2 NAHUM:    that's right government sector
 3 ANGELA:   alright and do you know whether or not you're a custom bill customer or not?
 5 NAHUM:    um now I've heard that word so I + is that relat- //+ is this\ a trick question?
 7 ANGELA:                                            /basically\\
 9 ANGELA:   not a trick //question at all\ [laughs]
10 NAHUM:                /no no okay\\
11 ANGELA:   we don't have //any trick questions\
12 NAHUM:                    /is that related to the\\ the um the billing?
13 ANGELA:   yes it is
14 NAHUM:    it is yeah then I think //we are yes\
15 AANGELA:                          /you think you are\\ okay good +
            and we're in the North Island today
            the company that I'm speaking to is Kamapene Māori
            I never get the //pronunciation right but I'm working on it\
19 NAHUM:                    /(actually) you said that quite well\\
20 ANGELA:   [laughs]
21 NAHUM:    you said that quite well
22 ANGELA:   if I keep on coming year after year I might get it right
            //[laughs]\
23 NAHUM:    /[laughs]: (oh okay):\\
```

Line numbers in this version are not consecutive so that the main text is on the same line numbers as the more detailed version of the transcript

---

An interactional sociolinguistic analysis can throw light on many different aspects of this interaction: e.g., self-consciousness regarding the recording, miscommunication, relative roles and statuses, and so on. I have chosen to focus here mainly on the signals of the changing interactional status relationship between the two participants.

Angela opens the interaction and constructs herself as the person in control of this interview with an initial opening 'now' followed by an utterance which requests confirmation of the sector which Nahum is representing. The need for confirmation is signalled not only by the phrase 'I understand' which is uttered slowly and followed with a hesitation and a pause, but also by the use of the modal 'would' signalling uncertainty and hypothesis, together with final rising intonation on 'sector' which clearly invites a verifying response. Despite this, the tone as well as the form of the request indicate she is constructing herself as in charge of this interaction.

Nahum responds with explicit confirmation 'that's right', followed by a word which he offers as a synonym for 'public', namely 'government' (line 3). His utterance also ends with a high rising terminal, but in this case his confident tone clearly signals that he is awaiting her next question rather than any uncertainty about his statement. She responds 'alright', accepting his synonym.

There follows an interesting miscommunication. Angela asks a question which begins 'do you know whether or not' (line 4). This type of question could indicate that she is checking Nahum's knowledge rather than seeking information from him. Nahum signals that he is unsure of what the terms mean by hesitating and then using a strategy to gain time 'um now I've heard that word so I' and then pausing (line 6). He seems to rethink and simultaneously with what appears to be the beginning of an attempt by Angela to explain ('basically') indicates by his utterance 'is this a trick question?' (line 7) that he has heard her question as a test question (such as teachers often use to check that pupils know information which they have been taught). At this point it appears Nahum is somewhat defensive and is constructing Angela as the expert by attributing knowledge to her which he is clearly unsure of. Angela responds reassuringly 'not a trick question at all' followed by a laugh which could signal embarrassment at Nahum's response or an attempt to defuse the tension caused by his suspicions (line 9).

Nahum is quick to accept this, overlapping her response in what sounds like a cooperative conversational style 'no no okay' (line 10). She repeats her reassurance invoking her institutional representative identity 'we don't have any trick questions' (line 11), and Nahum picks up the question he was about to ask with the exact same words ('is that relat-' line 7), before he became suspicious that he was being tested, 'is that related to the the um the billing?' (line 12), from which we can infer he has worked out what 'custom bill customer' most likely means. His repetition of 'the the' and hesitation 'um' indicate he is being cautious, perhaps suspecting he still could be wrong. Angela in response confirms very firmly 'yes it is' (line 13), a rather formal and explicit response which could be interpreted as a little condescending. After echoing her phrase, 'it is yeah', and thus accepting the reassurance, Nahum responds with a firmly uttered confirmation 'then I think we are yes' (line 14). Nahum's 'I think' is uttered confidently and thus supports an interpretation that he now feels reassured that he understands the financial status of his company. Angela then overlaps his response echoing its content 'you think you are', again suggesting she is being reassuring, cooperative and positive. She marks the end of this sequence with an evaluative 'okay good' (line 15).

There are many indications throughout this sequence then that Nahum perceives Angela as more knowledgeable than he is, and though Angela denies she is testing him she nonetheless takes on the role of reassuring and confident conversational partner. The excerpt thus progresses from confident interviewing by Angela with uncertain responses on Nahum's part to resolution and agreement signalled by the echoing of one another's utterances and cooperative overlapping.

At this point there is a striking shift in genre, namely the indication that the conversation is being recorded for a third party audience (or perhaps as a formal means of keeping a record of Angela's interviews). Angela's sudden shift from addressing Nahum to addressing some unknown non-present audience is very marked, not only by the lexico-grammatical structures which explicitly state where regionally the interaction is taking place, and the precise company that Nahum is representing, but also by the shift to a very formal and official tone: 'and we're in the North Island today the company that I'm speaking to is Kamapene Māori' (lines 16–17). The suddenness of the shift is especially apparent from the introductory 'and' which is not linked semantically to the previous utterance as might be expected but rather acts as a discourse marker introducing a new topic. The formality is also emphasised by the use of 'we' to refer to Angela's status as a representative of a (telecommunications) organisation, while the identification of her addressee as 'the company that I'm speaking to' explicitly identifies Nahum's role as a representative rather than as an individual.

Interestingly, this distancing strategy is followed by a self-denigrating comment which could be interpreted as an ameliorative strategy designed to soften the impact of the previous very formal utterance: 'I never get the pronunciation right but I'm working on it' (line 18).

With this utterance Angela puts herself in a one-down position in relation to Nahum, who she implies is an expert in pronouncing Māori. He confirms acceptance of this attributed expertise by explicitly contradicting Angela's self-denigrating comment: 'no you said that quite well' (line 19), and in response to her embarrassed or perhaps sceptical laugh he repeats this 'you said that quite well' (line 21). It is noteworthy that he uses the hedge 'quite' rather than an intensifier such as 'really' or 'very', thus implying that she has more progress to make, and this interpretation is confirmed by her wryly humorous response: 'if I keep on coming year after year I might get it right' (line 22). The humour as well as the content can be interpreted as a way of confirming solidarity with Nahum after the somewhat tricky earlier exchange when he had clearly felt on the back foot.

Hence while in the first part of the interview the contextualisation cues very clearly signal Angela as the person in charge of the interaction and the knowledgeable expert, following her genre switching utterance (lines 16–17), she reverses the roles by acknowledging Nahum as expert in the area of Māori pronunciation, a role he explicitly accepts with his evaluative comments.

CDS Analysis

by Veronika Koller

The critical analysis of discourse involves three levels (see Koller 2012 for more detail): the text itself, the discourse practice and the wider social or, as in this case, socio-economic context. While text analysis comprises both content analysis of who and what is represented, semiotic analysis, which is central to a linguistic approach to text and discourse, includes an investigation into *how* actors, events, actions and entities are represented. The findings from these descriptive analyses are then explained with recourse to the second context level: discourse practice captures who is communicating with whom and to what end, and what genre is realised by the text, as well as the conditions of text production, distribution and reception. Finally, the wider social context involves relevant historical factors and developments, wider systemic issues and dominant ideologies. Critical discourse analysts hold that all three levels influence each other: broad social and economic factors position participants in particular identities and relations, and affect who can, and indeed who has to, produce, distribute and receive particular types of text and talk. Ultimately, aspects of genre as well as identities, relations and discourse access influence the linguistic features used, and conversational behaviours exhibited, by writers and speakers.

The above outline indicates that analysis can proceed bottom-up, i.e., from the text via the discourse practice to the social context level, or top-down. For the extract above, we can start with the wider socio-economic context. Until the early 1990s, the New Zealand government held the monopoly on telecommunications and even after privatisation, the company that the market researcher in the extract represents was one of the country's largest corporations, with no serious competition. This economic background exerts an influence on the power relations and subject positions of the participants in the extract: while Nahum works for a public sector organisation that is nominally the customer of the company that commissioned the market research carried out by Angela, Nahum's organisation is to all intents and purposes a customer without a choice. What is more, the newly privatised telecommunications company was accused of obstructing competitors' access to its infrastructure, thereby damaging its image.

In terms of discourse practice, the excerpt represents the genre or activity type (Culpeper and McIntyre 2010) of a market research interview. The communicative purpose is therefore to gain and provide information. In the interaction, neither participant speaks in a personal capacity, but instead occupies the subject position of a representative of their respective employer, as indicated by their use of 'we'. The employee of the market research company in particular has a restricted role in the interaction, being obliged to cover a number of questions in a particular order. By contrast, the public sector employee, while to some extent constrained by the researcher's questions, has more leeway in his contributions.

How are these contextual factors at the socio-economic and discourse practice level reflected in the interaction itself? The relative power of Nahum as representing a customer of the telecommunications company – albeit one without much choice – is enacted and accommodated to at various points in the exchange. To begin with, Angela uses an indirect speech act to elicit information, phrasing her first question as a declarative with an additional modal marker, 'I understand ... that you would be in the public sector' (line 1), to avoid imposing on her interlocutor and thereby threatening his negative face. Her second question, while a direct speech act, enquires whether Nahum knows his employer's customer status rather than directly asking about that status, thereby leaving him the option to negate the question without too much of a threat to his own face.

In contrast, Nahum does not seek to mitigate the face-threatening act constituted by his suspicion of what motivates Angela's question, 'is this a trick question?' (line 5). This moment of potential conflict may well be a reflection of the telecommunication company's negative image and Angela is quick to reassure Nahum: she abandons the explanation she has just begun, 'basically', to repeatedly negate her interlocutor's suspicion 'not a trick question at all ... we don't have any trick questions' (lines 9 and 11), seeking to defuse the tension through laughter.

Later on in the excerpt, Nahum displays his relevant power by overlapping with Angela to favourably comment on her pronunciation of his company's Māori name, 'you said that quite well' (line 19); this could be read as a compliment and thus a positive politeness strategy but also has patronising overtones. For her part, Angela reinforces her relative lack of power by self-denigration, 'I never get the pronunciation right' (line 18). The joint laughter at the end of the excerpt may indicate some levelling of the power imbalance as the two participants co-create a humorous exchange.

In summary, we can see from this brief analysis how the wider social context of an interaction can influence both discourse practice and the conversational and linguistic features of talk itself. It should be noted though that cumulatively, instances of a genre or activity also have the potential to change discourse practices. For example, repeated deviations from expected forms and patterns in an interaction can over time change the norms for an activity type. Such a recasting may in turn play a part in how participants' subject positions in relation to each other – here as market researcher and customer – are defined against the wider economic backdrop and the values underpinning it, such as the primacy of customer choice and satisfaction. Any interaction, no matter how mundane or ephemeral, is therefore worth analysing.

Rapport Management Theory Analysis

by Helen Spencer-Oatey

Analysis of the 'Standing' Context

We always enter interactions with pre-existing expectations of various kinds. These are known in rapport management theory as the 'standing' context and it is often helpful to consider these first.

Participant Roles and the Communicative Event

The first thing to note about this extract is the people involved: one is a female market researcher (Angela) and the other is a male government employee (Nahum). Their role relationship is thus one of interviewer–interviewee and the interaction takes place at the beginning of a specific type of communicative event: a research interview. This awareness, which both participants align to, establishes some unspoken assumptions about their respective sociality rights and obligations. Given that Nahum has presumably agreed to be interviewed, these include the following:

- As interviewer, Angela has the right to control the line of questioning;
- As interviewee, Nahum has the obligation to respond to the questions asked;
- As interviewer, Angela has the obligation to restrict her questions to issues associated with her research topic, along with any 'polite' lead-ins;
- As interviewee, Nahum has the right to refuse to answer any questions that he deems outside the remit of the research interview.

Participant Relations

Angela and Nahum have never met before and are strangers. They therefore bring no interpersonal relational history with them into the meeting. They are distant in terms of the pragmatic variable of distance–closeness. In terms of hierarchical (power) relations, if we analyse it in terms of French and Raven's (1959) framework, a mixed picture emerges. They are equal in terms of legitimate (or status) power, but in terms of reward, coercive and expert power, Nahum is more powerful in that he has information that Angela wants (i.e., he has expert power), he can pass it on to her if he wishes (i.e., he has reward power) or he can withhold it if something annoys him (i.e., he has coercive power). This is likely to affect the way in which Angela conducts the interview.

Angela and Nahum seem to be ethnically different, although we are not provided with any details: Nahum is very familiar with Māori pronunciation, works in an organisation with a Māori name, and may be of Māori background. Angela acknowledges her poor Māori pronunciation and so may be of Pākehā background. If this is the case, this too may influence the way in which Angela conducts the interview.

Interactional Goals

Angela presumably has a very specific interactional goal: to obtain from Nahum the market information that she is seeking. In order to achieve this, she will be aware (from her training and/or her previous experiences of interviewing) that it is important to build good relations with interviewees. She needs them to co-operate with her and be as relaxed as possible, so that they will be open and honest and thereby provide her with valid and reliable data. In other words, Angela's interactional goal is primarily transactional (i.e., to obtain the market research information she requires), but she needs to manage rapport with Nahum in order to achieve this. We could expect, therefore, that her rapport orientation is one of moderate rapport enhancement.

Nahum, in agreeing to be interviewed, is representing his company, but it is likely that he was just being helpful and had no particular interactional goal of his own. His rapport orientation was probably one of maintenance (i.e., to co-operate with the interviewer, keeping things smooth and avoiding any behaviour that could cause any tensions), but it could also have been one of neglect (i.e., he might not care at all whether the interview went smoothly or not). However, given the Māori value of whanaungatanga (Holmes, Marra, and Vine 2011; Vine 2019), which emphasises the importance of good relations, the former is more likely. Nahum was also no doubt aware (from general knowledge or previous personal experiences) that sometimes interviewers ask trick questions in order to elicit information relating to a hidden agenda which interviewees are unaware of at the time. Given the historical background of Pākehā domination (Metge 2001), it is possible that Nahum is somewhat conscious about this.

Analysis of the Dynamic Unfolding of the Interaction

The interview itself proceeds in line with the sociality rights and obligations for this type of event, as described above.

Angela starts by seeking to confirm some background demographic information about her interviewee, Nahum. This is standard practice in research, but Angela is extremely hesitant in checking on this. Her first confirmation check concerns Nahum's sector, which seems fairly routine and it is unclear why she would be so hesitant about this. She then goes on to ask another background question: whether Nahum's organisation is a 'custom bill customer' (line 3). However, instead of simply asking 'Are you a custom bill customer?', she phrases it as 'Do you know whether you are a custom bill customer?' By wording it in this way, she seems to be showing sensitivity to Nahum's face, acknowledging the possibility that Nahum may be unfamiliar with the technical term 'custom bill customer'. This is less face-threatening than if she had asked him in a straightforward manner, as it treats any lack of knowledge on his part as normal rather than as something he has to proactively admit. Angela is thus managing rapport through being sensitive to Nahum's face needs.

Nahum indeed is unsure exactly what it refers to and he hesitates at first, trying to recollect uses of the term. Suddenly, though, he wonders whether it is a trick question and asks Angela explicitly (line 5). She dismisses this, accompanied by some laughter. Nahum does not laugh in response, but rather simply continues to check whether he has understood the term or not.

This initial phase of the interaction has thus turned out to be a little awkward and Angela next tries to move it onto a more positive footing by trying to pronounce the company's Māori name and then immediately acknowledging her inability to pronounce Māori words well. In admitting her pronunciation difficulties with Māori words, she displays modesty on the one hand, a value which Holmes, Marra and Vine (2011) maintain is important (for different reasons) to both Pākehā and Māori people, and on the other she admits to a lack of competence. This could act as a counterbalance to the lack of knowledge Nahum has just had to admit to. She goes on to say that she is working hard on improving her pronunciation of Māori words and hopes that if she comes back regularly enough, she will make progress. Through these exchanges she is thus trying to build common ground with Nahum, demonstrating that she too is interested in Māori culture and is committed to learning more about it and becoming more proficient in it. This is a rapport enhancement strategy on Angela's part, associating herself with his Māori affiliation, and the laughter that they both share together indicates that it has been successful.

In these ways, Angela seems to succeed in establishing a positive relational connection with Nahum that will provide a satisfactory foundation for the remainder of the interview.

Summary of Analyses

The CA analysis focused on the question and answer adjacency pairs and the importance of these to *doing* a market research interview. These are a prominent feature of this type of interaction, with the interviewer orienting to her right to ask questions and the interviewee to his obligations to provide answers. The slightly problematic talk that arose was also explored and the way this was repaired. The final aspect highlighted in this analysis was the functions of laughter in the excerpt and the role of laughter in building bonds. These factors all require a careful examination of the talk.

In exploring the way this section of the interview unfolds, the interactional sociolinguistics analysis highlighted the changing interactional status relationship of the two participants. The interviewer was clearly in control earlier in the excerpt, but her later use of self-denigrating humour serves to raise the interviewee's status and constructed him as the expert at this point. The focus here is on the status of the interactants and how this was negotiated throughout the excerpt. A careful examination of the transcript was supplemented by considering what was known about the participants.

With the CDS analysis, the focus moves explicitly to power and the significance of the wider social context on how the interaction plays out. The interviewer is asking questions on behalf of an organisation which has power within their industry, but the interviewee's company is the customer so this gives him a certain status which influences how the interviewer interacts with him.

The rapport management theory analysis explores the excerpt by focusing on the roles of the two participants and what this means in terms of their rights and obligations. In examining how this section of the interview unfolds, the orientation of the speakers, in particular that of the interviewer, to building and enhancing rapport was foregrounded.

Each of these approaches provides a different viewpoint on the excerpt, highlighting different aspects, although at times there is overlap. The approach taken needs to match the questions being asked, so these analyses have shown how one piece of data can be engaged with in different ways. Each approach produces useful insights.

Chapter Summary

This chapter has introduced some important background theories and concepts that inform research on language in the workplace, including **social constructionism**, which is an important social theory underlying approaches to communication in this area. Compatible with this is the **communities of practice** framework which provides useful insights when considering interaction in workplace teams in backstage settings.

Three approaches to data analysis have also been briefly introduced: **conversation analysis, interactional sociolinguistics, and critical discourse studies**. Each approach represents different perspectives and the understandings that arise from using the different approaches have been foregrounded. Approaches to the interpersonal or relational side of workplace interaction are also briefly highlighted, with a more detailed discussion of one theory, i.e., **rapport management theory**.

Conversation analysis, interactional sociolinguistics, critical discourse studies and rapport management theory all represent an underlying social constructionist ideology and they all focus on authentic workplace discourse. They all aim to explore how people *actually* interact and how communication at work is jointly constructed.

As you work through this book you will come across examples that have been gathered from research which draws on a range of approaches. One thing they have in common is their use of authentic interactional data.

Exercises

Read the excerpt below and then answer the questions. This excerpt comes from the same interview as the Sample Analysis Data Excerpt 2.A discussed above.

Excerpt 2.B (Source: LWP)

Context: A female market researcher, Angela, employed by a telecommunications company is interviewing a male government employee, Nahum, about services provided by the telecommunications company. Excerpt 2.B comes approximately 45 minutes into the interview.

ANGELA: mm now you mentioned right at the beginning
that you were a custom bill customer

NAHUM: mhm

ANGELA: er do you feel that that has improved or changed the way the bills are received?

NAHUM: um it has and um I I haven't um talked in depth with the finance people
but I I think overall they would should be happy
that the the billing is um done the way it is now than it was before

ANGELA: mm

NAHUM: so it's more manageable from their point of //view\

ANGELA: /mm\\

NAHUM: the way they receive the custom bill

ANGELA: okay + are there any ways you think
[telecommunications company name]
could improve the bills they send to your organisation?

NAHUM: um I don't think I can comment on that cos I don't +

ANGELA: not your area

NAHUM: not my area //yeah\

ANGELA: /mm okay\\
are there any other comments you would like to make
about the bills you receive from [telecommunications company name]?

NAHUM: yes they're too high

ANGELA: [sarcastically, laughing]: oh that's a unique comment: [laughs]

NAHUM: [laughs]: it is:

BOTH: [laugh]

1. Examine the transcript above from a CA perspective. What can you say about the turn-taking?
2. Now look at the excerpt from an interactional sociolinguistics perspective. Who is in control in this section of the interview?
3. From a CDS perspective, what do you think of the power dynamics as evident in this excerpt and how this relates to the wider context?
4. When examining from a rapport management theory perspective what rapport orientation do you think Angela and Nahum display at this point? What makes you say this?

. . . .

Further Reading

For more information on the theories, concepts and approaches covered in this chapter the following references provide excellent starting points:

- Social constructionism – Lazzaro-Salazar (2018);
- Communities of practice – King (2019);
- Conversation analysis – ten Have (2007) and Sidnell and Stivers (2013);
- Interactional sociolinguistics – Gordon (2011), Bailey (2015), Gumperz (2015);
- Critical discourse studies – Koller (2018);
- (Im)politeness theories – Culpeper, Haugh, and Kádár (2017);
- Rapport management theory – Spencer-Oatey (2002) and other publications by Spencer-Oatey and her colleagues.

Holmes (2014) provides a brief, practical description of the steps involved in undertaking discourse analysis, including collecting, transcribing and analysing data. If you are interested in multimodal data, exploring the unspoken aspects of interaction, Norris (2019) provides an introduction to conducting this type of research.

There are also many introductory textbooks on discourse analysis – see, for instance, Gee and Handford (2012), Jones (2012), Paltridge (2012), Johnstone (2018).

Another important issue in conducting research is ethics. Sarangi (2015) discusses ethics in relation to access, participation, interpretation and dissemination/intervention when researching.

What Are Some Key Topics in Workplace Research?

3 Directives and Requests at Work

CHAPTER PREVIEW

In this chapter, two aspects of primarily transactional talk are considered – directives and requests. The chapter covers:

- some definitions for **directive** and **request**;
- some ways to distinguish between **directives** and **requests**;
- the different forms these may take in different workplace settings;
- other contextual factors that may influence the use of different forms;
- ways people modify the force of directives and requests; and
- how people respond to directives and requests.

This chapter takes a functional approach, looking from the perspective of goals (or functions) that can be achieved through talk at work. Exploring directives and requests illustrates how people can achieve transactional goals in different workplace settings and the contextual factors that may influence their choices in terms of language strategies used to express and respond to these types of talk.

Directives and Requests: Introduction

Directives and requests are aspects of communication that have obvious roles when examining workplace talk: in order for transactional goals to be met, directives must be given (and followed), and requests need to be made (and granted). In all types of backstage settings we can find directives and requests. Interaction in frontstage settings also often involves directives and requests.

Consider the following example:

Example 3.1 (Source: LWP)

Context: A manager, Sonia, and a policy analyst, Genevieve, are deciding on a deadline for a report. Recorded in a government organisation in New Zealand.

SONIA: **make it** [false start]
GEN: the week //before the end of\ April
GEN: /the third of\\
SONIA: **hang on** here's my calendar
GEN: and um
SONIA: don't forget that April's a it's a terrible
         because you've got Easter
         and also school holidays
         but I think I'm the only one that's
         actually affected by school //holidays\ um
GEN: /mm\\
SONIA: so that's the week of Anzac week
         you've got Anzac on a Thursday
         and it's quite likely people will be taking leave on the Friday
         so you might need to put it out to the thirtieth
GEN: yeah I'm sure //I had it\ the eighth that um //I wanted\\ it
SONIA: /but that means\\   /okay\\
SONIA: **well how about then //(we'll) put it out?**
GEN: /the twenty\\ fourth
SONIA: **twenty fourth** (week-)
         so that's before //Anzac\ weekend
GEN: /mm\\
GEN: [tut] yeah //yeah\
SONIA: /or Anzac\\ day
GEN: yeah that would be good
SONIA: so due date //twenty fourth\
GEN: /twenty fourth\\
SONIA: **can you write a note on the on the notes**
         when you give it to me? so that I
GEN: yep

In this excerpt, the two women decide on a due date for a report which Genevieve is coordinating for the team. As the two women decide on the best date for the report deadline, we can see a number of directives from Sonia to Genevieve. These take different forms (see below for a discussion of form types). Her false start at the beginning of the excerpt is an imperative, as is the first full directive. Her next directive uses a declarative form, while the last two are interrogatives. This raises some interesting questions in terms of the way speakers issue directives and factors that may influence which forms they use. Obviously it is not enough to say that someone's role, who they are talking to, or the purpose of the meeting will account for all variation. Directives are contextually complex and in this chapter we will explore factors that influence the way people express directives and requests, while examining data from different workplace settings, different countries and different languages.

Definitions of *Directive* and *Request*

What are directives and requests?

A directive can be simply defined as an attempt by a speaker to 'get the hearer to do something' (Searle 1976: 11). This definition can also be applied to a request.

We can be more specific and say that with directives and requests a physical action is required rather than just a verbal response. So asking someone to write their name down may qualify as a directive or request, but just asking 'what is your name?' would not.

Directive and request are not defined according to form (a formal approach), rather it is acknowledged that they may take a range of forms and that a form which can be used to issue a directive can also be used to make a request (a functional approach).

How can we distinguish between *directives* and *requests* then?

If directives and requests can take the same forms, how can they be distinguished? There are a number of factors that have been used to distinguish between directives and requests. A common distinction is that with directives someone is 'telling' someone to do something, but with a request they are 'asking'.

How do we know if the speaker is 'telling' or 'asking'? In Example 3.1, when Sonia says 'can you write a note … on the notes when you give it to me?' what factors do we need to consider to decide if she is 'telling' or 'asking'? Her utterance takes an interrogative form so looks like a question, but is she really 'asking' or 'telling' Genevieve to do this? Two important questions to consider here are:

- what is the role relationship between the speaker and the hearer?
- what are the obligations of the interactants?

As a manager, a person is responsible for achieving certain workplace objectives. When they ask someone in their team to do something, their role means that they not only have the right to give a directive but they are also obligated to do this in order to make sure that goals are met. The lower level staff members that they issue directives to are also obliged to undertake the tasks required if the tasks fall within their responsibilities. It could be said therefore that with a directive someone in authority is 'telling' someone to do something, they have a right and obligation to do this, and the hearer has an obligation to carry out the proposed task. Taking this approach, because Sonia in Example 3.1 is Genevieve's manager, we can say that Sonia has given a directive when she says to Genevieve 'can you write a note … on the notes when you give it to me?'.

When the job roles and obligations of the people involved mean that a lower level staff member needs a higher level staff member to do something then the situation involves 'asking' rather than 'telling'. It can be argued that the speaker has the right and obligation to make requests of superiors, especially if the action required is necessary for them to undertake their own jobs, but because of the role relationships and who has authority, respect is required and so this is 'asking' and the situation therefore involves a request.

When equals interact it could also be argued that the role relationships mean that the speaker is 'asking' as they do not have the authority to 'tell' and so again this could be categorised as a request. An important question then is, does the speaker have the authority to 'tell' someone to do something? See Figure 3.1.

Consideration of role relationships and obligations gives rise to other questions, such as:

- is there an expectation of compliance?
- does the hearer have a right to refuse?

With a directive there is an expectation of compliance and there is not generally a right of refusal. If the task required is outside the hearer's normal job role and obligations, however, there is a right of refusal and there will not be the same expectation of compliance, even when the speaker is in a higher status position. In these cases, the speaker is 'asking' and not 'telling'. For instance, if Sonia asked Genevieve to

Figure 3.1
Distinguishing between directives and requests.

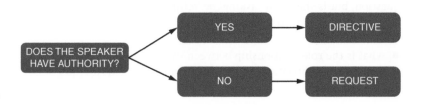

go and get her some lunch, a task which is not part of Genevieve's job, there is not the same expectation of compliance and Genevieve has a right to refuse. Sonia does not have the **authority** to 'tell' in this situation, so this would be a **request** rather than a **directive**. Authority does not always depend on job role therefore, but sometimes on other contextual factors.

What about frontstage settings?

In backstage workplace settings people have ongoing relationships along with generally clear role relationships and obligations. In frontstage settings where people do not interact regularly and may possibly only ever interact on one occasion, then we can still talk about obligations and the rights of the interactants. And once again, roles are important and although we do not talk about one or other person in, say, a service encounter as having authority, they do hold different types of power. A server has the power to refuse a request from a member of the public, but only in certain circumstances will they do this. As a rule they are there to grant requests and this may be a major part of their job. The requestor in these cases may also have power because they are, for instance, paying for services or items and if they do not get what they want they can take their business elsewhere. Because of these types of dynamics in frontstage settings, **request** is the term that is generally used.

The importance of these distinguishing factors varies between cultures. Hierarchy, for instance, is valued more in some societies than others, which will affect whether an utterance should be categorised as 'telling' or 'asking'.

The roles of those involved in some frontstage settings, however, may mean that a speaker does have the institutional authority and power to give a **directive**, for instance when a police officer tells a member of the public to show identification or a judge tells a defendant to stop talking and sit down.

Wherever you draw the boundaries, directives and requests both involve someone trying to get another person to do something and in the rest of this chapter both directives and requests are referred to since the discussion is relevant to both. A basic difference is perceived between directives and requests that depends on status, obligations and right of refusal because these factors can have important implications for how people express and respond to directives and requests in workplace settings.

Ways of Expressing Directives and Requests

What forms can directives and requests take?

Directives and requests can take any form. They may be non-verbal, e.g., a police officer directing traffic, or verbal.

When we talk about the form of an utterance, we look at the syntax. Example 3.2 shows some utterances that are directives or requests.

Example 3.2

a. Imperative: wait till they're done
                         (adapted from Mullany 2007: 128)

b. Interrogative: are dake chotto henkoo shite kureru?
                         would you change the deadline only for that one?
                         (adapted from Saito 2009: 119–20)

c. Declarative: you need to just check the travel booking
                         (adapted from Vine 2004: 70)

d. Sentence fragment: kaks vihreeta Smarttia
                         two green Smarts [i.e., a brand of cigarettes]
                         (adapted from Sorjonen and Raevaara 2014: 251)

In Examples 3.2a, b and c, the action required of the hearer is explicitly stated, 'wait', '*change*', 'check'. Example 3.2d involves a sentence fragment and because there is no verb it is less clear that an action is required and what that action is.

These utterances may also have other functions. Example 3.2a, for instance, may be a directive, request, advice or possibly an instruction on how to do something. In order to decide whether an utterance is a directive or request or is functioning in another way, we need to see it in context.

> If we distinguish between form and function we acknowledge the different ways that people use language. The same form may have many different functions, and may sometimes have even more than one function at the same time. We can also explore the different forms used to achieve the same goal and who uses these different forms and in what contexts.

Example 3.2 illustrates the basic forms that directives and requests can take. These utterances do not occur in isolation, however, and are put into context below. We will also examine a range of examples from different types of workplaces, different countries and languages and involving different types of role relationships, while also considering how directives and requests are expressed.

Imperatives

How and when do speakers use imperatives?

In this section, the focus is examples where the action required of the addressee is stated in the imperative form. Implied in the use of the imperative in languages such as English, but not often stated, is the subject 'you'. To begin, Example 3.3 shows the section of the meeting from which Example 3.2a was taken.

Example 3.3

Context: Jackie and Jane are discussing storage space in the department during a team meeting. Recorded in a manufacturing company in the UK.

JANE:	we could take them over there
	and the new ones could go in to Sharon
	and ask //(her to)\
PHYLLIS:	/either they\\ are //lost or\
CARRIE:	/**hold on a minute**\\
	wait till they're done
JANE:	well at the moment they're over there

Reprinted from Mullany (2007: 128)

Carrie is the Company Director and issues strong directives here. Phyllis has overlapped Jane's speech and tried to take the floor, and this is actually the second time she has done this during this part of the meeting. In order to stop her, Carrie first overlaps Phyllis's speech, saying 'hold on a minute', and then she tells Phyllis to leave the discussion of this issue to Jane and Jackie, 'wait till they're done'. Carrie's use of imperatives quickly and explicitly gets everyone's attention and stops Phyllis from taking over the discussion.

Example 3.4 also shows directives which require immediate compliance but which come from a different type of backstage setting.

Example 3.4

Context: A surgeon and assistant are conducting surgery. Recorded in France.

SURGEON:	**prends, lâche ça** ça sert à rien	*take drop that it's not useful*
	prends ça ...	*take this*
	reprends comme ceci voilà	*take again like that that's it*

Reprinted under STM guidelines from *Discourse Studies 16*, Mondada, Lorenza, 2014. Instructions in the operating room: How the surgeon directs their assistant's hands, p. 138.

In this setting, the directives issued by the surgeon to his assistant mainly take the imperative form. This is a situation where the directives are expected and the surgeon is entitled (and required) to issue them. Actions in this context need to happen in a timely and efficient manner and the results of a failure to comply can be high-stakes for the patient. Actions and gestures are also important in the way the assistant is directed, as is the fact that the two participants here are both engaged in a complex physical and collaborative task.

Example 3.5 also shows a directive in a setting where the participants are engaged in physical activity, with the directive this time aimed at a newcomer to the workplace.

Example 3.5

Context: A professional kitchen. Peter is a sous chef and interacts with a trainee, Max. Recorded in Singapore.

PETER: **come cut this**
[Peter takes a carrot, halves it, slices halves into strips.
He then lines the strips parallel to each other and cuts them into cubes.]
finish the rest

Reprinted with permission of the author, from Pang (2018: 9)

In this case, Peter tells Max to come and cut up carrots. Having got Max's attention and compliance with the first directive, 'come', he then demonstrates how he wants the cutting to be done by cutting up one carrot. He then directs Max to 'finish the rest'. Again, Peter wants the task to be completed immediately, although we could say that there is not the same urgency or high-stakes in relation to the outcome as when the surgeon is directing his assistant. There is still an expectation of compliance and Peter is entitled (and required) to issue directives and expects immediate compliance with minimal verbal interaction.

With Example 3.5, the directive is directed to a newcomer so Peter is very explicit in what he wants and how he wants this done. His actions in cutting up the carrot in a certain way also act as a directive, specifying how he expects the task to be completed. Imperatives are frequent in training situations, where the directives can also function as instructions on how to do something, as in Example 3.6.

Example 3.6

Context: A driving instructor and student are in a car having a driving lesson. Recorded in Germany.

INSTRUCTOR:	wo soll dein Auto?	*where should your car?*
	[student looks to the front window]	
INSTRUCTOR:	**guck mal nach //hinten**	*look* mal *backwards*
STUDENT:	/in die\\ Richtung	*in this direction*
INSTRUCTOR:	**guck mal nach hinten**	*look* mal *backwards*
	wo sell dein Auto hin	*where should your car go?*
	[instructor points to rear window]	
	[student looks to rear window]	

Reprinted with permission from Zinken, Jörg and Deppermann, Arnulf, A cline of visible commitment in the situated design of imperative turns: Evidence from German and Polish. In *Imperative turns at talk: The design of directives in action*, p. 43, © 2017, John Benjamins Publishing.

The instructor's directives not only direct the student on this occasion but also indicate what the student needs to do each time she drives. Example 3.6 also shows the importance of considering what else is going on. The student in this example is engaged in an ongoing activity when the instructor asks her a question. The student looks the wrong way in response to the question, and the instructor tells the student what they need to do to check, by looking behind them. The use of the imperative by the instructor at this point quickly and explicitly gets the student to modify her action and look in the correct direction.

So are imperatives only used when actions are required immediately?

Imperatives are not only used when the action requires immediate completion. Example 3.7 illustrates the use of imperatives when the actions will be undertaken at another time and in another place (see also Chapter 6, Example 6.3).

Example 3.7 (Source: LWP)

Context: Problem-solving meeting between a manager, Kiwa, and a policy analyst, Rawiri, in a government organisation. Recorded in New Zealand.

Kiwa:	**so that means that you'll need to ring [ministry]**
Rawiri:	yeah
Kiwa:	**ask for the person who's actually looking after those [slowly]: say: that we've got this ministerial**
Rawiri:	mm
Kiwa:	**s- suggest what our answer's going to be and then say we- and then ask them to send over the**
Rawiri:	some information about //(this\ okay)
Kiwa:	/right\\

Reprinted from *Journal of Pragmatics 41*, Vine, Bernadette, Directives at work: Exploring the contextual complexity of workplace directives, p. 1401, © 2009, with permission from Elsevier.

The first directive from the manager in this sequence is not expressed in the imperative form. As Kiwa outlines each aspect of the task, however, he uses imperatives, 'ask for ...', 'say that ...', 'suggest ...', 'ask them ...'. His use of imperatives acts as a summary of the required actions and he is detailed here in his instructions. Rawiri is relatively new to his position, so like Peter in Example 3.5, Kiwa provides more detail than he would if the addressee was a more experienced member of the team.

Imperatives in white collar contexts tend to occur in certain situations: when immediate action is required, where the addressee is not familiar with the tasks, when multiple tasks are required, or sometimes when the directive or request has been elicited. They are also frequent during interactions where the main purpose is task allocation or problem-solving. In the interaction Example 3.1 comes from, Sonia tended to use imperatives when giving directives to Genevieve when there had been an extended discussion of an issue. The imperatives act as a clear summary of decisions for action, as well as directing Genevieve to complete the required actions.

So are imperatives only used when the speaker has institutional authority?

All the speakers in the examples above are in higher status positions, so can we take organisational or institutional authority as a factor in who uses imperatives? The focus of a lot of workplace research in this area has been on the language of the higher status individuals in interactions, often because they are the ones who, because of their job roles and responsibilities, can frequently be seen to direct others to complete actions. The speakers in Examples 3.8 and 3.9 do not hold higher status positions in relation to their addressees. In Example 3.8, the shop assistant in a book store asks the customer to try his cash card again because the transaction failed the first time.

Example 3.8 (Source: LWP)

Context: Service encounter in a book shop. Recorded in New Zealand.

SERVER: two dollars fifty
           [Ben swipes card but it is declined]
BEN: oh ... okay [realises he used the wrong card]
           [server sets up the machine again so that Ben can try again]
SERVER: **try again**

The server in this case uses an imperative form to ask Ben to try the card payment machine again and the immediate nature of the required action means that the use of this form seems appropriate and does not stand out.

Example 3.9

Context: A home help worker has just arrived at an elderly resident's house accompanied by a researcher. Recorded in Sweden.

ELDERLY RESIDENT: stäng **stäng den //där\ dörrn**   *clo-* ***close that door //there***
RESEARCHER: /aa\\   /yes\\
HOME HELP: aa   *yes*
                     de ska ja göra   *I'll do that*
                     [Home Help closes the door]

Reprinted with permission from Lindström, Anna, Language as social action. A study of how senior citizens request assistance with practical tasks in the Swedish home help service. In *Syntax and lexis in conversation. Studies on the use of linguistic resources in talk-in-interaction*, p. 215, © 2005, John Benjamins Publishing.

The elderly resident here uses the imperative form to ask the visitors to close the door. Again, the speaker wants the task to be completed immediately, and the use of the imperative also conveys an expectation on the part of the speaker that she is entitled to make the request.

A number of factors have been found to influence the use of imperatives to give directives and make requests. The importance of considering a range of contextual factors has been highlighted by research in different workplace settings, different countries and on different languages. Who is interacting, where they are and what they are doing are all important.

Interrogatives

How and when do speakers use interrogatives?

Interrogatives can also be used to direct or request another person to complete an action. Example 3.10 gives the surrounding utterances and context for the interrogative form from Example 3.2b.

Example 3.10

Context: Takebuchi, a male superior from the manufacturing department of a company that makes dentistry products, is talking to Amano, a male subordinate from the sales department. Recorded in Japan.

TAKEBUCHI:	[slowly]: ano: mokee ga	*well the model [that I am working on]*
AMANO:	hai	*yes*
TAKEBUCHI:	nooki (henkoo) maniawanai n da	*[the model I am working on] cannot meet the deadline (change)*
AMANO:	hai	*yes*
TAKEBUCHI:	**are dake chotto henkoo shite kureru?**	***would you change the deadline only for that one?***
AMANO:	a wakarimashita ano nooki (boku) no hoo de ichioo settee shita dake na n de	*oh I got it # actually I just tentatively set up that deadline*

Reprinted with permission by the author, from Saito (2009: 119–20)

Again, we see a situation here where compliance with the directive is expected immediately. In this case an interrogative has been used instead of an imperative as Takebuchi asks Amano to change a deadline for him. In Example 3.11, the speaker also expects immediate compliance to her request.

Example 3.11

Context: Lindy has been making a complaint at an airline counter but is unhappy with the response she has received from the woman at the counter. Data from a British television documentary.

LINDY:	**can you get me a manager?**
AIRLINE REP:	I can do but he'll say exactly the same
LINDY:	**can you get me a manager?**
AIRLINE REP:	yes I can er if you
LINDY:	good
AIRLINE REP:	give me a minute
LINDY:	yeah

Reprinted from Geluykens and Kraft (2016: 182)

Lindy is not getting the response she wants from the airline representative at the desk so asks to speak to someone with more authority. Asking a question usually suggests the addressee has a choice, but in Example 3.11 when the airline representative does not immediately agree to get a manager, Lindy repeats her request, showing that she expects the woman to comply with her request.

Both Examples 3.10 and 3.11 require the action to be completed immediately, although there is not the same urgency to comply as there is with for instance Example 3.4. Example 3.12 does have a degree of urgency and shows another context where modal interrogatives have been found.

Example 3.12

Context: An afterhours phone call to a doctor's office. Recorded in the UK.

Doctor: hello
Caller: hello is that the doctor?
Doctor: yes doctor [name] speaking
Caller: i- (yeah) **could you (call) and see my wife please?**
Doctor: yes
Caller: she's breathless she can't get her breath

From *Research on Language and Social Interaction 42,* Curl, Traci S. and Drew, Paul, Contingency and action: A comparison of two forms of requesting, p. 139, © 2008, reprinted by permission of Taylor & Francis Ltd.

The caller here describes the problem in a way that shows that the doctor needs to come to visit the caller's wife at home. He is in no doubt that the problem is serious enough and that he is entitled to request the doctor's presence. The two are not interacting face-to-face and this is also an influence on the form used. A question requires a response and when the speaker cannot see non-verbal responses this is a useful strategy to adopt.

In Example 3.1, Sonia used a modal interrogative when the action required needed to be completed in another time and place, 'can you write a note … on the notes when you give it to me?'. When a directive required an additional task beyond what had already been decided, or did not involve discussion, Sonia often used interrogatives or declaratives to give directives rather than imperatives.

A conventional way to make a request in English is to use a modal interrogative, with for instance 'can' as in Examples 3.1 and 3.11. Although the literal meaning of these utterances is to question the ability of the addressee to complete an action, i.e., to write a note or to get a manager, these types of interrogatives are used so often to make requests and issue directives, that this has become the conventional interpretation. They are referred to as being 'conventionally indirect'. For the literal interpretation regarding ability to be understood in these cases, there needs to be an indication that this is the intended meaning: the speaker either says something or there is a contextual factor that means that the literal meaning is intended and an action is not required. From the addressee's point of view, the modal interrogative format is used so frequently for directing and requesting they can assume that this is the function. This gives the speaker a form that is easily understood to be a directive or request, but which is generally less syntactically forceful than using an imperative.

How and when do speakers use more complex questions?

The way someone words a directive or request can show that they are orienting to a potential obstacle or barrier which may prevent the addressee from completing the required task. In Example 3.13, the requestor embeds her request in a question about whether the hearer has time to do something, while in Example 3.14, she embeds her request for action within a question about the addressee's willingness to complete the required action.

Example 3.13 (Source: LWP)

Context: A finance clerk, Clare, is asking a manager, Sonia, to come and approve a payment. Recorded in a government organisation in New Zealand.

CLARE: **do you think you'll have time to come and approve the [payment]?**
one payment that Yvette's bonus payment
it has been paid it hasn't been paid yet
SONIA: okay

Clare is asking someone of higher status to complete an action and the action also involves a higher level of imposition than most of the examples above. It is a requirement of Sonia's job to approve payments but she will need to go to another location to do this.

The request also opens this part of the interaction, with no previous build up to the request, apart from the fact that Clare does not often come to see Sonia and when she does it is always in relation to finance issues of some kind given her role as a finance officer in the organisation.

Example 3.14

Context: Care recipient asks for help from the home care provider who has cooked her lunch. The care provider has just walked back into the room. Recorded in Denmark.

CARE RECIPIENT:	det dejigt stegt	*it's lovely cooked*
HOME HELP:	det v da godt	*well that's good then*
CARE RECIPIENT:	**ve du godt være sød å**	***would you please be kind enough***
	stoppe den ned te mig?	***to tuck it down to me?***
	[Care recipient points at napkin]	
	[Home help stops, turns and looks at Care recipient]	
CARE RECIPIENT:	[slowly]: det: falder ned hele	*it falls down all the time*
	//tiden\	
	[Home help moves towards Care recipient]	
HOME HELP:	/m\\ k]a du ikk selv	*but can't you get the arm*
	få armen derop da?	*up there yourself then?*
CARE RECIPIENT:	nej	*no*
HOME HELP:	nå	*right*
CARE RECIPIENT:	det ka jeg ikk	*that I can't ++*
	[Home help tucks napkin in and moves away]	
CARE RECIPIENT:	tak	*thanks*

Reprinted from *Journal of Pragmatics 38*, Heinemann, Trine, 'Will you or can't you?': Displaying entitlement in interrogative requests, p. 1085, © 2006, with permission from Elsevier.

Again, there is a higher degree of imposition here as the care recipient wants the home help to divert from what she is doing to come and help her. Embedding her request and using a form of 'will' rather than 'can', she is showing more deference to the home help, while also acknowledging that the home help may refuse her request. There is some negotiation here before the home help does complete the required action for the care recipient.

In Examples 3.13 and 3.14, although embedded, it is still clear what action is required and who the speaker wants to complete the action. Examples 3.15 and 3.16 illustrate the use of interrogatives where the action required of the hearer is not explicitly stated.

Example 3.15 (Source: LWP)

Context: A customer has just ordered coffee in a café. Recorded in New Zealand

BEN:　**and do you have one of those loyalty cards that you just stamp?**
　　　yeah [laughs] I just realised I don't have one

The customer here has just ordered a cup of coffee and now asks for a loyalty card. He does this by asking if the server has one. It is enough for him to ask if they have them for the server to know that he wants one. The way the customer words his request also highlights a potential obstacle to compliance, because it allows for the fact that the object the speaker wants the hearer to give him may not be available.

Example 3.16 (Source: LWP)

Context: A manager, Kiwa, and a policy analyst, Eve, having a meeting in a government organisation in New Zealand.

KIWA:　this is a good report this Eve
EVE:　　yeah I haven't read it yet
　　　　but //um yeah it's\
KIWA:　　　/mm I just\\ I started last night
　　　　so Jan like [voc] would like a copy
　　　　have you got a spare cop- a few spare copies?
EVE:　　no but I'll get I'll run off another copy for her
KIWA:　… would be useful eh

Kiwa introduces a new topic to the discussion here. He comments that a report is 'good' and mentions that his boss, Jan, would like a copy before asking Eve if she has any spare copies. Eve does not, but immediately offers to make another copy for Jan. Kiwa's question about whether she has any more copies is enough to direct her without a more explicit question or statement telling her to complete the task.

When considering less direct ways to express directives and requests, non-modal questions can be very useful. In many settings, asking 'do you have?' or 'have you got?' an item gives the expectation that if the hearer does have the item they will provide it and not just answer 'yes'.

A number of factors have been found to influence the choice of interrogatives to give directives and make requests. The importance of considering a range of contextual factors has once again been highlighted by research in different workplace settings, different countries and on different languages. Who is interacting, where they are and what they are doing are all important.

Declaratives

How and when do speakers use declaratives?

Declaratives can also be used when giving directives and making requests. Example 3.17 shows a longer section of the interaction from which Example 3.2c came.

Example 3.17 (Source: LWP)

Context: Sonia, a manager, is catching up with her personal assistant, Beth, who has just returned from leave. Recorded in a government organisation in New Zealand.

SONIA: I'm travelling down south
BETH: that's right here it is here [laughs]
SONIA: now am I going I am going on- on er
BETH: what was that was that a travel?
SONIA: yeah **you need to just check the travel booking ++**

Sonia informs Beth that she will be travelling for work and Beth locates the paperwork for this. Sonia then tells Beth to check the travel booking, using an explicit declarative, 'you need to just check the travel booking'.

Declaratives that use 'need', or 'want' as the main verb, or 'need to' and 'want to' as auxiliary verbs, are common forms to use when expressing directives and requests. Sometimes, as in Example 3.17, the person who 'needs to' carry out the required action is explicitly stated.

How and when do speakers use more complex declaratives?

As with interrogatives, speakers at times also use embedding with declaratives. Example 3.18 illustrates a common type of embedding found with directives and requests.

Example 3.18

Context: A university lecturer, Jim, is asking the department secretary, Liz, to have a meeting with him. Recorded in the UK.

JIM: **I was wondering if ... you and I could possibly this week**
       at about eleven o'clock on Thursday morning
       reinforce each other half an hour on-
       just to look //through\ [name of journal]
LIZ: **/yes**
JIM: **and see where we are**

Jim wants Liz to come and have a meeting with him on Thursday. 'I was wondering if' or 'I wonder if' suggests that the proposed action is only a possibility. Wording a directive or request in this way shows an orientation to the addressee's right to refuse and to contingencies, i.e., orienting to factors that might affect the addressee's ability to complete the action. The speaker does not suggest the same level of entitlement to make the request or directive when using this type of form as opposed to a more direct and explicit type.

Another embedded form that is frequent with directives and requests in some situations involves the use of a variation of the form in English 'if you + modal + verb + it would be good' as illustrated in Example 3.19.

Example 3.19 (Source: LWP)

Context: A policy analyst, Brenda, is talking on the phone to an analyst in another organisation, Garth, about arrangements for an upcoming meeting that they are organising together. Recorded in New Zealand.

BRENDA:	… anyway um now the minutes
	I've polished up the minutes from the last meeting
	and I'm working on the minutes for this meeting
	now do you want eight copies of those or shall I mail them out myself?
GARTH:	oh yep **if you could mail //them that would be\ really good** yeah
BRENDA:	/shall I ( )\\
BRENDA:	sure okay

Example 3.19 shows two people from different organisations interacting, but they work closely on this particular issue. Brenda elicits the request here, having asked Garth what he wants her to do. The 'it would be good' part of the construction is present in this example although it is not always stated and when it is it may be at the beginning or end of the utterance. Again, the use of an 'if clause' suggests that the task is only a possibility and makes the directive or request sound more tentative. In this case, Brenda has offered to do this, so Garth accepts her offer and chooses this action on her part rather than the alternative she has also proposed.

Example 3.20 shows a similar 'if clause' in another language.

Example 3.20

Context: Hata is instructing new employees, Kato and Nishi, on how to manage email messages. Recorded in a company in Japan.

HATA:	meeru saitee demo ichinichi	*as for email messages*
	ikkai wa mite henshin ga hitsuyoo	*check them at least once a day*
	na mono wa dekiru dake hayaku	*for those that require a response*
	henshin o suru yoo ni suru to	*it is good if you respond to them*
	ii desu yo	*as soon as possible*

In Example 3.20, Hata uses the conditional *to* clause ('if clause') to issue his directive. As with the English examples above, the 'if clause' in Japanese makes the directive tentative.

With Examples 3.17 to 3.20 the action required and who the speaker wants to complete the action is evident in the utterances, even when embedded as in Examples 3.18, 3.19 and 3.20. In Example 3.21, these aspects are not explicitly stated.

Example 3.21

Context: Service encounter data collected in a print shop in the US.

SERVER:	how can we help you?
CUSTOMER:	I hope so
	[approaches and places papers on the counter]
SERVER:	oh yeah
CUSTOMER:	**we need three copies of this by three three thirty today**
SERVER:	three copies of this big [slowly]: huge: stack
	[straightens body, maintains gaze]
CUSTOMER:	yeah there's two stacks
SERVER:	okay

From *Language in Society 37*, Moore, Robert J., When names fail: Referential practice in face-to-face service encounters, p. 390, © 2008 Cambridge University Press.

The customer here expresses her request with a statement about what 'we need'. Given the setting and the services that are provided in this shop, this is enough to make a request for the employee to copy the papers (or arrange for another employee of the print shop to carry out the required task). Example 3.22 is similar, although there is more embedding. The focus again is on what outcome is required, rather than the action needed to achieve this outcome and who will do it.

Example 3.22

Context: A caller has rung up an emergency line to request an ambulance. Recorded in Denmark.

CALL-TAKER:	alarmcentralen	*the emergency centre*
CALLER:	ja dav …	*yes hello*
	det fra [by] kirke	*it's from [town] church*
	vi vil gern ha	*we would like to have*
	en ambulance herop	*an ambulance sent up here*
CALL-TAKER:	[by] kirke det på [ø] ikk å	*[town] church that's on [island] right*

From *Research on Language and Social Interaction 46*, Larsen, Tine, Dispatching emergency assistance: Callers' claims of entitlement and call-takers' decisions, p. 216, © 2013, reprinted by permission of Taylor & Francis Ltd.

Again, the speaker here states what they need and, given the hearer's role, the hearer knows what they need to do in order for the speaker to get what they need. Both the speaker and the addressee know the addressee has the power to grant what is required. The use of a modal declarative has been seen to indicate that the speaker feels that they are entitled to make the directive or request, as with the modal interrogative in Example 3.12. Modal declaratives are also, like modal interrogatives, so often used to make directives and requests that they are an easily understood form to use in such situations, even when the focus has shifted away from the action and agent to the outcome.

A number of factors have been identified which influence the use of declaratives to give directives and make requests. Again, the importance of considering a range of contextual factors has been highlighted by research in different workplace settings, different countries and on different languages. Who is interacting, where they are and what they are doing are all important, as well as what else is going on.

Sentence Fragments

How and when do speakers use sentence fragments?

With sentence fragments like Example 3.2d no action is stated. Example 3.23 provides the context for Example 3.2d.

Example 3.23

Context: A customer is buying cigarettes in a convenience store in Helsinki, Finland. The seller and the customer are looking at each other as the customer moves towards the counter.

SERVER:	//hei\	*hello*
CUSTOMER:	/hei\\	*hello*
	kaks vihreeta Smarttia	*two green Smarts* [brand of cigarette]

Reprinted with permission from Sorjonen, Marja-Leena and Raevaara, Liisa, On the grammatical form of requests at the convenience store. Requesting as embodied action, p. 251. In *Requesting in social interaction*, © 2014 John Benjamins Publishing.

At the beginning of Example 3.23, the two participants exchange greetings. This opens the transaction, showing acknowledgement of the customer by the server, and allowing the customer to make the request. The request takes the form of a sentence fragment with the requestor just stating what they want, 'kaks vihreeta Smarttia [two green Smarts]'. The setting is important here and this is a context where gaze and gestures are also used. The location of the customer has also been identified as a key factor: in Sorjonen and Raevaara's (2014) dataset interrogatives and declaratives rather than sentence fragments were used to make requests if the customer had more distance to cover to reach the counter when they started speaking.

Examples 3.24 and 3.25 show fragments without a stated agent or action which function as directives from a white collar workplace.

Example 3.24 (Source: LWP)

Context: A manager, Ruth, and a policy analyst, Jo, are discussing changes needed to a letter to an outside group that Jo has written to on behalf of their organisation. Recorded in a government organisation in New Zealand.

Jo: so probably what then-
          shall I go go back and have another go at the letter
          //saying\
Ruth: **/just this\\ bit here**

After discussing the issue covered in the letter, Jo offers to go back and rewrite the letter. At this point Ruth overlaps her saying 'just this bit here' meaning 'change/rewrite just this bit here'. Her directive at this point comes in response to Jo's offer to rewrite the letter and she pinpoints the part of the letter that needs changing. In situations such as this all that is needed is specification of the object since the agent and the action are already understood.

In Example 3.25, another manager issues two directives to a policy analyst.

Example 3.25 (Source: LWP)

Context: A manager, Sonia, is in a meeting with someone else but sees Eloise outside her office with a piece of paper. Recorded in a government organisation in New Zealand.

Sonia: **is that the final Eloise?**
          [Eloise comes in]
Eloise: well this is to go with the briefing notes
          for the minister
Sonia: oh good one **yes please**

The first directive comes in the form of a question about what Eloise is holding, which has the effect of directing Eloise to enter Sonia's office in order to answer the question. Eloise explains what she is holding and Sonia directs her to give it to her by simply saying 'yes please', leaving out the 'give it to me', or similar, since what she has said is enough to convey her directive.

> The use of shortened forms acknowledges the addressee as someone who knows what needs to be done. The action and who the speaker wants to complete the action do not need to be stated.

Effectiveness and Modification of Directives and Requests
So are some forms more effective or polite than others?

This really does depend on the context. What works well in one setting may not be appropriate in another, due to a whole range of potentially influential contextual factors, such as those highlighted above. For instance, the surgeon in Example 3.4 does not have time or a need to say

'I was wondering if you could take this'. In this context *'prends ça* [take this]' is an appropriate and efficient way of expressing his directive.

It is generally thought that using an interrogative or declarative is more polite than using an imperative to issue a directive or make a request. However, deciding whether the way someone has expressed a directive or request is polite or not is not simply a matter of looking at the basic form they have used. We need to go beyond this and consider a range of factors that influence the perceived (im)politeness of an utterance. The surgeon in Example 3.4 is not being impolite when he says *'prends ça* [take this]', using an imperative, as this is an appropriate and efficient way of expressing his directive in this context.

Different types of interrogatives and different types of declaratives can also vary greatly in terms of how polite they are. The declarative in Example 3.21, 'we need three copies of this by three three thirty today' is not as polite as the one in Example 3.19, 'if you could mail them that would be really good'.

Also, when considering the basic form of utterances, a high degree of politeness has at times been equated with a high degree of indirectness. The two concepts, however, do not neatly map onto each other. Being very indirect may not be as polite as using a conventional form that is recognised and accepted as an appropriate way to make a directive or request in a particular setting.

There are also a whole range of ways that people modify the force or politeness of their directives or requests, and these can be used with different basic forms.

How and why do people modify the force of directives and requests?

Directives and requests can be softened or strengthened in a range of ways, and speakers may see a need to strengthen or soften them for a range of reasons. Wanting to be polite and maintain good relations with the addressee is a possible reason, but sometimes a need for clarity or urgency may be more important. At other times the speaker may be concerned to enact an appropriate professional identity.

Features of the context can soften a directive or request, or at least mean that there is not the same need to mitigate the force. If the addressee is expecting to be told or asked to do something, especially when immediate compliance is required and their role means they have an obligation to undertake the task, then softening may be unnecessary, or at least a lack of softening may not be marked. Another situation where this would be the case is when the addressee has directly elicited the directive or request. On the other hand, when the directive or request is unexpected for some reason then a lack of softening may attract attention and cause problems on a relational level between the speaker and hearer.

Softening of directives and requests is more common in settings and situations where there is not a sense of urgency and immediacy. Directives and requests in white collar meetings are frequently mitigated, with attention being paid to maintaining ongoing relationships. Frontstage interactions also frequently involve mitigation of some type as people who are not necessarily familiar with each other may negotiate access to goods or services.

Modification of directives and requests can be non-verbal or verbal. Gestures, physical actions, touch, posture, body language, eye contact and facial expressions on the part of the speaker can soften or strengthen a directive or request. Smiling as you request to see the manager rather than banging your fist on the counter will have very different effects on your addressee, even if the utterance used in each case is the same.

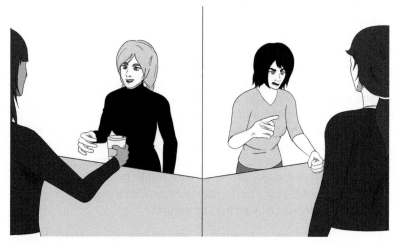

© Jacynta Scurfield 2019

Other aspects of non-verbal communication can also soften or strengthen directives and requests. Tone of voice, rate and volume of speech, rhythm, intonation and stress can all have an effect.

Verbal softening or strengthening can be either:

- internal to the directive or request utterance; or
- external to the directive or request utterance.

How do people internally modify directives and requests?

Internal modification involves the devices that someone can use within an utterance to mitigate or strengthen the force. Imperatives are generally considered the most forceful basic forms used to give directives and make requests, and to ask a question and use an interrogative form is often perceived as less forceful than expressing your directive or request with an imperative, for instance saying 'can you write a note?' (Example 3.1) rather than 'write a note'. Directives and requests are always context-bound, however, so their force needs to be considered in their social and discourse context. An imperative can be perceived as softer than an interrogative when said with a more even tone of voice and in a situation where this form is expected and appropriate. Different forms are appropriate in certain situations so expressing a strong forceful directive may simply involve using a form that is unexpected in that context.

Directives and requests can also be internally softened or strengthened in a range of ways. This can be syntactic or lexical. The examples above illustrate some ways people do this. Some types of **internal syntactic modification** include:

1. Use of (different) modal verbs
   The use of modals (e.g., *can, will, should, might*) or marginal auxiliaries (e.g., *need to, have to*) can soften or strengthen the force of a directive or request. The use of auxiliary verbs is common when expressing directives and requests without using an imperative. The precise modal or marginal auxiliary used can either soften or strengthen the force.

   Modals and marginal auxiliaries can be divided into those that express permission, possibility or ability (e.g., *can* and *might*), volition and prediction (e.g., *will*), and those that express obligation and necessity (e.g., *should, need to*). The use of auxiliary verbs from this last category tends to strengthen directives and requests the most, e.g., 'you need to just check the travel booking' (Example 3.17) rather than 'you might just check the travel booking'. In Example 3.14, it was noted that using a form of 'will' rather than 'can' generally shows more deference to the addressee, while also acknowledging that the addressee may refuse the request.

   you might   you could   **you should**   *you must*

2. Use or absence of embedding
   Embedding the directive within a question about whether the addressee will have time to do something (Example 3.13), or in a statement using 'I was wondering if ...' (Example 3.18) typically softens the strength of the request or directive. Directives and requests without embedding tend to be more forceful.
3. Focusing on the object or outcome rather than the action or agent
   Indirect questions or declaratives that focus on the object or outcome required and leave the action and the agent implicit tend to be less forceful than utterances where these aspects are stated. In Example 3.18, the customer says 'we need three copies ...' rather than 'copy these' or 'you need to make three copies ...'. The focus on the outcome of an implied action distances the action required and the addressee as agent of the action since these aspects are not explicitly stated.

   Internal modification may also be **lexical**, including:

1. Use or absence of 'please' or equivalent
   Adding 'please' can soften (or sometimes strengthen) a directive or request: 'could you call and see my wife please?' (Example 3.12)

is softer than 'could you call and see my wife?'. If there has been negotiation it may strengthen. The use of *please* in English in many backstage settings is infrequent. In some frontstage settings, however, it is common.

2. Use or absence of hedges

   Adding hedges such as *just* in English can soften (or also sometimes strengthen) a directive or request, e.g., 'you need to **just** check the travel booking' (Example 3.17). *Just* can make an action seem less of an imposition. This may intensify the directive or request in some cases, however, especially when there has been negotiation between the speaker and the addressee about completing the action required.

3. Use of different pronouns

   Pronoun use is another way directives and requests can be softened or strengthened. Using 'we' rather than 'you' for instance can soften the force of a directive; see Example 3.26 below. 'You' is understood in these cases to be part of the 'we' that is specified. 'We' can also strengthen a directive, since if it means 'we' the organisation, for instance, it can highlight the importance of the action to wider workplace goals.

4. Use or absence of discourse markers

   Discourse markers such as 'so' often occur at the beginning of a directive or request (e.g., Examples 3.1 and 3.7). They indicate that the directive or request is the logical conclusion of any discussion or arguments that have preceded so can have a softening effect. They can also alert the addressee that they are about to be asked or told to do something.

How do people externally modify directives and requests?

External modification involves the things that someone can do outside the directive or request utterance to mitigate or strengthen the force. Again, the examples above illustrate a range of ways people do this. Some of the ways speakers can externally modify their directives and requests include:

1. Giving reasons or not for the action

   Several of the examples above show speakers giving reasons for the required action. In Example 3.12, for instance, the caller provides a reason that he wants the doctor to come and see his wife. In Example 3.14, as well as internally mitigating her request, the care recipient also softens it externally by explaining why she needs help with the napkin, saying 'det falder ned hele tiden' [*it falls down all the time*].

2. Attempting to develop or maintain rapport (or not) with the addressee

   Example 3.14 also illustrates another way a speaker might soften a request or directive. Here, the care recipient compliments the home help at the beginning of the exchange on the meal she has prepared for the care recipient. This gets the attention of the home help, but can also be seen as an attempt by the care recipient to develop rapport with the addressee, which may in turn make the home help more receptive to helping her. A speaker may also use small talk or humour to develop or maintain rapport with their addressee and this can soften directives and requests (see Chapter 4).

3. Repeating the directive or request

In Example 3.11, Lindy asks to see a manager twice. This strengthens her request, since it seems unclear if the airline representative is going to grant the request from her initial response to being asked to get the manager. Repetition can also soften a directive or request. In Example 3.26, Sonia's first utterance is more direct, but she immediately tones it down when she repeats it.

Example 3.26 (Source: LWP)

Context: A manager, Sonia, and a policy analyst, Aroha, are having a problem-solving meeting. Recorded in a government organisation in New Zealand.

AROHA:	does anyone have the latest copy
	of the questionnaire that they used
	do you know?
SONIA:	that's a good question I don't think we do ++
AROHA:	okay
SONIA:	**you should ask**
	maybe we should ask that ++

'Should' is a strong modal of obligation and necessity and Sonia has also been explicit about who 'should ask'. In repeating the directive, Sonia still uses 'should', but hedges it with 'maybe' as well as changing 'you' to 'we'.

Repetition may not always be immediate. It may occur at different times in an interaction, for instance, during a discussion and then at the end as the participants get ready to leave. Repetition may also occur over multiple interactions. The repetition in this case may just reinforce a directive or request where the addressee is expected to complete a task by a later date, or may act as a reminder for an action that the speaker may have wanted the addressee to have completed already.

The ten ways highlighted above that speakers can modify the force of directives and requests are not the only ways to soften or strengthen. The focus here has been mainly on ways speakers can do this in English. You might want to think of other ways directives and requests can be internally and externally modified in English and how they can be modified in other languages you know. What about the use of negation, pragmatic markers or laughter?

There are many ways that directives and requests can be softened or strengthened. These include non-verbal as well as verbal aspects. Verbal modification may be internal to the directive or request utterance, or external. Often more than one layer of softening or strengthening may be present. The reasons why people soften or strengthen directives and requests are as complex as the reasons they may use one form or another.

Responding to Directives and Requests

The examples above show a range of ways that people respond to directives and requests in workplace settings. Responses require an action, so when immediate compliance is required, the action tends to be completed immediately. Sometimes there is also a verbal acknowledgement and acceptance of the directive or request. When the action required will be completed at another time and/or place there may be verbal acceptance or the addressee might acknowledge the directive or request by writing a note or nodding.

There are some examples above where the addressee does not immediately comply or agree to comply. In Example 3.11, the airline representative initially implicitly refused the request to get a manager. Because a modal interrogative had been used to make the request, 'can you get me a manager?', the addressee responded verbally to the question and did not move to complete the action, saying 'I can do but he'll say exactly the same'. The customer can see that the airline representative is not complying and repeats her request. The airline representative then answers 'yes' and moves to comply and asks the customer to wait.

In Example 3.14, the home help also initially did not comply with the request, questioning the care recipient instead about whether she could complete the action herself without help. Only when the care recipient replied 'nej [*no*]', did the home help complete the action. Again, an interrogative form had been used to make the request, showing an acknowledgement on the speaker's part of the possibility of negotiation or refusal.

Some forms of directives and requests are easier to refuse than others. Because the interrogative form, and in particular modal interrogatives, question and suggest the addressee has a choice, it is easier for the hearer to say 'no' or to question the need for the proposed action. Modal interrogatives that use a form of 'will' rather than 'can' have been regarded as easier to dispute (Heinemann 2006). In Example 3.14, the care recipient uses a modal interrogative and words her request in a way that suggests she is not entitled to make the request and as such cannot necessarily expect compliance. The home help responds in this case by challenging the care recipient about the need to do the action for her.

Sometimes negotiation occurs because the addressee needs more information or is unclear about aspects of the directive or request. In Example 3.22, the call-taker's response is to seek more information about where the ambulance needs to go, although this in itself serves as an acceptance of the request as the call-taker focuses on clarifying precisely what other information they need in order for the request to be granted.

It is much easier to comply with a directive or request than to refuse, or at least to agree or seem to agree to comply. And even when someone in a higher status position refuses a request from someone of lower status, they tend to mitigate their refusals. In Example 3.27, a policewoman refuses a request from a member of the public.

Example 3.27

Context: Interaction in a police station reception between a policewoman and a member of the public. Recorded in the UK.

MAN:	I've lost me key … and I'm scared of somebody sort of breaking in there today
POLICEWOMAN:	hmm
MAN:	**so I was wondering if it's not put you out too much if er you know send a chap round sometime during the check we've still got all our furniture you know [laughs]**
POLICEWOMAN:	well wouldn't it be advisable to get a locksmith to put you a new lock on?
MAN:	yeah me dad and me brother have got a key you see they're both at work and er
POLICEWOMAN:	yes but if somebody else has got the key your key is no good is it ( )
MAN:	that's right yeah that's right [laughs] this is the problem yeah … [outlines possible places his key might be] …
POLICEWOMAN:	**well I'm afraid all the men are out on a murder inquiry at the moment //and\ all the men are wanted**
MAN:	/I see\\
MAN:	fair enough no no okay that's fair enough
POLICEWOMAN:	**er no way we could guarantee that we could watch the premises at this particular time**
MAN:	I see no that's fair enough //okay\ fine
POLICEWOMAN:	/yeah\\
POLICEWOMAN:	**it takes priority I'm afraid**
MAN:	oh yes (it does) I understand

Reprinted under STM guidelines from *Text & Talk 23*, Harris, Sandra, 2003. Politeness and power: Making and responding to 'requests' in institutional settings, pp. 38–9.

This is a situation where the interactants do not know each other. The policewoman has institutional power, but does not refuse the request in a direct, brief way. Her refusal is complex and develops over several turns. Initially, she suggests the man gets a locksmith to change the lock. If he had accepted this suggestion she would not have had to directly refuse his request. However, he rejects the suggestion and explains at length why he does not want to do this. The policewoman then refuses the request, but softens this in various ways, such as prefacing her refusal with 'well I'm afraid' and by providing justification for her refusal.

© Jacynta Scurfield 2019

The Contextual Complexity of Directives and Requests

What factors can affect the way directives and requests are expressed and responded to?

A range of factors may influence the way someone phrases a directive or request, as well as how they respond. These factors all relate to the context, and may not be necessarily independent of each other. They can be summed up by considering five main questions and related sub-questions. The examples above demonstrate the importance of many of these factors.

1. What features of the speaker and hearer(s) may be important?
   - what are their specific roles?
   - is one person in a position of authority?
   - how well do they know each other?
   - are they part of a team with established norms?
   - are they likely to meet again?
2. What features of the physical setting may be important?
   - where are the speaker and hearer(s)?
   - is the environment noisy?
   - are they interacting face-to-face?
   - does the speaker need to get the hearer's attention?

3. What about features of the particular type of speech event or activity they are engaged in?
   - what is the goal of the interaction?
   - are the participants engaged in (joint) physical actions?
   - is the interaction high-stakes for one or more of the participants?
   - is the speaker talking to a group or to only one or two others?
   - is there an audience?
4. What about what else is going on in the interaction?
   - is the addressee expecting a directive or request at this time?
   - is the speaker moving or engaged in an action?
   - are the participants already engaged in a joint action?
   - does the addressee accept, refuse or negotiate?
5. What about factors related to the specific action required?
   - is the action required immediately?
   - is there a need for urgency?
   - is there a high level of imposition?
   - are there potential obstacles that might make granting of the request or directive difficult?
   - is this the first time the speaker has issued this directive or made the request?
   - is the likelihood of compliance high or low?
   - has the directive or request been elicited?
   - is the requested action routine?
   - has the addressee done the task before?

Understanding why someone expresses or responds to a directive or request in a particular way is therefore not simply a matter of considering the relationship between the participants or thinking about where they are. Directives and requests are contextually very complex.

Directives, Requests, Power and Identity

How does power affect the way directives are expressed and responded to?

As already discussed above, people in positions of power need to issue directives in workplace interactions in order for transactional goals to be achieved. Superiors have the right to make demands on workers and insist that work gets completed. This does not mean that they will necessarily express directives strongly and explicitly by, for instance, using imperative forms. And even if they do use imperatives, they may soften their directives in other ways. They are also likely to soften their refusals.

There are a range of ways someone might choose to lead (see Chapter 6) and leadership style will affect how someone issues directives and responds to requests. For instance, adopting a leadership style of being a good mate or a good bloke may mean a person's directives are less direct, relying on people's understandings of their roles to complete tasks without too much explicit direction. They are also likely to grant requests (within reason) or mitigate refusals. Someone with a more authoritarian leadership style may use bald imperatives and more explicit ways of directing staff and responding to requests.

When subordinates ask superiors to do things, they need to do this in a way that manages the power relationship, while also taking into account other contextual factors such as whether urgent compliance is required. Depending on the norms of the culture, workplace, or team, they may also use different strategies to mitigate their requests, for instance, using small talk as a precursor to a request (see Chapter 4). Their responses will also tend to be mitigated.

When explicitly considering power we can identify goals that may affect how directives and requests are expressed and responded to. Does the speaker want to:

- mitigate power?;
- assert power?; or
- challenge power?

In Example 3.18, the university lecturer is in a higher status position than his addressee. However, he expresses his directive with an embedded declarative in a way that mitigates his power. The policewoman in Example 3.27 also mitigates her power in the way she refuses the request from a member of the public.

In contrast, in Example 3.28, the speaker asserts his power when he issues directives.

Example 3.28 (Source: *Soldiers to Be* documentary)

Context: A platoon sergeant reprimands an army recruit. Recorded in the UK.

Sᴇʀɢᴇᴀɴᴛ: Downes … come here … stand there look at me listen

Reprinted with permission from Bousfield, Derek, *Impoliteness in interaction*, p. 151, © 2008, John Benjamins Publishing.

This is a workplace setting where hierarchy differences are acknowledged and reinforced in the way people interact and in this situation the sergeant uses direct imperatives with no internal or external mitigation.

In Example 3.29, the nurses use imperatives to a doctor, challenging the power difference between him and them.

Example 3.29 (Source: LWP)

Context: Two staff nurses, Tracey and Rebecca, are talking in the nurses' station on a hospital ward as André, the doctor, walks in. Recorded in New Zealand.

Rᴇʙᴇᴄᴄᴀ: gonna be a busy week isn't it
            I might have a wee look [7 second pause]
            hello André [pause]
            the man of the moment [laughs]
Tʀᴀᴄᴇʏ: [slowly]: André:
Rᴇʙᴇᴄᴄᴀ: **come here André**
Tʀᴀᴄᴇʏ: **come hither**
Rᴇʙᴇᴄᴄᴀ: [laughs]

From Holmes and Major (2003: 16)

The nurses have been waiting for the doctor, André, who was supposed to be at the ward an hour earlier. While they were waiting, Tracey said she would have a word with him about time management. When Rebecca sees him coming she calls him over using an imperative, 'come here André'. Tracey repeats this but jokingly uses an archaic word 'hither'. The nurses do not 'tell' André off for his lateness but they do tease him and the use of imperative forms challenges the power difference between them and him. Later in the interaction when André asks them to do a ward round, Tracey refuses and Rebecca then also takes her side and refuses as well, again challenging the power difference.

How does the way directives and requests are expressed and responded to relate to the enactment of identity?

Expressing directives in an indirect way with mitigation has typically been associated with a more feminine style of speech (see Chapter 7). As we have seen above, though, there are many contextual factors that may affect how directives and requests are expressed, and we have seen both men and women using both internal and external mitigation. When they do this they enact a professional identity in a way that constructs them as empathetic, considerate and reasonable. Men and women may also utilise more direct forceful styles to present themselves as decisive, and confident, depending on their communicative goals in each situation.

Takano (2005: 657) argues that for Japanese women in positions of authority using more polite and indirect styles than men enables them to empower themselves and control workplace power dynamics. This allows them to perform their institutional role as superiors. Other research in Japan has also shown that in formal workplace contexts, men use honorifics in the same way as women. This is not perceived as a gendered style, but rather enables the men to construct a professional identity (see Saito and Cook 2018: 206).

A competent professional identity for those not in leadership positions may also be enacted through the use of certain types of language. Being a competent surgeon in the operating theatre, whether interacting with an assistant or with other surgeons, for instance, requires a certain type of interaction style with the use of imperatives and actions to issue directives and make requests, and where compliance with directives and requests entails minimal (if any) verbal responses. In other settings, being a competent worker may require a completely different style.

The way directives are expressed and responded to may also highlight other aspects of identity, such as ethnicity. For instance, one of the men in the LWP database, Greg, uses indirect directives to avoid asserting his status in keeping with Māori cultural values. This therefore helps him enact leadership in a culturally appropriate way.

The enactment of status and of professional identity is influenced by cultural values. Cross-cultural research comparing Asian data to Western data, for instance, suggests that there are different expectations and norms in different cultures when it comes to directives. Not all cultures share the same values in regard to the importance of hierarchy, for instance, and this can influence acceptable ways to express directives and requests. In Example 3.30a, Yin, a Chinese worker, issues a directive to a subordinate, while in Example 3.30b he makes a request to a superior.

Example 3.30

Context: Meeting of government officials. Recorded in China.

a. YIN: wai er Lem Fong da dinwa beih   *hey er Lem Fong*
         Cungzei men keur gemyed lo fan ceh mei   *call Cungzei and ask him*
                                                   if he's got the car back today

b. YIN: ngo nidou gong gong xin ne   *I'll speak first alright?*
         hou m hou?

Reprinted under STM guidelines from the *Journal of Language and Social Psychology 14*, Pan, Yuling, 1995. Power behind linguistic behavior: Analysis of politeness phenomena in Chinese official settings, p. 467.

Yin's directive in Example 3.30a is very direct, as were the directives from other superiors in this study and Pan (1995) argues that this is because hierarchical relations are the norm between superiors and subordinates in China, and it is neither necessary nor desirable to treat subordinates as if they have equal status. When speaking to superiors, workers soften requests, as Yin does in Example 3.30b.

In some cultures, age is an important social variable and this may then be a factor in how directives and requests are expressed and responded to. Cultures also differ in terms of the level of directness that is considered appropriate in certain settings.

If people come from different cultures with different expectations and norms then there is potential for misunderstandings and even for conflict talk when they interact (see Chapter 5). The way directives and requests are expressed and responded to can cause problems if the speaker and addressee have different expectations and understandings of what is appropriate. Culture and language at work is explored in Chapter 8.

Chapter Summary

This chapter has explored the achievement of transactional goals, and in particular how people express and respond to directives and requests. Directives and requests are important types of talk when considering interaction in a range of workplace contexts, and may be expressed in a range of ways. There are many factors that can influence how they are expressed: aspects of the physical context (where they are and what they are doing), discourse context (what else is going on in the interaction), and social context (including relative power, status, and role responsibilities of the participants), all contribute to speakers' choices of directive and request strategies. Different workplaces, teams and cultures may also have different expectations and norms regarding appropriate ways to express and respond to directives and requests and these can add another layer of contextual complexity.

Exercises

The two excerpts below come from different types of workplace settings. Consider the data and answer the questions that follow.

Excerpt 3.A (Source: LWP)
Context: Rick, a work experience student, and Tom, a qualified builder, are working on a residential construction site. Recorded in New Zealand.

RICK: do you want the top bit done?
TOM: er I just just want that corner done
        cos then we can put this angle thing on +
        you see what I mean
        you've got see how we've put that one on down there

Excerpt 3.B (Source: LWP)
Context: Service encounter recorded at a café in New Zealand.

CLEMENTINE: //hi\
KIM: /hey\\ um can I have a regular cappuccino please?
CLEMENTINE: mhm
KIM: um with cinnamon on top [pause]
CLEMENTINE: (   ) three dollars and eighty cents
KIM: oh I actually have a free one
CLEMENTINE: oh //nice\
KIM: /so\\ [laughs] can I have another card //please\
CLEMENTINE: /yes\\ of course thanks
KIM: thank you

1. What basic form does the speaker use to issue the directive or make the request?
2. What features of the context do you think may affect the form they use? Consider the five questions from pages 23–4:
    i.   What features of the speaker and hearer may be important?
    ii.   What features of the physical setting may be important?
    iii. What about features of the particular type of speech event or activity they are engaged in?
    iv.   What about what else is going on in the interaction?
    v.   What about factors related to the specific action required?
3. How do the speakers modify the strength of the directive or request?
4. Does the addressee respond verbally? If they do, is their response softened or strengthened in any way and how?

Further Reading

For much more in-depth discussions of the use of imperatives in a range of languages following a conversation analysis approach see Sorjonen, Raevaara and Couper-Kuhlen (2017). Also taking this approach, Drew and Couper-Kuhlen (2014) contains papers that explore directives and requests across a range of settings, including workplace settings. Saito (2011) examines Japanese directive discourse, demonstrating how male managers manipulate gendered language, while Vine (2004) explores various concepts that researchers should consider when conducting research on directives and requests.

4 Social Talk, Humour and Narrative at Work

CHAPTER PREVIEW

In this chapter, three aspects of primarily relational talk are considered – social talk, humour and narrative. The chapter covers:

- some basic definitions of **social talk**, **humour** and **narrative**;
- the functions that these can serve in different workplace settings;
- why these types of talk are important in workplace discourse.

This chapter examines some language strategies, and explores the functions that these can achieve in talk at work. Exploring social talk, humour and narrative illustrates how people can support the achievement of transactional goals in different workplace settings while paying attention to relational or interpersonal goals.

Social Talk, Humour and Narrative at Work: Introduction

Social talk, humour and narrative are all aspects of communication that may not at first glance appear to be important to consider when examining workplace talk. Research on workplace interaction, however, suggests otherwise. While the roles of directives and requests are obvious in workplace contexts, what roles do social talk, humour and narrative play?

Consider the following example:

Example 4.1 (Source: LWP)

Context: Pre-meeting talk before a management team meeting in a private New Zealand organisation.

JASON: well I traced the Hadyns back to the year seventeen hundred
EVAN: oh yeah?
JASON: yeah there's a pirate in there and er
EVAN: [laughs]
JASON: a whole chain of um pubs in Wales + they owned
EVAN: is Hadyn a Welsh name?
JASON: [coughs] no it's not but um that's where the most recent history is
MARSHALL: pirate start the pubs or escape from the pub?
JASON: I think they used to go there from time to time
            and chat up the girls //[laughs]\
                              /[laughter]\
EVAN: /yeah after a after a hard day's swashbuckling\\
            [laughter]
JASON: [laughs] where's my pirating outfit [laughs] ++
STEPHEN: and you're still doing it
            [laughter]

This excerpt of talk comes from a workplace interaction, but could as easily have occurred in a non-work setting. It starts off with social talk from Jason about tracing his family roots and is part of an ongoing discussion around this topic, where other participants have talked about their ancestry. There is a narrative aspect as Jason reports what he found and then the conversation becomes humorous.

The example comes from pre-meeting talk before a management meeting. Just after this the managing director asks who they are waiting for and the meeting then begins. It is therefore at the boundary of the transactional talk; so does this mean that such talk is unimportant and irrelevant to the workplace's goals? Let's begin by considering social talk.

Social Talk

Definition of *Social Talk*
What is social talk?

In workplace contexts, we can define social talk as talk where the content is not work-related. This can include minimal greetings and exchanges, often referred to as **phatic communion**. Another term used is **small talk**. **Small talk** in a workplace context is talk that is defined as not being core business talk. In the introduction to her edited book *Small Talk*, Justine Coupland (2000a: 1) notes that the term **small talk** includes **gossip, chat and time-out talk**, 'a range of supposedly minor, informal, unimportant and non-serious modes of talk'.

Holmes (2000) defines **small talk** as covering a range of talk at the end of a continuum which does not focus on core business issues: see Figure 4.1.

Small talk in this approach includes minimal exchanges which are the prototypical cases of **phatic communion** and more extended sequences of talk where interactants discuss non-work related topics. Small talk can fall at different points on the continuum shown in Figure 4.1. Holmes proposes a number of criteria that define the two ends of the continuum: see Figure 4.2.

It is not always easy to position talk on the continuum as business talk and social talk sometimes intertwine.

What are typical topics of social talk and where do we find social talk at work?

Exchanging greetings is one type of social talk, as is saying 'goodbye' at the end of the day. The topics that are discussed and the level of detail involved are affected by the relationships between interactants (along with other factors). Weather is an example of a safe, ritualised topic which even people who have not met before and do not know each other can

Core	Work	Social	Phatic
business talk	related talk	talk	communion

<-------SMALL TALK--------->

Figure 4.1
Small talk continuum
Reproduced from Holmes, Janet, Doing collegiality and keeping control at work: Small talk in government departments, p. 38. In *Small talk*, 1st ed., edited by Justine Coupland, published by Routledge, © Pearson Education Limited 2000. Reproduced with permission by Taylor & Francis Books UK.

CORE BUSINESS TALK --	PHATIC COMMUNION
Relevant "on-topic" talk	Atopical talk
Maximally informative	Minimally informative
Context-bound	Context-free
Transactional	Social

Figure 4.2
Criteria for distinguishing business talk from phatic communion
Reproduced from Holmes, Janet, Doing collegiality and keeping control at work: Small talk in government departments, p. 37. In *Small talk*, 1st ed., edited by Justine Coupland, published by Routledge, © Pearson Education Limited 2000. Reproduced with permission by Taylor & Francis Books UK.

converse about, although Crystal (1987) notes that this is not universal. Other common topics include ritual inquiries about someone's health, 'how are you?', comments on someone's appearance or an achievement, sport, social activities, and family. Topics may vary from one group to another, and safe topics differ between cultures.

Social talk is typically found at the boundaries of interactions. Example 4.1 comes from pre-meeting talk and this is a common place to find social talk as a group of people gather for meetings. It can also occur after a meeting finishes as people prepare to leave. Although not as common, social talk can also occur during work-focused interactions. Below are some examples which occur both at the boundaries of and during core-business talk. These examples illustrate functions of social talk in a range of workplace contexts.

© Jacynta Scurfield 2019

Functions of Social Talk

What functions can social talk have?

If social talk is not on core-business topics and tends to be minimally informative, we would expect to find it at the boundaries of work talk. But the question can still be asked: why does it occur at all in a workplace context, even at the boundaries? The term **small talk** implies that the talk is unimportant, but as we will see this type of talk has important functions.

Consider the role of social talk in Example 4.2:

Example 4.2 (Source: LWP)

Context: Service encounter recorded at a café in New Zealand.

SERVER:	//hi how are you?\
CUSTOMER:	/hi hi\\ good thanks could I have a a peppermint tea to have here thank you?
SERVER:	can I grab your name?
CUSTOMER:	yeah Sasha
SERVER:	Sasha?
CUSTOMER:	yep
SERVER:	er so that's three fifty
CUSTOMER:	thank you
	[pause while Sasha pays with her debit card]
CUSTOMER:	busy afternoon?
SERVER:	yeah it's been very steady yeah
CUSTOMER:	for this for this time of the year?
SERVER:	yeah definitely
CUSTOMER:	that's everything isn't it
SERVER:	do you want your receipt?
CUSTOMER:	no I don't need it thank you
SERVER:	thank you

At the beginning of Example 4.2, the two participants exchange greetings and the server asks the customer how she is, both classic phatic communion types of social talk. This opens the transaction, showing acknowledgement of the customer by the server, and allowing the customer to make her request. The social talk later in the interaction fills time while the server and customer wait for the electronic payment to go through. It also establishes rapport as the customer shows interest in the server's work. We can see that the customer's comments at this point are certainly not related to the current transaction and there is minimal informational content as she just asks the server if she is having a busy afternoon, an issue which is unlikely to be of genuine interest to her.

Often social talk occurs at the beginning of meetings while participants are waiting for everyone to arrive and for the meeting to begin, as in Example 4.1. Again, this could be regarded as a time filler. The additional aspect in these situations though is that the participants know each other and have ongoing relationships so this time provides an opportunity to pay attention to these relationships.

An important way to build solidarity in the workplace is through the use of social talk. Engaging in social talk at the beginning of an interaction can help people begin work in a positive mood, and at the end of a meeting it can ease the transition from work talk as people get ready to leave. If a meeting has involved heated discussion or disagreement, social talk at the end can help defuse tension, reaffirm connections and help end the meeting on a positive note.

Researchers have examined the use of small talk during sections of primarily transactional talk, or what Koester (2006: 58) refers to as **relational episodes**. The use of the term 'relational' here highlights the role that such 'episodes' may play. Mullany (2006), for instance, looks at the interweaving of small talk into business talk by women managers to create solidarity and collegiality. The use of social talk during transactional talk may serve a number of other functions. It may also be used to relieve tension or embarrassment, as in Example 4.3.

Example 4.3

Context: Interaction between a medical provider and a patient in the USA.

PROVIDER: are you doing okay?
PATIENT: [laughs] alright [slowly]: yeah: +++
PROVIDER: <u>not</u> always the <u>best thing</u> to do is it
PATIENT: [laughs] //[laughs] (a little)\
PROVIDER: /<u>never</u> (just the)\\ <u>thing</u> to spend your after //noon\
PATIENT: /[laughs]\\
           I can think of <u>a lot</u> of other <u>things</u> [laughs]
PROVIDER: [laughs] oh [slowly]: yes:
PATIENT: definitely=
PROVIDER: =[laughs]

Reproduced from Ragan, Sandy L., Sociable talk in women's health care contexts: Two forms of non-medical talk, p. 276. In *Small talk*, 1st ed., edited by Justine Coupland, published by Routledge, © Pearson Education Limited 2000. Reproduced with permission by Taylor & Francis Books UK.

This extract comes from a medical examination and can be seen to ease the tension inherent in the situation. Ragan (2000) notes that the rapport that develops through the playful small talk here eases the patient's embarrassment and discomfort and encourages her to relax.

In the following example, a typical topic of social talk, the weather, allows participants in a service transaction to disclose more personal information and develop friendly relationships.

Example 4.4

Context: An agent helping a customer book tickets in a travel agency in Cardiff, UK.

CUSTOMER: so (winter is the best time do) you reckon?
AGENT: er no I was out there in the summer I went out there August +++
CUSTOMER: that's the trouble isn't it all the exotic locations for <u>us</u>
           are in the wrong time of year //(probably)\
AGENT: /yeah\\ [laughs]

Reproduced from Coupland, Nikolas and Ylänne-McEwen, Virpi, Talk about the weather: Small talk, leisure talk and the travel industry, p. 175. In *Small talk*, 1st ed., edited by Justine Coupland, published by Routledge, © Pearson Education Limited 2000. Reproduced with permission by Taylor & Francis Books UK.

Coupland and Ylänne-McEwen's (2000) examples of weather talk from travel agency interactions reveal a variety of ways in which the topic of weather is treated by participants, ranging from phatic communion and shared experience, to acting as a bridge to more intimate, personal self-disclosure, and as a commercialised topic within the transactional talk of the travel industry.

Social talk may also be used as a way of creating an informal atmosphere during more task-focused activities. One manager from the LWP database who actively and explicitly encouraged a very informal culture in his workplace was Daniel. One of the ways he did this was through his use of social talk. Frequently he would insert and encourage small talk during business meetings. In Example 4.5, Daniel checks with Maureen during a meeting of the management team that everything is lined up for the company's Christmas lunch:

Example 4.5 (Source: LWP)

Context: Management team meeting in a government organisation in New Zealand.

DANIEL: so everything's all lined up for that day then Maureen?
MAUREEN: yep
DANIEL: okay + what are we eating?
MAUREEN: [quietly]: spit roast:
DANIEL: spit roast eh we got a pig lined up +++
            I'll have you know I only put on a hundred grams while I was away

The Christmas lunch is an item on the agenda that Daniel wants to check. Maureen confirms that everything is ready for the lunch. Daniel acknowledges this and after a pause asks what is on the menu. The important thing is that everything is organised. His enquiry about the food is not necessary to being able to tick this item off the agenda. He then takes the social talk even further by commenting on the fact that he did not put on weight while recently away on a business trip.

To sum up, social talk can:

- act as a time filler
- relieve tension
- create an informal atmosphere
- mark the boundary/transition to/from business talk
- create bonds
- build rapport
- enhance relationships

Social talk may often do more than one of these things at once.

Why Is Social Talk Important in the Workplace?

There is a popular view that social talk is distracting or irrelevant in the workplace, but as many researchers have noted small talk is not in any way 'small' as the name suggests. In filling time, relieving tension, creating an informal atmosphere, marking boundaries, creating bonds, building rapport, and enhancing relationships, social talk in the workplace is an important device for paying attention to interpersonal aspects of workplace interaction. This important relational function furthers transactional goals by facilitating interaction across a range of workplace contexts.

In frontstage interactions, rapport building can help the transaction go more smoothly, leaving customers feeling happy and satisfied with the level of customer service they have received. They are then more likely to use the service provider in the future. In frontstage interactions such as in healthcare contexts, the participants may have ongoing relationships so the rapport developed, as in Example 4.3, also has a wider function in the way it contributes to longer-term patient/medical professional relationships. The provider is showing concern for her patient which Ragan (2000) argues can create a 'climate of trust' which promotes patient co-operation, both in the immediate context of the examination and in the longer-term context of following medical advice. In backstage interactions, rapport building means that employees feel valued and colleagues can create a strong team. Research has shown that happy employees and strong teams are more productive and efficient.

Social Talk, Power and Identity
What role does social talk play when we consider power differences?

Social talk contributes to the construction of power relationships in the workplace. It can be used as a less direct, more covert way of doing power. People in positions of power tend to be the ones who manage the social talk at work. Superiors have the right to minimise the small talk or cut it off and get (back) to business. After the excerpt in Example 4.1, it is the senior manager who asks if everyone is there, with a view to getting the meeting underway. Superiors can also actively encourage social talk, as in Example 4.5 with Daniel, and use it as a device to reduce social distance and create an informal atmosphere. The medical provider in Example 4.3 is also in the position of having expert power, so her use of small talk mitigates the inherent power difference between her and the patient.

Mullany (2006) sees power as a fundamental issue when considering the role of small talk in the workplace, 'even when interactants appear to be using small talk to display collegiality and solidarity' (Mullany 2006: 62). The higher status women in her study used small talk in powerful ways, to reduce social distance between them and their subordinates, but also as an in-group identity marker between women, excluding the men present and creating social distance.

When considering professional roles, social talk has been seen as an important device for effective leaders in paying attention to relational goals and presenting themselves as good leaders. The fact that leaders engage in social talk is important here, although topics are also relevant.

In the New Zealand context, a range of leadership styles have been identified. If a leader is adopting a motherly or fatherly style of leadership then attention to personal situations is part of this. If a manager adopts a leadership style of being a good mate or a good bloke (guy) then possible topics of small talk may be rugby (an important aspect of identity for many New Zealand males), other sports or topics they know will interest their subordinates and that are valued by men. In Example 4.5, Daniel uses small talk to help create an informal atmosphere in his meetings. As a leader he tends to project the image of a good bloke (guy) and his informal style is a big part of this, including his use of small talk. The extent of his use of social talk (on a range of topics) contributes to his style of leadership.

Subordinates may also use small talk as a device to manage the power relationship. They may use it for instance as a precursor to a request or as a way of resisting power. In Example 4.6, a subordinate resists a superior's repression of social talk by repeatedly talking about her personal situation.

Example 4.6 (Source: LWP)

Context: Anne, a computer adviser, talking to Kate, a senior policy analyst, in a government organisation in New Zealand.

ANNE: yeah it was a real bummer me not coming in yesterday
//but I was absolutely wrecked\
KATE: /oh don't worry I worked it out\\ for myself and I didn't need to use it
ANNE: I got up and I I just was so exhausted and I thought gee I just wanted to cry
KATE: oh you poor thing

Kate's initial response to Anne's social talk is to overlap and to focus on transactional issues. She is asserting her power. Anne's social talk then involves personal disclosure as she asserts her right to personal consideration, and Kate responds sympathetically at this point.

So when explicitly considering power we can identify additional functions for social talk. It can:

- mitigate power; but also
- assert power; and
- challenge power.

How does social talk relate to the enactment of identity?

Social talk is one device that a leader can draw on to enact their leadership identity. It can also serve this purpose when equals are interacting or when subordinates are interacting with people of higher status. Many aspects of identity may be evident in the content of small talk. For instance, drawing on North American data, Koester (2006: 141) gives an example where the speakers build a picture of themselves as cosmopolitan and knowledgeable of European culture. In Mirivel and Tracy (2005: 20) the topics of small talk (and other pre-meeting talk) directed at the staff assistant – coffee, bagels and the agenda – affirm her identity as the assistant.

Social talk is one linguistic device which has typically been associated with women's speech (see Chapter 7). As mentioned earlier, Mullany (2006) notes its use as a tool to mark in-group identity by women managers with other women. Holmes (2006a: 91) identifies small talk as being associated more often with feminine communities of practice. Again, topics of small talk are important here. Example 4.1 comes from a predominantly male workplace and is one where the managers, in particular Jason, make a great deal of use of social talk in order to enact the relational aspect of leadership (see Chapter 6). Another example from Jason can be seen in Example 4.7. This excerpt comes from an interaction where Jason and Paul discuss a potential employee who formerly played regional rugby. They are trying to work out when it would have been.

Example 4.7 (Source: LWP)

Context: Meeting between two men in a private organisation in New Zealand.

JASON: yeah yeah well Mehrtens has been there for a quite some time though eh
          so that it does put it back quite a bit

Being a 'good kiwi bloke' (see Phillips 1987), Jason shows he is knowledgeable about regional rugby. In both Example 4.1 and 4.7, the topics that Jason discusses highlight aspects of identity valued by men, such as alluding to pirates in his ancestry as well as being knowledgeable about rugby. Women are less likely to talk about sport in our LWP database, unless it is a topic that is important within the community of practice in which they work. Topics of social talk may also highlight other aspects of identity, such as ethnicity or age.

Daniel, as noted above and illustrated in Example 4.5, uses small talk to help create an informal atmosphere in his meetings. The extent of his use of social talk (on a range of topics) contributes to his style of leadership. Of relevance here is also the fact that he is Māori and leading a Māori company. LWP research has shown how in the Māori workplaces we worked with social talk was more frequent within the meetings than it was within the meetings from Pākehā organisations (Holmes, Marra and Vine 2011). Social talk was skilfully integrated into transactional talk, frequently furthering the transactional goals. Daniel's use of social talk therefore is not marked within his meetings and helps him enact leadership in a culturally appropriate way.

Social talk is valued in different ways in different cultures and researchers have found cultural differences in both the use and perception of social talk. Cross-cultural research comparing Asian data to Western data has noted that in Asian societies there is a greater tolerance for and valuing of silence, and therefore small talk is not used in the same way to avoid silence as in Western cultures (Yamada 1992, Chan 2005, Murata 2011). When comparing Japanese and New Zealand meetings, Murata (2011) also observed another difference: the social talk in the New Zealand meetings was constructed co-operatively, while in the Japanese meetings some participants would talk, but others would remain silent. This suggests that there are different expectations and norms in different cultures when it comes to social talk and meetings (see Chapter 8).

If meeting participants come from different cultures with different expectations and norms then there is potential for misunderstandings. During pre-meeting talk in a welcome meeting held by a British company for Chinese visitors, Spencer-Oatey and Xing (2003) note that the British meeting participants introduced themselves and engaged in small talk. There were many occurrences of silence, however, and the British seemed very uncomfortable with the silence and actively initiated small talk. From a British point of view, the social talk was seen as primarily a time filler to avoid embarrassing silence, while from a Chinese point of view, the social talk was seen as a valued opportunity for relationship building. In a second meeting which started without an extended pre-meeting phase, both groups were unhappy with the outcomes of the meeting. A number of factors were influential here, including the lack of opportunity for pre-meeting small talk.

Other intercultural studies have examined successful interactions between negotiators from different cultures. Planken (2005), for instance, explores rapport management in English lingua franca role-played negotiations, analysing the use and function of small talk. Planken found that small talk about 'interculturalness' (e.g., language difficulties, experience with the other's culture) was used as a safe topic. She argues, however, that this type of 'professional safe talk' is not aimed at maintaining rapport, rather serving to embed and develop transactional goals and reinforce a negotiator's professional identity.

Ladegaard (2011b) found similar results when investigating service encounters between a Danish customer and mainly Chinese servers in Hong Kong. His data shows the use of small talk as an icebreaker and to create an informal atmosphere, but Ladegaard argues that because of the context this is a strategic use of small talk to further transactional goals. Both groups, however, were happy with the outcomes since they understood the transactional function of the social talk in this context.

In examining another frontstage context, counsellor/student interaction, Erickson and Shultz (1982) noted that when the people interacting had very different backgrounds (in terms of a range of factors including ethnicity, race and social class) it was necessary to spend more time engaging in social talk in order to establish connections. The topics covered needed to be about 'more universally shared commonalities among people' (Erickson and Shultz 1982: 199). When participants are able to make connections, rapport is more likely to be established, and whatever the work context, transactional goals may then be more likely to be met.

Social talk serves important functions across a range of workplace contexts. It plays a role in helping people achieve relational and transactional goals, as well as enabling them to enact various aspects of identity. In the next section, the role of humour is considered.

Humour

Definition of *Humour*

What is humour and where do we find humour at work?

There are many different definitions of **humour** in the literature. For the purposes of this chapter, humour occurs when a speaker says or does something amusing, and when one or more interactant perceives it as amusing. An important aspect of the definition used here is the interactional nature of humour, acknowledging the importance of the audience as well as the speaker(s). Humour may involve a single utterance or action from one person or may develop collaboratively, but even when it does not develop collaboratively, the audience is important.

Humour may be intentional or unintentional, and may be successful, but may also fail. Different types of humour have also been identified. These include the use of irony, teasing, the telling of anecdotes, fantasy humour, wordplay, and self-deprecating humour.

Like social talk, humour can be found at the boundaries of interaction. Humour can also occur frequently during work-focused interactions, depending on the culture of the workplace, the participants and the goals of an interaction. In the next section some examples are presented which occur both at the boundaries of and during core-business talk. These examples illustrate the functions of humour in a range of workplace contexts.

Functions of Humour

What functions can humour play in workplace contexts?

In Example 4.1 we saw participants in the pre-meeting stages of a meeting engaged in social talk and joking around. The humour in the example is repeated below as Examples 4.8a and 4.8b. The humour arises after Jason says that some of his ancestors were pirates and owned pubs. The participants joke about this.

Example 4.8a (Source: LWP)

Context: Pre-meeting talk before a management team meeting in a private organisation in New Zealand.

[laughter throughout – not always marked in transcript]
MARSHALL: pirate start the pubs or escape from the pub?
JASON: I think they used to go there from time to time
           and chat up the girls //[laughs]\
                         /[laughter]\
EVAN: /yeah after a after a hard day's swashbuckling\\
          [laughter]
JASON: [laughs] where's my pirating outfit? [laughs] +++

Marshall's humorous question about whether the pirates started or escaped from the pubs evolves from the social talk preceding it. This then leads on to others adding their own humorous comments. Jason comments that the pirates used to go to the pubs to chat up girls. Evan adds that this would be 'after a hard day's swashbuckling'. Jason expands on this, suggesting that like his ancestors he is a pirate.

Again, this humorous exchange fills in time before the meeting starts and the collaborative nature of the humorous comments from Marshall, Jason and Evan builds rapport and enhances relationships. It also amuses and entertains.

After Jason's rhetorical question 'where's my pirating outfit?' there is a three-second pause before there is one final comment, Example 4.8b.

Example 4.8b (Source: LWP)

Context: as in 4.8a.

STEPHEN: and you're still doing it
            [laughter]

This one-liner from Stephen, also adds to the humour, but his comment here is less collaborative as he teases Jason that like his ancestors he chats up girls. Stephen has a strong relationship with Jason so the tease is unlikely to damage this, instead building solidarity. Teasing can be hostile however and is one type of humour that can have a negative effect.

In Example 4.3, social talk was used to relieve tension in a medical examination, and again this example involved humour. Daniel's social talk in Example 4.5, which contributed to the informal atmosphere in this workplace, also contains humour as he jokes that he only put on one hundred grams while he was away. As a part of sequences of social talk, humour can also mark the boundaries to and from business talk, create bonds, build rapport and enhance relationships.

In Example 4.9, humour is used to help socialise a newcomer to the workplace. Emma is the newcomer and Gavin and David are her mentors who are teaching her to use a computer program in this interaction.

Example 4.9

Context: Interaction between Emma, a migrant worker from the Philippines, and her mentors. Emma is a newcomer to the Hong Kong office of a company.

EMMA: oh I under-tick the ( ) box
DAVID: what? //this\
EMMA: /yeah\\ yeah I find out the problems oh
DAVID: oh you tick it ( ) give you zero (point) one minute
GAVIN: you make it //[laughs]\
DAVID: /[laughs]\
EMMA: /oh <u>help</u>\\ (5) I leave that flower box blank is it?
GAVIN: yeah …
EMMA: okay ( ) other two minute
GAVIN: two minutes
DAVID: [laughs] thirty second
GAVIN: twenty sec twenty seconds
DAVID: [laughs] thirty [laughs] oh not more than twenty
EMMA: ten times of it
        [all laugh]

David and Gavin, the mentors, playfully tease Emma, the newcomer, suggesting that she can fix the problem quickly, in 'zero point one minute'. Emma responds to their humour, 'oh help', followed by a five-second pause. However, later in the interaction, Emma suggests she can fix it in two minutes and the men tease her again. Emma plays along with it by joking that she needs 'ten times' their suggested time, and they all laugh. Humour during mentoring can ease tensions and create an informal atmosphere for learning, but it also provides newcomers with opportunities to socialise. Emma fails to respond humorously initially, highlighting her newcomer status. Through joining in with the humour later in the interaction, however, she demonstrates that she is transitioning to becoming a core member of the workgroup.

Humour can also be used as an in-group identity marker between people, and boundary-marking humour builds solidarity when the speaker(s) and their audience all belong to the same in-group that is being referenced: see Example 4.10.

Example 4.10 (Source: LWP)

Context: Talk during morning tea in a New Zealand government organisation (only women are present).

ELLEN: I like your chair
NELL: yes I do too …
CAROLE: … aspirations for
          //c[hief] e[xecutive] got the chair next\ step the job
NELL: /aspirations for c[hief] e[xecutive]\\
NELL: [laughs]: ne- //next step: the\ the ( ) [laughs]
KATE: /[laughs]\\
KATE: what you need is golf clubs though
ELLEN: yeah you gotta have a BMW and some golf clubs
NELL: oh no we're working on the BMW
          even if it is rented for a week [laughs]

Reprinted with permission from Vine, Bernadette, Kell, Susan, Marra, Meredith and Holmes, Janet, Boundary marking humour: Institutional, gender and ethnic demarcation. In *Humor in interaction*, p. 132, © 2009, John Benjamins Publishing.

The humour arises from social talk here, as in Example 4.8. Ellen has commented on Nell's new office chair. Carole then sets a humorous tone by joking that now Nell has a fancy chair she has aspirations for the chief executive's job. Nell supports Carole's humour by repeating her words, extending the humour, with Kate and Ellen then joining in as the humour is collaboratively further developed. Kate and Ellen bring in status symbols associated with male power and wealth, making a point about women's ways of behaving compared to men's. The women distance themselves from these symbols, which in turn reinforces their membership of a group that does not value these things, although Nell's final comment endorses the BMW.

Humour can also reaffirm group solidarity when it has been tested or challenged in some way. In the next example the team leader of a factory packing line has been telling the group off for not checking their work properly. Mistakes when documenting packing codes have caused serious delays.

Example 4.11 (Source: LWP)

Context: Team meeting in a factory in New Zealand.

GINETTE: check the case … make sure you check them properly
           cos like I said it's just one person's stupid mistake
           makes the whole lot of us look like eggs

Ginette uses direct imperative forms and repeats her point several times to reinforce it. To mitigate and soften, however, she also uses humour, saying it makes them all 'look like eggs'. This reaffirms her solidarity with the group (she'll be one of the 'eggs'), while also playing down her status as the team leader whose job it is to make these types of demands. This type of jocular abuse was a common feature of the interactions in this team. Being the brunt of such humour, as well as being an instigator, signalled membership of the team.

One last example here involves self-deprecating humour, i.e., rather than putting someone else down, the humour is self-directed.

Example 4.12 (translated from Cantonese)

Context: Team meeting in Hong Kong. Benjamin, a junior clerk, has taken a phone call. He looks annoyed and angry as he finishes the call quickly. Liu is the team boss.

BENJAMIN: [puts down his mobile phone]
LIU: *yeah excuse me Benjamin + don't be so angry*
BENJAMIN: *oh no no-*
LIU: *w- w- we //we've been having this meeting for too long*
BENJAMIN: */( ) my father\\ my father //urged\ me*
LIU: */yeah*
BENJAMIN: *asked me whether //I am going home for dinner*
LIU: */talking to your father\\ in such an impolite manner*
           how //can you do this?
BEN: */[laughs softly]*
                    /[soft laughter]
           [Benjamin smiles through Liu's utterance]
LIU: *{you} can be impolite to your boss*
           {you} can't be impolite to your father
           //don't you know?
           /[louder laughter]

Reprinted from *Journal of Pragmatics 43*, Schnurr, Stephanie and Chan, Angela, When laughter is not enough. Responding to teasing and self-denigrating humour at work, p. 28, © 2011, with permission from Elsevier.

Benjamin's boss Liu adopts both teasing and self-deprecating humour as he reprimands Benjamin for his impolite manner in speaking to his father on the phone. Using these types of humour softens his reprimand. Self-deprecating humour can enhance social cohesion and contribute to team collegiality, as in this case. People can also use it to disarm criticism that may be coming their way.

In summary, social talk can include humour and even when not part of social talk, humour may also serve the functions identified for social talk. It can:

- act as a time filler;
- relieve tension;
- create an informal atmosphere;
- mark the boundary/transition to/from business talk;
- create bonds;
- build rapport;
- enhance relationships.

Some additional functions that humour may serve (and which may be relevant for social talk too) are to:

- amuse/entertain;
- help socialisation of newcomers;
- identify/assert commonalities;
- mitigate potentially problematic interaction;
- reaffirm group solidarity when it has been tested or challenged.

Humour can also have negative functions when it isolates or makes fun of others in a hostile way. It can exclude, mock, criticise and challenge, as well as include, show acceptance, co-operation and support.

The most obvious role that humour plays in any context is to amuse, but like social talk it will often serve more than one function.

Why Is Humour Important in the Workplace?

Like social talk, humour has been considered distracting or irrelevant in the workplace, but the range of functions that humour may serve make it an important device for creating solidarity and building good relationships. As with social talk, the relational functions of humour further transactional goals by facilitating interaction across a range of workplace contexts.

In frontstage interactions, humour can help the transaction go more smoothly. In frontstage healthcare contexts the participants may have ongoing relationships so the rapport developed through humour once again has a wider function by contributing to longer-term patient/medical professional relationships. In backstage interactions, rapport-building humour means that employees feel part of the team and colleagues can create strong and productive workplace relationships. The team involved in Example 4.11 was the most productive team at the factory where they worked, and humour was a salient feature of their interactions.

Humour, Power and Identity

What role does humour play when we consider power differences?

Humour also contributes to the construction of power relationships in the workplace. It can be used as a less direct, more covert way of doing power. People in positions of power may be the ones who manage the humour. As with social talk, superiors have the right to minimise humour or cut it off and get (back) to business. As noted earlier, after the excerpt in Example 4.1, it is the senior manager who asks if everyone is there, with a view to getting the meeting underway. Superiors can also actively encourage humour and use it as a device to reduce social distance and create an informal atmosphere. The medical provider in Example 4.3 is also in the position of power, so as with her use of social talk, her use of humour mitigates the inherent power difference between her and the patient. Ginette's use of humour in Example 4.11, also mitigates her powerful status as team leader.

Because humour can mitigate and assert power, it can be a useful resource for leaders. Humour is seen as an acceptable strategy for a superior to use in maintaining a position of power. It can be used to soften directives and criticism, although underlying this softening and apparent enactment of solidarity there is still the enactment of power. Leaders may be the ones who instigate humour during work-focused talk, and humour has been seen as an important device for effective leaders in paying attention to relational goals and presenting themselves as good leaders. Stephen, the managing director of the company in Example 4.8b, did not often initiate humour, but did contribute and allowed humour in his meetings. Leaders who use and encourage humour are generally seen in a positive light and the use of humour can create an image of being reasonable and approachable.

Both superiors and subordinates can also use humour as a distancing device which emphasises boundaries between the speaker and the target of the humour. Humour, therefore, can be a powerful device for superiors to assert power. Humour is not always about building rapport. Consider the function of the humour in Example 4.13:

Example 4.13 (Source: LWP)

Context: Meeting in a private organisation in New Zealand.

Neil: and when you start thinking
         about driving accountability profitability
         and all these sorts of things
         then th- these are very subtle signals
         you're sending to these guys …
Victor: they're not subtle at all
         they're quite direct [laughs] …
         you're identified as part of the id- talent pool
         and you're not
Neil: you're not
Victor: that's a pretty direct signal
Neil: yeah it is …

Reprinted from Schnurr (2009b: 109)

Here Victor, the director of the company, challenges what Neil is saying in a humorous way. He pretends to select people as being 'part of the talent pool' or not. He expresses disagreement through his humour and this allows him to display his power and exert control.

Teasing is a type of humour that has been identified as functioning as both a playful expression of solidarity, while at the same time it can display and reinforce the speaker's power and control.

Alternatively, humour can serve as a valuable strategy for subordinates to challenge power structures and subvert repressive or coercive discourse from superiors. The advantage of using humour in this way is that it gives the speaker the option of saying they were 'just joking'. Example 4.14 is an example where a subordinate uses humour in a challenging way, in this case teasing a newcomer, as well as allowing the speaker to make a point to his boss.

Example 4.14 (Source: LWP)

Context: Neil is an HR consultant who has just started working at the company. Victor is the company CEO and Shaun is a manager. Recorded at a private organisation in New Zealand.

SHAUN: people do need to know who that guy with bad tie taste is around the office //(   )\
NEIL: /[laughs]\
VICTOR: that's <u>very</u> rich coming from you
          (speaking of eccentricity) [laughs]

Reprinted from *Journal of Pragmatics 41*, Schnurr, Stephanie, Constructing leader identities through teasing at work, p. 1129, © 2009, with permission from Elsevier.

Shaun's comment here teases Neil, but also challenges his boss, since Victor has not yet introduced Neil to the other staff. The use of humour allows Shaun to highlight Victor's failure to introduce Neil without directly challenging Victor.

© Jacynta Scurfield 2019

So when explicitly considering power we can once again identify specific power-related functions for humour. It can:

- mitigate power; but also
- assert power; and
- challenge power.

How is humour used to enact different aspects of identity?

As well as creating an image of being a 'good sort', humour is a device that speakers use to construct different facets of identity. Boundary-marking humour plays an obvious role in the presentation of aspects of identity, with different in-groups and out-groups being referenced. It can mark institutional, gender, age or ethnic boundaries, thereby reinforcing various shared aspects of identity.

Sometimes the use of humour enables speakers to highlight aspects of their own identity that separate them from their workmates, and this may of course be positive: see Example 4.15.

Example 4.15

Context: American research participant, David, and the researcher are chatting at lunch in English. Japanese colleagues of David hear him speaking English with the researcher and tease him about this. Recorded in a workplace in Japan.

YAMAMOTO:	[looking at David]: eigo perapera na n da:	*(your) English is fluent!*
DAVID:	so ssu [slowly]: ne:	*that's right*
MORITA:	[laughs]	
DAVID:	perapera desu hi- hisshi-ni	*I'm fluent*
	renshu shiteru n da kedo	*I've been practicing intensely*
YAMAMOTO:	[laughs]	
DAVID:	nakanaka muzukashii desu yo	*it's very difficult*
YAMAMOTO:	uso da joozu	*that's not true (you're) very good*
ALL:	[laugh]	
DAVID:	arigato arigato arigato ne	*thanks thanks thank you*
	eikaiwa yatteru to kizu //kimashita ka\	*did you realize I'm running an English class?*
ALL:	/[laugh]\\	
YAMAMOTO:	[slowly]: ah: //[laughs]\	
ALL:	/[laugh]\\	

David's workmates are used to hearing him speak Japanese. Teasing him about his English demonstrates that he is an accepted member of their team. David joins in and collaborates with Yamamoto in joking about his proficiency in English as if he were not a native speaker, but this is humorous because he is. It highlights an aspect of his identity that separates him from the group.

Humour can help a manager enact a particular type of leadership identity. In Example 4.16, a Middle-Eastern female manager enacts a motherly style.

Example 4.16 (translated from Arabic)

Context: Team meeting in a company in Bahrain.

FATIMA: *do you want me to get you anything from Japan?*
           I myself don't know what's there
           [laughter]

From Baxter, Judith and Al A'ali, Haleema, *Speaking as women leaders. Meetings in Middle Eastern and Western contexts,* p. 65, published 2016 Palgrave Macmillan. Reproduced with permission of SNCSC.

Fatima is going to Japan on a business trip and everyone has been wishing her well for the trip. At this point she plays the role of mother as she asks her team if they would like her to bring them back anything from Japan. Al A'ali considers this a significant moment, as the team engage in an intimate family farewell (Baxter and Al A'ali 2016: 108). She sees Fatima as empowered by the co-construction of her as a mother figure to the group.

Another type of leadership identity that the use of humour can contribute to is the image of being a good mate. This aspect can also be exploited by others in the way they enact their professional identity, some people actively take on the role of the joker, i.e., the person who can always be relied on to lighten the atmosphere with a bit of humour. Others may not want to be perceived as being too light-hearted in their approach at work, although they are happy to join in humour, signalling that they are part of the team.

The identities that a person enacts may at times be contradictory and humour is a strategy which can help reconcile tensions between apparently conflicting identities, e.g., for women leaders who wish to 'do femininity' and achieve their leadership objectives. Example 4.17 shows the Chair of the Board of Directors of a company using humour to control the Managing Director and to get the meeting back on track.

Example 4.17 (Source: LWP)

Context: Board meeting of a private organisation in New Zealand. Jill is Chair of the Board.

SAM: (the) customer service (is a bit)
           keep hitting (him) with a stick
JILL: //yeah\
DONALD: /that's\\ that's my job
           Ann's job is to massage them and she's and
           that's that's where it's working well
           it's working very //well at Ann's\

JILL:	/Donald's perfecting the\\ good cop bad cop
	um process of managing //customers\
DONALD:	/[laughs\\
JILL:	but can we move on I've got Dave Bruce coming in at one

Reprinted from Schnurr (2009b: 111)

In this example, Jill cuts Donald off but she does this with humour, so builds solidarity as she jokes that Donald is 'perfecting the good cop bad cop process of managing customers'. It is clear from her next turn that she is doing this also to keep the meeting on track as she has another meeting to attend after the current one. In her role as Chair of the Board she has the right to do this, and her use of humour enables her to manage this in a way that pays attention to Donald's relational needs.

In Example 4.15, David, an American and an accepted member of a Japanese work team, jokes with them about his outsider status. Here the humour arises when his workmates cast him as one of them, i.e., as a native Japanese speaker, when he obviously is not. It draws attention to his outsider status, while also showing how his workmates accept him as part of the team. Focusing on 'interculturalness' (e.g., language and cultural differences) was found to be a safe topic for social talk (see above), and this also provides topics that can work for humour. In the following example, a New Zealand Pākehā mentor teases his Chinese intern. Isaac has earlier confided in him that he is not used to using a fork and finds it easier to use chopsticks. Leo then teases him about this on a number of occasions.

Example 4.18 (Source: LWP)

Context: Leo is talking to Isaac, an intern, about how well he feels Isaac has done while he has been completing his internship, including making an effort to attend social functions. Recorded in a New Zealand organisation.

LEO:	and you came to lunch and yeah
	I know they didn't have chop sticks but er //[laughs]\
ISAAC:	/[laughs]\\

Humour is a device that may smooth interaction in a workplace context when the participants come from different cultural backgrounds. But, it may also cause problems. Different cultures value different types of humour, and in some cultures humour is not considered to be an appropriate part of serious business talk. In comparing New Zealand and Japanese business meetings, Murata (2011) found that the Japanese used humour less frequently in meetings. She also found that in the Japanese meetings it tended to be the meeting moderator and the CEO who initiated humour during the core business phase of the meetings. In the New Zealand data, anyone could and did instigate humour.

In examining intercultural meetings in Hong Kong involving people with a range of different cultural backgrounds, Rogerson-Revell (2007) found that humour was largely associated with the dominant speakers in each meeting. The majority of these were Western male managers, although humour was also used by the highest ranking Chinese manager. As in Murata's Japanese data, there was a relationship between the use of humour and the status of speakers. Rogerson-Revell concluded that the humour had both positive and negative sides, feeling that this 'polarity' was potentially problematic in an intercultural context 'where a specific interactive mix may result in one individual or group becoming more influential than another' (2007: 24). As well as bridging cultural gaps, it could also widen them.

As with social talk, participants with different cultural backgrounds can use humour to make connections and establish rapport, and this can aid with transactional goals. This needs to be balanced, however, with consideration of cultural values as to the appropriateness and acceptability of using humour during meetings or other workplace interactions (see Chapter 8).

> Humour serves important functions across a range of workplace contexts. It can help people enact aspects of their identities, as well as aiding in the achievement of relational and transactional workplace goals. In the next section, the functions of narrative are explored.

Narrative

Definition of *Narrative*
What is narrative?

A basic definition of a narrative is that it is a story, a spoken or written account of something that happened. The telling of the story is generally removed in time and place from the action recounted, so is displaced temporally and spatially.

Researchers have investigated the structure of narratives, with Labov's (1972) work being very influential. He identified six key components of a prototypical narrative:

1. **Abstract**: a brief summary of the general propositions the story will make. It usually occurs at the beginning of the story;
2. **Orientation**: essential background information like time, place and people involved;
3. **Complicating action**: the key events;
4. **Evaluation**: highlighting and evaluating the point;
5. **Resolution**: how the crisis/complicating action was resolved;
6. **Coda**: closing or concluding remarks.

Not all narratives contain all components, but the **complicating action** and an **evaluation** or **resolution** are important.

Consider the following example:

Example 4.19 (Source: LWP)

Context: Management team meeting in a New Zealand government organisation. Greg, the CEO, has just been talking about an upcoming work trip he is going on to Europe, which he is combining with a holiday as he will be attending a wedding while away. Blake had joked that Greg might get sick.

> [minimal feedback/overlapping speech omitted from transcript]
> BLAKE: oh well somebody was just telling me that um +
> what fun they'd had
> they'd been where had they been? oh ++
> [sighs]: in the States: and somewhere in Europe
> it was jus- just recently they've come back
> and did you have a great time?
> [puts on humorous voice]: oh just great:
> and they'd contracted some sort of a + bug
> and it had cost them <u>days</u>
> and that was all it was a of their holiday

Blake's story has most of Labov's narrative components. It has the **abstract** 'oh well somebody was just telling me that um + what fun they'd had'. There is the **orientation** 'they'd been … in the States and somewhere in Europe … just recently they've come back', the **complicating action** about how he'd asked them about their trip and it turned out they had been ill. Blake's **evaluation** of the events was that the illness 'had cost them <u>days</u>' and had taken up all of their holiday.

An important part of the story here is that it has a **trajectory**, i.e., that it 'goes somewhere'. Narratives generally need to have some narrative development as well as what has been referred to as **tellability**, i.e., they need to be interesting in some way. Thornborrow and Coates (2005b: 11) argue that to achieve tellability, 'a story needs to reach a moment where the unexpected and unusual erupts from out of the mundane and predictable'. This helps distinguish them from business reports in a workplace context.

Another characteristic of narratives is that they have a teller (or tellers) and the teller is always important. Fasulo and Zucchermaglio (2008) argue that even when there is only one teller, audience members become co-participants in the development and interpretation of narratives.

As with humour, there are different types of narratives. Some workplace researchers distinguish between narratives which occur in pre-meeting and other social talk in workplaces from those that are found during core business talk. In the next section, a range of functions that narratives can have in both social workplace talk and during core-business talk are considered.

Functions of Narrative

What functions can narrative have?

Like social talk and humour, the use of narrative in the workplace can also have a range of functions. Sometimes social talk includes narratives and at times narratives may be humorous so the overlap here is clear. A primary function of narratives, as with humour, is to amuse and entertain. Narratives can fill gaps during pre-meeting talk, while also amusing, creating bonds and building rapport. When meeting participants do not know each other, narratives and anecdotes can also work as icebreakers.

Narratives can provide an outlet for negative feelings, such as frustration and dissatisfaction. Example 4.20 comes from social talk in a medical context, where three nurses commiserate with each other about how tired they are. This builds solidarity as the teller, Ruth, relates a brief incident that those present can all relate to.

Example 4.20

Context: Two female nurses and one male nurse complain about the rota and how often they have to work. Data recorded in a hospital in Northern Ireland.

RUTH: but I think we're psychologically traumatized because of
        a long day + we wouldn't be this tired if we were off at two
BEA: no … see when it hits three o'clock on our ward I hate it #
        from about three to five is terrible …
RUTH: I remember one day last week when I was doing the pills
        and I was trying to talk to people on the phone and listen to the
        voice and I was trying to listen … it's like what? what did you say?
BOB: [laughs]: (   ): +++ that's right and of course
        look who's working on Monday + and on a bank holiday +
        it just seems like we're always working on holidays

Republished with permission of Taylor and Francis Group LLC Books, from McDowell, Joanne, Men's talk in women's work: Doing being a nurse, p. 366. In *The Routledge handbook of language in the workplace* © 2018; permission conveyed through Copyright Clearance Center, Inc.

Ruth's brief narrative about what happened to her the previous week is something that all three of the nurses understand. They are all tired because they work long hours and her story highlights what this can mean in terms of doing their jobs, that even trying to listen to someone on the phone can be difficult and that they must frequently multi-task. The sharing of this story reinforces her position in the group, contributing to team cohesion.

In Example 4.21, the narrative helps create an informal atmosphere and, like Example 4.20, it builds solidarity. Since it occurs during a business meeting it also appears to provide a welcome digression from the core business talk.

Example 4.21 (Source: LWP)

Context: Planning meeting attended by six women in a New Zealand government organisation.

LEILA: didn't you hear my little story
        about coming back from somewhere and seeing this little dirty
EMMA: I haven't actually seen it (   )
LEILA: v- van I saw this little dirty v- van
        and on the back it had flying filing squad
        //and I was trying to drive\ round to [laughs]: see who it was:

XW: /I think I have seen them\\
LEILA: and I was cos they didn't have their phone number
        on the back only on the //side of the van\
ZOE: /yeah that's there's\\ a lot that do that
EMMA: (for)=
LEILA: =mhm no well they were in front of me [laughs]: you see:
        //so just at our corner\ you know like
KERRY: /flying filing squad\\
LEILA: just at the point they were going up Brooklyn hill
        and I was proceeding up Aro [laughs]: Street: or into Willis
        and I was trying to sort of edge round
        and I was [laughs]: stretching this way in the //car: [laughs]\
                              /[laughter]\\
LEILA: //I was a wee\ bit like (   ) [laughs]
EMMA: /(they must have) thought you were a maniac\\
LEILA: you must have been away the day that I told this
XX: [laughs] //[laughs]\
LEILA: /that I'd found\\ these funny people
        and er Zoe tracked them down

In this workplace anecdote, Leila, the team manager, tells the story in a way that makes her seem a little ridiculous and in doing so shows she does not take herself too seriously. The anecdote provides a moment of diversion from the serious topics of the meeting, although it is not unrelated to workplace goals in that it is about a company that they have employed to help out with filing.

In Example 4.20, Ruth's brief narrative added to a feeling of in-group membership. Another way that workplace narratives can reinforce in-group cohesion is when they bring colleagues together as a group by contrasting them with an out-group, much in the way that boundary-marking humour does. In Example 4.22, Paul's narrative marks the team as a group separate from the French team he talks about.

Example 4.22 (translated from Danish)

Context: Paul, IT support team leader, during a focus group discussion with his support team in a company in Denmark.

PAUL: *I can provide a very specific example from France*
        where I was in a meeting with three or four colleagues and their boss
        and we were discussing how they could estimate prices
        when they sell to their customers
        and er of course I had to know how they wanted that done
        so I could set up the system to handle all the regulations they had
        and er it was the boss who er presented their er terms and conditions
        and told me how everything worked types of customers etcetera etcetera
        and those three or four colleagues they just sat there nodding
        and were completely passive
        and er he was very convincing
        and I was like okay I took notes and then he left

and the four colleagues stayed behind
and then they told me 'now we'll tell you how it really is'
and then we started all over
[general laughter]

Paul uses the story to convince his audience that the way the French interact and allow their boss to dominate the discussion makes things difficult, especially when the French team know that their boss does not understand how things work. This draws on negative stereotypes of the French and creates them as the out-group. They are contrasted with the Danish team who work for an organisation with a flat management structure where this would not happen.

Narrative can be a way to share workplace norms and expectations to help newcomers understand the workplace, and as reinforcement of norms and expectations for employees who are not new. Paul's narrative, for instance, does reinforce the way his company operates in contrast to French companies, so may also have this additional function of reminding the current team of their values and reinforcing the benefits of the way they do things.

Other practical outcomes that narratives can achieve in workplace contexts are justifying actions, educating and providing information. In Example 4.23, a doctor tells her patient about how she took a stronger dose of a drug than normally prescribed.

Example 4.23

Context: Interaction between a doctor and a patient in the USA.

DOCTOR: we just happened to have some of the eight hundred milligrams at home
          from the drug rep sent us so I took that for this and I
          I don't know if I should even be telling you this
          because a typical dose is two hundred five times a day
          but I took that I took one of those
          and it just knocked it out

In recounting this incident to the patient, she justifies her suggestion that they try a higher dose of the drug to knock out the infection. The personal disclosure also builds rapport with the patient at the same time so has both a transactional and a social function here.

Narratives may have a wider reach and at times may be primarily transactional in function, for instance, when they provide information or justify actions. In some workplace contexts they play a crucial role in the transactional goals of a workplace, for instance in legal settings where narratives are an integral part of evidence giving and gathering. Even when primarily social, as with social talk and humour, they can achieve transactional functions; in creating bonds and building rapport, narratives can help further transactional goals.

Narratives can therefore (like social talk and humour):

- act as time fillers;
- relieve tension or tediousness;
- create an informal atmosphere;
- mark the boundary/transition to/from business talk;
- create bonds;
- build rapport;
- enhance relationships;
- amuse/entertain;
- help socialisation of newcomers;
- reinforce workplace culture and corporate values;
- reinforce in-group cohesion;
- reaffirm group solidarity when it has been tested or challenged;
- mitigate/soften.

They may also have some more practical functions:

- justifying actions;
- providing information;
- educating;
- expressing preoccupations/perspectives/feelings;
- making complaints;
- disagreeing;
- making accusations.

As with social talk and humour, narratives may often do more than one thing at once.

Narrative, Power and Identity

What role can narrative play when we consider power differences?

Given that social talk can involve narrative, and that narratives may contain humour, it follows that narrative can contribute to the construction of power relationships in the workplace. Personal stories can be hard to refute and so provide a way for individuals at different status levels and in different workplace contexts to challenge, contest, assert and mitigate power.

Narrative is another device which the manager from Example 4.5, Daniel, frequently uses in creating an informal atmosphere and building solidarity in his meetings. The importance of narrative as a tool for leaders to build solidarity is a factor which has been picked up by business consultants. Unlike social talk and humour, which have been viewed negatively, narrative is seen in a positive light. Gargiulo (2006: 62) goes so far as to state that '(f)or leaders strategically focused on the critical nature of relationships, the capacity of stories to help people bond is one of the greatest tools they have at their disposal'.

When we consider Example 4.21, we can see Leila, the manager, uses her narrative to make herself seem a little ridiculous. This has the effect of creating solidarity and mitigating the authority she has as the team's leader. Another woman leader from a different workplace context, however, uses stories in a quite different way in order to enact her position as leader. In Example 4.11, we saw Ginette using abusive humour to mitigate directives. In the next example, she is a participant in the story she tells, but as an observer of ridiculous behaviour by someone else.

Example 4.24 (Source: LWP)

Context: Ginette, team leader, talking to a member of her team on the packing line in a New Zealand factory.

GINETTE: yesterday + afternoon Christian and I were standing at the end
by the elevator over there talking
and David was coming round with the vacuum by the two kilo
elevator + …
and then he went over to clean that trail of powder + alongside the
wall + what he did h- he disconnected the hose off + off the end piece
and then he walked over
and he swept [voc] + the trail [laughs]: of powder up with that:
HELENA: how stupid

Reprinted with permission from Holmes, Janet and Marra, Meredith, Narrative and the construction of professional identity in the workplace, p. 207. In *The sociolinguistics of narrative*, © 2005, John Benjamins Publishing.

© Jacynta Scurfield 2019

In this story then, David is the one who is held up for ridicule, while Ginette constructs herself and, by association, the person she is interacting with, as the smart ones. She builds solidarity then, but in quite a different way from that seen in Example 4.21.

Superiors can use narratives in their own talk, as well as actively encouraging others to provide narratives. They can also cut them off, as we saw Kate try to do with Anne in Example 4.6. Anne's insistence on continuing with her narrative also shows how subordinates can use narrative to challenge power.

The content of narratives can also play this role, as individuals can use their stories to highlight issues they want to contest. In Example 4.25, Peter and Niels have been criticising the company and Natalie uses her narrative to disagree with them.

Example 4.25 (translated from Danish)

Context: Natalie, Head of Sales and Project Proposals, in a meeting with Peter and Niels, engineers who work in another department. Recorded in Denmark.

NATALIE: *you know I lost this guy*
            Hans Christian Nissen he worked for me
            you know the guy who died
PETER: *really? oh my goodness*
NATALIE: *Sunday it was didn't you see it on the news channel? …*
            [slowly]: er: his wife called me Monday morning
            yesterday it was and she told me he was dead
PETER: *okay*
NATALIE: *and she was confused of course right and didn't know who*
            she should talk to she'd like to talk to somebody from PFA [Pension Fund]
            you know so I promised I'd call HR and ask
            and you know HR were just absolutely amazing
            they just took over completely
NIELS: *really?*
NATALIE: *and found the names and took care of everything you know*

Natalie uses her narrative as an indirect disagreement strategy. Her story contests Peter and Niels's negative opinions of the company and presents the company as one which cares about its workers. Using narrative allows Natalie to do this in a way that challenges their views, while making it difficult for them to contest hers.

So when explicitly considering power we can identify additional functions for narratives. They can:

- mitigate power; but also
- assert power; and
- challenge power.

How does telling stories help people enact other aspects of identity?

As with social talk and humour, various aspects of identity may be expressed through narrative and narrative can function on several levels at once. Narratives reflect personal, social and professional identities and because narratives tell stories, they are a useful device in constructing and enacting identity. When identity is viewed as dynamic and as something that emerges and is negotiated through talk, then narratives 'tell who we are: they are central to our social and cultural identity' (Thornborrow and Coates 2005b: 7). Storytelling can be used as a creative and socially acceptable strategy for expressing both personal and professional identity in a workplace context.

Differences have been found in the ways men and women tell stories, so not only can the topics of stories help men and women enact their gender identity, but this can also be evident in the way the narratives are told. Men tend to prefer solo-narrative, while women's stories are more likely to be told collaboratively (Coates 2005: 89).

Narrative is considered a universal that applies across all social and cultural groups, but different cultures have different conventions for storytelling. In some cultures, for instance, it is quite acceptable to tell 'hero stories'. In these narratives, the teller is depicted as doing something commendable or wonderful. In cultures where modesty is valued, telling hero stories can create problems for the teller, who may be perceived as overly confident and boastful. In this type of culture it is more likely to find stories where the teller plays up the role of others and plays down the importance of their own role, as in Example 4.26.

Example 4.26 (Source: LWP)

Context: General staff meeting in a private Māori organisation in New Zealand. Yvonne, the managing director, is giving her monthly report.

YVONNE: yesterday I talked I had to give a
          presentation ( ) conference
          I was invited by [name] …
          I felt the presentation wasn't that good
          because my briefing was about
          a two-second phone [laughs]: call:
          [laughter]

Yvonne here tells how she gave a presentation at a conference on behalf of the company. She criticises her performance, and makes a joke out of the situation. Her self-deprecating story here shows her presenting herself in a way that is consistent with Māori cultural values of being humble; she does not present herself as the hero. However, it is acceptable for others to give praise, as one of her employees who was present at the conference does shortly after Yvonne's assessment of her own performance. Yvonne does not lack confidence and is a strong leader, but does not sing her own praises.

Since the norms and expectations for the use of narrative vary between cultures, this can have implications when people from different cultures interact. Yvonne's story in Example 4.26, for instance, when viewed from a Western perspective, would suggest that she is not a confident leader, when we know that she is (from our extensive recording and observation) and that she is expressing herself here in a way that is consistent with her cultural values.

For people planning to work in a different country, there can also be serious implications when their norms for telling narratives differ. In an analysis of job interviews for low-status positions in the UK, Roberts (2013) found that applicants with immigrant backgrounds were usually not successful in securing employment because they were unable to produce appropriate narratives. Failure to understand the norms and expectations of telling and interpreting workplace narratives in a new culture, therefore, means that migrants may suffer exclusion. Reissner-Roubicek (2010) found similar results in interviews for professional positions in New Zealand.

> Narratives serve important functions across a range of workplace contexts. They can help people enact various aspects of their identities, as well as playing a role in the achievement of relational and transactional workplace goals.

Chapter Summary

This chapter has explored the achievement of primarily relational goals, and in particular the use and functions of social talk, humour and narrative in workplace interaction. Social talk, humour and narrative have all been regarded as dispensable in workplace contexts. They are often off-topic, but this does not mean that they are irrelevant or unimportant. Teambuilding and relational work are essential across a range of workplace contexts, and social talk, humour and narrative can all play key roles in these processes. In fulfilling relational goals at work, social talk, humour and narrative further transactional goals. Narrative may also serve transactional goals, having a role more explicitly at the cross-over between transactional and relational talk.

When considering power we can identify additional functions. Social talk, humour and narrative can:

- mitigate power; but also
- assert power; and
- challenge power.

Exercises

Use the excerpt below to answer the questions.

Excerpt 4.A (Source: LWP)

Context: Management team meeting in a private organisation in New Zealand. The team have been discussing problems with products and service provided to them by another organisation. Stephen and Jason have had a meeting with two men, Jack and Lenny, from the other organisation to try and get their complaints addressed, and will be going to meet them again.

> [Laughter throughout – not noted in transcript]
>
> STEPHEN: but Jack knows he is gonna get absolutely hammered [*criticised forcefully*] +
> the last time this happened it was in front of his boss as well
> but he's just such an idiot he needs it
> he got his business card out
> and started writing the complaints on the back of his business card
> and he ran out of space ++
> and Lenny Lenny head honcho kept saying haven't you got a pad
> haven't you got a pad get a pad ...
> and he kept writing on this //card\
>
> JASON: /and\\ then Stephen says and then another thing
> and then he goes you're gonna run out of business //[laughs]: cards soon:\
>
> STEPHEN: /that's what he said
> and then he said make sure you \\ don't put them in
> and give them to someone + (all those complaints on them)
> I said to Jason we should cut down a little tiny pad + about that big
>
> JASON: a really thick pad [laughs]
>
> STEPHEN: give it to him and tell them to take some note
> because we've got some big problems

Exercise 4.1 (social talk aspects)

1. What do you think is going on here?
2. Is this social talk, core business talk or somewhere in-between?

Exercise 4.2 (humour aspects)

1. What functions does the use of humour have here?
2. What image does this humour create of the other organisation?
3. What does the way the humour develops suggest about the relationship between the two speakers?

Exercise 4.3 (narrative aspects)

1. Can you identify Labov's narrative components in the excerpt?
   Abstract: a brief summary of the general propositions the story will make. It usually occurs at the beginning of the story;
   Orientation: essential background information like time, place and people involved;
   Complicating action: the key events;
   Evaluation: highlighting and evaluating the point;
   Resolution: how the crisis/complicating action was resolved;
   Coda: closing or concluding remarks.
2. Why is this story tellable?
3. How do the speakers create a line between their own company and the other organisation in the story?

....

Further Reading

To further explore the topic of social talk, the chapters in Coupland's edited book *Small Talk* (Coupland 2000b) provide an excellent starting point. Two recent papers which explore small talk in medical settings are Benwell and McCreadie (2016) and Van De Mieroop (2016). Holmes and Stubbe (2015) includes chapters on small talk and humour, while Schnurr (2009b) provides a useful introduction to humour in business meetings. Holmes (2006a) covers humour, social talk and narrative in relation to gender. De Fina and Georgakopoulou (2015) provide comprehensive coverage of research on narrative, while the chapters in Thornborrow and Coates (2005a) analyse the use and functions of narratives in a wide range of contexts, including the workplace (Holmes and Marra 2005).

5 Complaints, Disagreement and Conflict Talk at Work

CHAPTER PREVIEW

In this chapter some potentially problematic aspects of workplace talk are considered: complaints, disagreement, and conflict talk. The chapter covers:

- some basic definitions of **complaint**, **disagreement** and **conflict talk**;
- how people manage these types of talk in a range of workplace settings;
- what factors influence how complaints and disagreement are expressed and responded to;
- what distinguishes conflict talk from complaints and disagreement.

This chapter takes a functional approach, looking from the perspective of goals (or functions) that can be achieved through talk at work, and in exploring complaints and disagreements illustrates how people can achieve transactional goals while managing interpersonal ones. At times this can lead to conflict talk and the management of this type of talk is also examined.

Complaints, Disagreement and Conflict Talk: Introduction

Chapter 4 considered some aspects of talk that can be used to maintain good relationships in workplace contexts: social talk, humour and narrative. It was also noted how, at times, these can be used to contest power relationships and to express disagreement. Using social talk, humour and narrative in such contexts is generally regarded as a socially acceptable way to manage difficult situations. In this chapter, the focus is more explicitly on potentially problematic talk, namely complaints, disagreement and conflict talk, and how these types of talk are handled in workplace interaction. They may be managed through the use of social talk, humour and narrative, but what other strategies do people use?

Consider the following example from an interaction between two women in a government organisation. The section manager, Jocelyn, and IT administrator, Antonia, are discussing Antonia's work and engage in problem-solving. Jocelyn has asked Antonia to think about producing instructions for employees on using a new scanner and the main ways it will be used.

Example 5.1 (Source: LWP)

Context: Jocelyn, a manager, and Antonia, an IT administrator, discussing work issues. Recorded in a government organisation in New Zealand.

```
ANTONIA:   I'll try and suss out the main things like just scanning a text //document\
JOCELYN:                                                              /mm\\
           [tut] cos that is what people are //going to be\ doing here=
ANTONIA:                                     /but\\
ANTONIA:   =yeah=
JOCELYN:        =well
ANTONIA:   but there's a lot of other things
           like putting in a picture
           and then bringing your document
           and putting the picture into the document
JOCELYN:   but we're=
ANTONIA:           =that's quite complicated=
JOCELYN:                           =s- but seriously
           what documents are we going to be producing here with
           pictures in + we aren't in the business of picture documents
ANTONIA:   people might //create\ their own newsletter
JOCELYN:                /no\\
ANTONIA:   don't they have a [newsletter name] newsletter or something
           //along those lines\
JOCELYN:   /they're not\\ going to do that
ANTONIA:   they're not gonna //do\ that? [laughs]=
JOCELYN:                      /no\\                =certainly not in the near future
```

In this extract Antonia suggests some tasks for which employees may need technology support when using the new scanner. Jocelyn agrees with Antonia's first idea, but when Antonia suggests people will want to put pictures into documents, Jocelyn explicitly disagrees with this. She does this by directly challenging Antonia, 'but seriously what documents are we going to be producing here with pictures in?' Antonia goes on to suggest a reason people might need to do this, 'people might create their own newsletter', but Jocelyn overlaps her, saying 'no'. Antonia provides some more reasons and justification but Jocelyn continues to disagree emphatically.

Activities such as problem-solving may involve expressing differing views and are a key type of interaction found in many workplaces. Disagreement may arise and this can be helpful in reaching a satisfactory outcome: effective problem-solving often involves disagreement and the presentation of opposing ideas. At other times, disagreement may result in more direct conflict, which can undermine the goals of a workplace. Complaints can also threaten the achievement of both transactional and relational goals. To begin, we examine complaints and consider how this potentially problematic aspect of talk may be managed.

Complaints

Definition of *Complaint*

What is a complaint and where do we find complaints at work?

A complaint is when someone expresses dissatisfaction about an issue or with an item, an action or with something someone has said. Complaining can challenge, contest, and criticise. Because a problem may have practical implications within workplace settings, it is important for complaints to be made and problems to be brought to the attention of the people who can fix them.

The complaints considered in this section are ones where the person or organisation who is the target of the complaint is the recipient (or addressee) of the complaint. These have been referred to as **direct** complaints. Of course people also often complain about things to someone who is not the target and who has no power to fix the problem, for instance, when a worker goes home and complains to family members about a colleague. These complaints are known as whinges, third party or indirect complaints and will not be considered below. In the following discussion, the terms **direct** and **indirect** refer to the use of strategies by speakers to either explicitly or implicitly express and respond to complaints rather than a type of complaint.

Complaints can potentially be found in any workplace setting. Wherever a problem can arise, complaints may be made. However, there are some settings and activity types where complaints may be an expected part of the interaction. One major role of customer enquiry desks in shops and telephone help lines is to handle complaints and help solve customer and client problems.

Across a range of workplaces, there are also types of interactions where complaints may be an expected part of the interaction, or if not expected then there is always the potential for complaints. This includes team briefing meetings at the beginning or end of the day where any problems from the previous work shift may be highlighted so that they can be avoided on the next shift. Work performance reviews are another context where complaints may arise, again with the aim of addressing any problems and improving a worker's output or performance. We begin by considering some examples of complaints from backstage settings.

Expressing and Responding to Complaints
How are complaints expressed and responded to in backstage settings?

Complaints can be expressed in many ways. Chapter 4 illustrated how humour may mitigate complaints. In Example 4.11 for instance, Ginette, a factory team leader, used humour to soften her criticism of her team as she urged them to check their work. In Example 5.2, she is engaged in a one-to-one interaction, complaining to a worker who has not been checking the product boxes properly on the factory production line.

Example 5.2 (Source: LWP)

Context: Interaction between Ginette, team leader, and a member of her team. Recorded on the packing line in a factory in New Zealand.

GINETTE: [picks up a box and pats it] you know when you check these right
            you're supposed to look at the carton to make sure it's not leaking
            not like this? [pats box and looks away]
SAM: [sarcastically]: oh that's that's good checking:
GINETTE: //[humorous tone]: you're not going to see anything if you're like this:\
SAM: /that's all right that's all right\\ that's all right
GINETTE: oh my gosh [smiles]
SAM: [laughs]

Ginette makes a complaint, as is necessary in this situation. The boxes need to be checked to ensure they are not leaking; if they leak the stock cannot be sold and will be sent back, which will cost the company money. Ginette handles this in a way that makes a joke of the way the packer has been checking without looking carefully at what he is doing.

Sam responds to the complaint in a positive way. He sarcastically notes that Ginette's checking performance is 'good' when it obviously is not, and acknowledges her point that in order to check the boxes you need to look at them carefully.

This example shows one way a complaint can be softened. Making a complaint is a situation where disagreement and conflict can arise, which is why people often express complaints in a way that defuses tension, as in Example 5.2, where the complainant uses humour.

In other cases, someone might handle a complaint or criticism by aiming it at a group rather than an individual: see Example 5.3.

Example 5.3 (Source: LWP)

Context: Team meeting in a government organisation in New Zealand. Hera is the manager.

```
            [minimal feedback not marked in the transcript]
HERA:    which leads me onto one other item
            which I haven't got on the um agenda
            madam chair is it alright if I?
RIPEKA:  (mhm) yep
HERA:    and that's the um issue of writing [inhales] um +
            when [slowly]: um: whenever you er are drafting
            I've noticed a couple of mistakes creeping into our work
            and that's stuff that e- that even that I've signed out
            and I notice it because the letters get circulated through
            all all the letters that go out of the ministry get circulated through
            the what's called the day file through er each manager
            as well as our own [unit name] file
            and I've suddenly as I'm rereading I spot a spelling mistake
            which I didn't see the first time round or a grammatical mistake …
            I really make a plea for all of you
            to make sure that you take it to one other person
            at least + to um to peer review before you
            before either you sign it out
            or even when you send it to me to sign out
            okay must be peer reviewed by others #
            course when you're doing a big chunk of work
            then that's normal for us t- we always do that peer review
            but just simple letters even +
            make sure that they're peer reviewed
            it's so easy to overlook just a simple mistake
            and the less mistakes we send out on our + the better
```

In this example the manager of the group, Hera, is complaining that the staff have been sending out documents with mistakes in them. She downplays the extent of the problem, saying she has noticed 'a couple of mistakes', and also takes some of the blame onto herself, 'that's stuff that e- that even I've signed out'. Having identified the problem she then outlines her solution. She makes this an issue for the whole team (including herself), rather than focusing on the one or two people who may be the main culprits. This example also illustrates the way complaints tend to develop. They are not usually restricted to one or two utterances but emerge through longer turns of talk.

The responses of the team are not noted here but there is some minimal feedback and agreement and people nod as she talks. The fact that the complaint is being made to the group rather than in a one-to-one situation is one reason that the responses are not extended.

Example 5.4 illustrates an indirect way that a complaint can be made. On the surface, the complainant appears to be asking her Branch Manager for advice. Again, the complaint emerges over a number of utterances.

Example 5.4 (Source: LWP)

Context: Claire, a policy analyst, is talking to Tom, her branch manager. Recorded in a government organisation in New Zealand.

CLAIRE:	yeah I want to talk to you about um
	oh it's a personal issue um +
	well the decision to make Jared acting manager while Joseph is away +
	and I wanted to get some-
TOM:	mm
CLAIRE:	well I've been overlooked quite a few times
	//but\ I wanted to find out specifically how
TOM:	/mm\\
CLAIRE:	what I could do to help myself be considered next time
	[Tom answers phone] …
	(well) I just want to talk to you about it
	and I suppose I just wanted to get some ideas
	on what I could do to actually be considered
	favourably next time
TOM:	yeah I don't think it's a it's a question of er favourability
	I mean it was a question more practicalities more than anything else
	um I was in urgent need of someone to fill in and
	Jared had done that in the past already …

Reprinted under STM guidelines from *Discourse Studies 5*, Stubbe, Maria, Lane, Chris, Hilder, Jo, Vine, Elaine, Vine, Bernadette, Marra, Meredith, Holmes, Janet and Weatherall, Ann, 2003. Multiple discourse analyses of a workplace interaction, p. 381.

Claire begins by saying she wants to talk about a 'personal issue', and then refers to 'the decision' to give someone else the acting manager job. The trouble has been raised but in an indirect way. She further develops this indirectly when she explicitly says she wants some advice, 'to get some ideas' on what she could do so that she will be given the acting manager position in the future.

As the extract shows, Tom reads Claire's **advice seeking** as a complaint and orients to this, providing justification for why the acting manager position went to Jared rather than Claire. His justification actually extends for quite some time (not shown here), in part because Claire's responses do not indicate that she is convinced by his arguments (see Stubbe et al. 2003). The indirect raising of a complaint, as in this example, has been considered an effective way to highlight a problem, without explicitly referring to it. The other participant in an interaction then has the option of orienting to the complaint and if they do the complaint is co-constructed.

These three examples are all taken from backstage settings. In such settings, ongoing relationships are an important consideration for people in how they express and respond to complaints. People generally want to avoid conflict and maintain relationships, so complaints tend to be softened or expressed indirectly and the recipients of the complaints generally accept the complaint. The following example comes from a different type of backstage setting, and shows a complaint expressed explicitly without any mitigation.

Example 5.5

Context: Sergeant addressing recruits following the morning's barrack room inspection. Data from a British TV documentary.

SERGEANT: but worse than not achieving the standard
              you just have not even tried
              you have not bothered
              I do not expect you to get it right
              but I do expect you to give me a hundred percent +
              you have not done that
              and I warned you right at the beginning if you cannot motivate yourself
              I will motivate you …

Reprinted with permission from Bousfield, Derek, *Impoliteness in interaction*, p. 124, © 2008 John Benjamins Publishing.

The complaint here is expressed very directly as the sergeant criticises the recruits. This setting is one in which this direct type of talk is expected, and also one where the recipients of the complaint are expected to accept the complaint in silence. This does not of course mean that the recipients perceive an explicit complaint like this as legitimate, but they are still expected to accept it.

Example 5.5 highlights the importance of norms and expectations in different settings. Such explicitly expressed complaints would be inappropriate in many white collar Western settings and there are certainly no complaints like this in the white collar data from the Wellington Language in the Workplace Project database. The lack of attention to interpersonal aspects of communication here would have a very negative effect on the working relationship between the complainant and the target of the complaint. In many types of workplace settings and in many countries confrontational behaviour of this type is not the norm and nor is it an acceptable way of interacting.

> Complaints in backstage settings are often softened or expressed indirectly. The recipients of complaints are generally quick to acknowledge problems and either accept complaints or justify themselves. Complaints are co-constructed by participants in an interaction with complainants often indirectly introducing complaints and the people they are interacting with quickly

orienting to the issues being raised. There are some settings and contexts where the norms mean that complaints are expressed explicitly. The recipients of complaints in these settings are not expected to object, but to accept complaints.

How are complaints expressed and responded to in frontstage settings?

What happens when complaints are made in frontstage settings? Ongoing relationships are not always an issue in such cases, and the complainant may be interacting with a person they have not talked to before. This can influence how complaints are expressed and responded to. Example 5.6 illustrates one way that a customer deals with a problem with her order.

Example 5.6 (Source: LWP)

Context: Service encounter in a café in New Zealand.

> [A customer realises that although she specifically asked if bean sprouts are an ingredient in the noodle soup and then requested that they be omitted from her order, her order contains bean sprouts. She does not say anything to the staff at the café]

The customer avoids the problematic situation altogether by picking the bean sprouts out and she does not complain to the staff at the café. She commented that she felt uncomfortable about making a complaint so did not make one. This is one way that a complaint may be dealt with.

In Example 5.7, the complainant makes two complaints. This excerpt comes from an interaction between a nurse and a patient in a hospital ward.

Example 5.7 (Source: LWP)

Context: A nurse and a patient interacting in a hospital ward. Recorded in New Zealand. The nurse arrives to check the patient's blood pressure, not realising that the patient has buzzed her for attention.

PATIENT: hi
NURSE: hi + just gonna check your + //blood pressure and things\
PATIENT: /did you know I called you?\\ +
NURSE: oh no
PATIENT: [slowly]: oh:
NURSE: did you give me a buzz?
PATIENT: first time I've used my //buzzer\
NURSE: /your\\ buzzer I didn't know you'd called me
PATIENT: since I've been here //+ and you didn't even know\
NURSE: /[laughs]\\ no I didn't what were you wanting?
PATIENT: [softly]: oh my hand's really sore from that //last one\ you did mm:
NURSE: /[softly]: oh:\\
NURSE: okay we'll have a look

From Holmes and Major (2003: 15)

In this example the patient first complains because she rang her buzzer but no-one answered. She makes her complaint by asking the nurse if she knew that she had buzzed her. From the way the nurse has greeted her, it is clear to the patient that she has not come because the patient summoned her. The nurse then asks if the patient buzzed her, orienting to the topic of the complaint, and the patient then ruefully comments that it was the first time she used the buzzer and the nurse did not even know. The nurse laughs in response to the patient's wry tone and then acknowledges that she did not hear the buzzer. The patient then complains that her hand is really sore after a previous treatment that the nurse did. In response to this complaint the nurse immediately orients to the topic of the complaint, reassuring the patient and moving to find a remedy for the problem.

In Examples 5.6 and 5.7, the particular frontstage settings examined involve face-to-face interaction. In call centre interactions, callers are not interacting face-to-face and generally deal with a representative of an organisation rather than directly with the person who may be responsible for the problem. An important role of telephone call centres can be to deal with complaints. Example 5.8 comes from a call centre.

Example 5.8

Context: Call to a call centre which organises and ensures the transportation of dialysis patients from home to hospital. Recorded in Italy.

CALLER:	[inhales] sono Gadeni qui dall emodialisi	it's Gadeni here at the haemodialysis department
	[inhales] e i pazienti oggi domani non liandate a prendere	er the patients today tomorrow don't you go and pick them up?
CALL-TAKER:	ah io ho il programma qua ed è	it er I have the schedule here and it's
	c'è stato un grave errorre perché hanno messo tutto per domani	there's been a serious mistake because they wrote all down for tomorrow
	e oggi nessuno	and nobody today
CALLER:	ah ué io ho Golsemi oggi	er c'mon I have Golsemi today
CALL-TAKER:	Golsemi adesso lo andiamo a prendere	Golsemi now we're gonna pick him up
CALLER:	l'andante a prendere	are you gonna pick him up?
CALL-TAKER:	si va bene	yes alright

Reprinted from *Journal of Pragmatics 41*, Monzoni, Chiara M., Direct complaints in (Italian) calls to the ambulance: The use of negatively framed questions, pp. 2468–9, © 2009, with permission from Elsevier.

The caller here is a doctor. She has rung the call centre because the patient she was expecting has not arrived. She expresses her complaint in an indirect way though by asking the call-taker if they pick up patients. She knows the answer to this question so her question introduces the problem and because of the negative form it takes, rather than saying 'do you go?' the caller has said 'don't you go?', Monzoni (2009: 2469) argues that this immediately identifies a failure on the part of the service provider. It may be indirect therefore, but is also a strong way of expressing a complaint.

The call-taker does immediately orient to the question as a complaint and acknowledges the problem, while shifting the personal blame to someone else. She also says that the problem will be rectified and the company will go and pick the patient up.

In frontstage situations then, such as Examples 5.7 and 5.8, the recipient of a complaint typically quickly acknowledges the problem and seeks to remedy it. People working on telephone help lines are encouraged not to respond in a confrontational way when callers are making complaints. They are expected to remain neutral while helping to solve any problems. This neutrality may cause problems however if a complainant does not feel their complaint is being taken seriously.

In the next example, the caller has rung a travel and accommodation helpline in order to complain about the accommodation she and her husband have been allocated. In doing this she asks the criterion for allocating the accommodation, and so the recipient of the complaint addresses this question.

Example 5.9

Context: Call to a travel and accommodation helpline. Recorded in Latin America.

CALLER:	[slowly]: e: bueno yo como no estoy conforme cómo es el condominio quisiera saber cuál es el criterio por el cual nos adjudicaron la unidad que tenemos y demás …	*[slowly]: um: okay so since I'm not satisfied with the way the condominium is I'd like to know the criterion why we were allocated the unit that we have and that …*
AGENT:	si viajan dos personas le damos una unidad de dos personas ya? entonces en este caso el operador que le atendió le debe haber preguntado con quién viajaba usted le dijo con mi esposo etonces viajan dos personas se le dió una habitación que es para tres	*if two people are travelling we give them a unit for two people right? so in this case the agent that served you he must have asked you who you were travelling with you told him with my husband so two people were travelling and you were given a room for three people*
CALLER:	está bien //suena-\	*alright //it sounds-*
AGENT:	/lo que\\ habia disponible era este complejo usted se le ofreció [slowly]: em: me imagino que habrá tenido la oportunidad de verlo aunque sea en el directorio o por internet	*/what\\ was available was this resort it was offered to you [slowly]: um: I'd imagine that you had had the opportunity to see it at least in the directory or in the internet*
CALLER:	no no no no no lo vimos porque yo confié que me iban dar por lo menos algo similar a lo que yo tengo	*no no no no we didn't see it because I trusted that I was going to be allotted at least something similar to what I've got*
AGENT:	sí	*yes*

CALLER:	entonces ahora yo estoy en un- nosotros somos dos personas grandes nos dieron tipo duplex así que subo y bajo escaleras para el dormitorio	*so now I'm in and we are two mature people they gave us a kind of duplex so I've to go up and down steps to the bedroom*
AGENT:	sí	*yes*

Reprinted from *Journal of Pragmatics 57*, Marquez Reiter, Rosina, The dynamics of complaining in a Latin American for-profit commercial setting, pp. 236–7, © 2013, with permission from Elsevier.

The caller states that she is not happy with the accommodation she has been allocated. The agent knows this is a complaint, but since the caller then explicitly asks about the criterion for allocating accommodation, the agent orients to this question and provides the criteria. She also then asserts that the caller will have had the opportunity to see the accommodation prior to accepting it. In responding like this, the agent has not accepted responsibility for the problem. She redirects the blame for the problem back onto the complainant by pointing out that the problem has arisen because of some action (or lack of) on the part of the complainant. Call centre agents are encouraged not to directly accept responsibility, since if they do callers may insist on compensation of some kind.

Often when a complaint is made in a frontstage setting, the complainant must deal with someone who represents the organisation or institution rather than the person who made the mistake or caused the problem. Company representatives are often quick to acknowledge problems, although tend to redirect the blame. As with backstage complaints, frontstage complaints are co-constructed by participants in an interaction. Complainants often indirectly introduce complaints or signal that there is a problem and the people they are interacting with are quick to orient to the issues being raised.

Complaints, Power and Identity

How do power relationships influence the way complaints are expressed and responded to?

One of the reasons Claire resorts to such an indirect strategy in Example 5.4 to make her complaint is the role relationship between her and Tom. Tom is the branch manager of the unit where she works, while Claire is a policy analyst. In being indirect, Claire can deny that her comments were meant as a complaint, although in this case she does not do this. Expressing a complaint indirectly can allow people in lower status positions to manage these types of situations. Indirectness and humour are two strategies that those in lower positions can generally use without negative consequences.

In Chapter 4, Example 4.14, a complaint from a lower status individual was directed at his boss. The example is repeated below as Example 5.10.

Example 5.10 (Source: LWP)

Context: Neil is an HR consultant who has just started working at the company. Victor is the company CEO and Shaun is a manager. Recorded at a private organisation in New Zealand.

SHAUN: people do need to know who that guy with bad tie taste
        is around the office //(   )\
NEIL: /[laughs]\\
VICTOR: that's <u>very</u> rich coming from you
        (speaking of eccentricity) [laughs]

Reprinted from *Journal of Pragmatics 41*, Schnurr, Stephanie, Constructing leader identities through teasing at work, p. 1129, © 2009, with permission from Elsevier.

Shaun's comment here teases Neil, but also challenges his boss, Victor. He complains that Victor has not yet introduced Neil to the other staff. The use of humour allows Shaun to do this without directly challenging Victor. In responding to this, Victor ignores the implied criticism and takes the humour at face value, turning it back on Shaun and teasing him about his eccentric dress sense.

Often it is a higher status person who is in a position to make a complaint explicitly: the responsibility for ensuring work is completed or that jobs are done correctly falls back to those in supervisory roles. In order to maintain rapport and manage the relational aspects of ensuring a productive team, leaders will often use humour or express complaints in a way that mitigates the face threat, as in Examples 5.2 and 5.3.

The complaint from the military training setting, Example 5.5, is expressed very directly. This context is one where the status differences between the complainant and the recipients of the complaint are high. This is also a setting where the culture of such workplaces is not typified by attempts to minimise status differences: workplace hierarchies are acknowledged and directly reinforced in the way people communicate in these settings. The higher status person is institutionally sanctioned to express complaints directly, while the lower status person is expected to receive the complaint in silence.

In frontstage settings, the institutional power is with the recipients of the complaints, who are generally representatives of companies. They have power because they can fix the problem, or possibly provide compensation. Because the institutional representative has this power, complainants will again often indirectly introduce complaints or at least mitigate the way they express them.

How is the expression and acceptance or rejection of complaints related to the enactment of identity?

The way that people express and respond to complaints is influenced by the way they want to be perceived by others. Expressing complaints indirectly, with humour or with hedging, are useful strategies for leaders in enacting leadership in a way that makes them appear as reasonable, non-authoritarian leaders. Complaints are a problematic aspect of work talk, but avoiding them when in a leadership position can create more problems. Dealing with them in an indirect or mitigated way allows rapport to be maintained while enacting a leadership style that acknowledges the importance of team relationships. This is seen as a desirable way to enact leadership in many cultures.

For lower or equal status individuals the expression of complaints may be avoided in many cases. When an issue is important enough to bring to the attention of colleagues or superiors, the expression of a complaint indirectly or with mitigation helps people enact their identity in a way that presents them as logical and rational individuals, who do not complain for no reason nor in a direct and aggressive manner. In Example 5.4, the way Claire makes her complaint shows her enacting her identity as a professional who wants to improve herself and develop her skills.

Responding to complaints in backstage settings in a positive rather than a defensive way enables the recipient of a complaint to demonstrate that they are focused on transactional goals and they do not let personal feelings interfere with their work. This is important for leaders, subordinates and equals when wanting to enact a professional and competent workplace identity.

Mitigation, negotiation and indirectness are strategies for managing interaction which are stereotypically associated with feminine interaction styles. Masculine interaction styles are perceived as being more direct. In indexing gender identity therefore women are more likely to use indirectness to soften complaints and responses. Because these features can also be associated with appropriate ways to enact professional identity in many contexts, men may also use this style of interaction (see Chapter 7).

Cultural considerations are also always relevant. In many cultures and contexts, acceptable ways of expressing and responding to complaints require mitigation and negotiation, particularly if a person is interacting with someone who has power over them in some way. In other cultures it is acceptable to be more direct, particularly when in a leadership position (see Chapter 8). Norms and expectations at a number of levels may be important.

Factors Influencing the Way Complaints Are Expressed and Responded To

So what factors influence the way complaints are expressed and responded to?

The examples in this section highlight a number of contextual factors which affect the way complaints are expressed (or not) and how they are responded to. When examining complaints we need to consider a range of questions:

- do the participants have ongoing relationships?
- how well do they know each other?

- what are the participants' roles? (e.g., a manager complaining to a worker, or vice versa);
- are they interacting face-to-face?
- are other people present?
- what is the current purpose of the interaction?
- how important is the problem?
- what are the norms for the workplace setting or within the community of practice?
- how might cultural norms be important?
- what about factors related to the enactment of gender or other aspects of a person's identity?

Another important feature of complaints noted above is that they are co-constructed in interaction. In many cases a complainant will bring up the trouble in an indirect way and the person (or people) they are interacting with will then respond in such a way that either the complaint is clarified or the potential trouble is diverted or redirected somehow.

Because complaints have an effect on relationships, they are often expressed and responded to in ways that minimise the damage to rapport, particularly in backstage settings. When complaints are handled with humour or in a way that pays attention to the addressee's face needs, i.e., to relational aspects, then they are less likely to have long-term effects and they are also less likely to be rejected. When a person makes a complaint they are also generally wanting a problem to be fixed or rectified in some way. Paying attention to relational aspects in expressing complaints means therefore that they are more likely to achieve a satisfactory outcome.

When complaints are made, there is always the potential for the recipient of the complaint to disagree. In Examples 5.4 and 5.9 the complaints were rejected, with the recipients of the complaints disagreeing with the complainants. In the next section, disagreement is examined in more detail.

Disagreement

Definition of *Disagreement*
What is disagreement and where do we find disagreement at work?

Disagreement involves the expression of opposing views. This typically involves one person making a claim and another then refuting that claim. The recipient of a complaint may disagree with the complaint, but disagreement can also involve challenges to someone's point of view or opinion on something, or the factual content of a statement. This may involve a single utterance, or several turns of talk.

There are different types of disagreement and we can imagine them as existing on a continuum: see Figure 5.1. At one end of this continuum is unmarked disagreement, while at the other we have marked disagreement. Unmarked disagreement is when the disagreement does not stand out.

unmarked disagreement <--------------------------------------> marked disagreement
expected   unexpected
acceptable   unacceptable
appropriate   inappropriate

Figure 5.1
Types of disagreement.

In problem-solving interactions for instance, as seen in Example 5.1, disagreement may be an expected and therefore an unmarked part of the process. Disagreement tends to be marked when it is unexpected in some way. It may also be marked when it is expressed in a way that is inappropriate or unacceptable for the context in which it occurs.

Normally, when someone makes a claim, the expected response to this claim would be to agree. This is referred to as a 'preferred response' (see Chapter 2). The disputing of a claim and the expressing of disagreement is therefore a 'dispreferred response'. In disagreement sequences there is what has been called 'preference reversal', so instead of agreeing with a claim, the norm is that someone disagrees with it. If disagreement is expected and allowed in certain settings such as debates and in some legal contexts, then disagreement becomes the preferred response. This may have implications for how disagreement is expressed and responded to.

Disagreement can potentially be found in any workplace setting. However, there are some settings and activity types where disagreement may be an expected part of the interaction. In backstage settings, problem-solving is an activity where disagreement may be expected and this can lead to robust decisions and solutions. This does depend on the community of practice, however, as collaborative problem-solving may be the norm in some workplaces or work groups. Peer feedback sessions where a colleague reviews another person's work and gives feedback is another type of backstage interaction where disagreement could be expected.

There are also some frontstage settings where disagreement is expected, for instance in legal contexts. In such contexts, the discourse has been found to be highly rule-governed so that disagreement is carefully managed. Other frontstage contexts where we expect to find disagreement include negotiations, mediations and political debates. Calls to telephone call centres are also a place where there is the potential for disagreement. Again, as with legal discourse, these contexts are ones where institutional representatives tend to carefully manage any disagreement.

We begin by considering some examples of disagreements from backstage settings.

Expressing and Responding to Disagreement
What does disagreement look like in backstage settings?

Like complaining, disagreeing is something that people may approach indirectly. In disagreeing, it is common to have delays in responding, or hedging and other types of responding which do not directly and immediately address the first speaker's claim. At other times the disagreement may be prefaced by something like 'yes but'. This looks like an acceptance of the claim, and therefore a preferred response, but the use of 'but' immediately following an agreement token introduces the rejection or qualification of what has just been said. In Example 5.11, Tricia, the manager, has been outlining what will happen when an outside group comes and does training within an organisation. A prior survey of staff has raised some issues that the trainers will help to address, although she has also asked the training group to help identify problems.

Example 5.11 (Source: LWP)

Context: Management meeting in a New Zealand IT organisation. Tricia is the manager.

TRICIA:	I mean one of the ones that came out in that issues thing that um Isabelle raised was er that we we make decisions or overturn staff decisions
SERENA:	mm
TRICIA:	and so one of the things that I've asked them to do is do a proper thing about what they think the actual problem is
SERENA:	mm
TRICIA:	and then come back with recommendations on how it could be fixed and that's not just recommendations for us that's recommendations for them as well
SERENA:	yeah but I think that's people being confused about their level of authority isn't it
TRICIA:	that's some of it is that it's there's a whole mix of things I mean some of it is that we haven't got standards set some of it's that we do make changes and that they have to recognise that that will occur … [continues to outline the issue]

Serena disagrees with Tricia, prefacing her differing opinion with 'yeah but I think'. This signals and softens her disagreement with the idea that they need an outside group to identify a problem for them. Staff have been complaining about not being consulted in decision-making, and Serena sees the issue as clear: the staff complaining are not acknowledging management's right to make decisions. In disagreeing with Serena's assessment, Tricia begins by acknowledging Serena's point and accepting it as true, 'that's some of it is that', but goes on to elaborate that there is more to the problem than this.

Example 5.12 shows a variation on this pattern. In Example 5.12, Zoe looks like she is going to agree with Leila as her initial utterance in this excerpt consists of 'right'.

Example 5.12 (Source: LWP)

Context: Team meeting. Leila is the manager. The team are discussing the need to get their filing sorted. A suggestion is to bring in an outside company to help, The Flying Filing Squad. Recorded in a government organisation in New Zealand.

LEILA:	now when I did say earlier that we had the um solutions here I mean I was actually thinking

> I was incorporating the Flying Filers in that
> as //well\ not just thinking of us as
> ZOE: /right\\
> ZOE: well it just seems to me um a bit silly to bring in the Flying Filers
>   if all they're gonna do is file for us when we know
>   we can get Robyn to do it + …

From Holmes and Stubbe (2003: 67–8)

Zoe initially says 'right' and then disagrees in her next turn. She signals with 'well' that she is going to give her view and then hedges with 'just' and 'a bit' as she brings up her objection to Leila's idea. In this case the discussion actually extends for quite a while longer as Leila seeks to get everyone, including Zoe, to agree to her proposed solution to the problem.

Instances of disagreement such as those illustrated in Examples 5.11 and 5.12 have been referred to as **weak disagreements** (Pomerantz 1984). With a **weak disagreement** there is partial agreement. In Example 5.11, Serena uses the agreement marker 'yeah' before qualifying this with 'but I think'. In disagreeing with Serena, Tricia begins by partially agreeing with Serena 'some of it is that' before going on to raise several other relevant issues that Serena may be overlooking. In Example 5.12, Zoe's 'right' signals agreement, although her next statement expresses a differing point of view. Weak disagreements may also involve silence and there is often a delay before the person disagreeing speaks, as in Example 5.13.

Example 5.13 (translated from Cantonese)

Context: Team meeting. Anthony, the production manager, has explained some production procedures. Liu, the boss, makes fun of Richard's allegedly sudden trust in Anthony, whose decisions he normally challenges rather than supports. Recorded in a Hong Kong workplace.

> LIU: *no need to take a look*
>   *he trusts him now*
> RICHARD: *[sighs]*
> LIU: *{he} suddenly has so much confidence in (him) +*
> RICHARD: *[sighs] {I've} already got used to {it}*
> LIU: *already got used to {it}*
>   *good …*

Reprinted from *Journal of Pragmatics 43*, Schnurr, Stephanie and Chan, Angela, When laughter is not enough. Responding to teasing and self-denigrating humour at work, p. 25, © 2011, with permission from Elsevier.

Richard is being teased by his boss here for not disagreeing with Anthony. Richard expresses his disagreement with the idea that he now trusts the colleague whom he normally disagrees with by sighing and remaining silent for much of the exchange.

In Examples 5.14 and 5.15 there is **strong disagreement**, the disagreement being directly expressed. The data in Example 5.14 comes from a leaderless research team in a university setting.

Example 5.14

Context: Meeting of a university research team. They are discussing the presentation of results in a research paper the team are writing. Recorded in the UK.

SCOTT:	(　　) where you have two dimensions and
	//the (　　) plot\
DAN:	/it doesn't make\\ any sense
YLVA:	(　　) figure you showed the other day with (　　)
BEE:	that makes sense
SCOTT:	well it's shown in the data
SARAH:	yeah I can do that
BEE:	no the scatter plot makes makes sense
YLVA:	//(　　)\
BEE:	/yeah\\
DAN:	the scatter plot's okay it's the circle that doesn't make sense
BEE:	no the circle does make sense too
DAN:	no it doesn't
BEE:	yes it does
SARAH:	[laughs softly]
DAN:	you can write an infinite number of circles [label]
	there's ninety five percent inside it and five percent outside
YLVA:	but the the the this probability's
	//(　　)\
BEE:	/but\\ anyway we can leave the circle out it doesn't matter
DAN:	yeah you can show the plot if you want

Reprinted under STM guidelines from *Discourse Studies 16*, Choi, Seongsook and Schnurr, Stephanie, 2014. Exploring distributed leadership: Solving disagreements and negotiating consensus in a 'leaderless' team, p. 9.

Most of the disagreements in this extract are expressed strongly. They do not contain agreement tokens and contrast directly with the claims they are disputing. Dan begins by explicitly criticising the visual presentation of some of the results, overlapping Scott's speech as he does this. The example also shows the speakers using what is referred to as an 'opposition format'. This means that the speaker disagreeing takes the first speaker's words and negates them. There are several variations on Dan's initial disagreement phrase 'it doesn't make any sense' which use an opposition format, e.g., Bee saying 'the circle does make sense too'.

Example 5.14 comes from a problem-solving meeting and Choi and Schnurr (2014: 20) note that the disagreement is expected. Because it is expected, disagreement in problem-solving meetings may be expressed and responded to more directly, as with directives in certain contexts (see Chapter 3). The disagreements are resolved smoothly in the meeting that Example 5.14 comes from, once everyone has had a chance to disagree. Choi and Schnurr (2014: 20) note that in this community of practice, quite explicit and direct ways of disagreeing are part of the established norms.

In Example 5.15 the disagreement is also expressed strongly without any agreement markers like 'yes', 'yeah' or 'right'. There are no delays in responding and no hedging and there is also overlapping speech.

Example 5.15 (Source: LWP)

Context: Management team meeting in a private organisation in New Zealand.

JASON:	I think the other thing too to note is
	that we're actually not even already
	judging these guys we don't
	we're not saying that they're doing it wrong
	we're saying that they're really that's
	they're doing the best they can
	//+ but it's not that no but we no we said\
ROB:	/oh no I'm saying they're doing it wrong [laughs]\\
	//[laughs]\
JASON:	/hear me out we're saying they're\\ doing the best they can
	but that's not gonna be good enough
	when [business name] comes along
	because we're gonna be able to offer
	such a better system such a better service
STEPHEN:	they just don't know any better do they?
JASON:	they just don't know any better

Jason was not expecting Rob to disagree with him in this case, so Rob's disagreement is marked. It is also expressed strongly: Rob and Jason overlap, there are no agreement markers and Rob's disagreement uses an 'opposition format'. Jason has said 'we're not saying that they're doing it wrong' and in refuting this Rob says 'oh no I'm saying they're doing it wrong'. Jason responds forcefully as well and insists that Rob hears him out. Jason also repeats the last part of his statement from before Rob interrupted, 'they're doing the best they can' as he disagrees with Rob. Stephen, the managing director, also supports Jason, explicitly siding with Jason and disagreeing with Rob. In doing this, Stephen says 'they just don't know any better do they?' and Jason explicitly reinforces this by repeating Stephen's words, 'they just don't know any better'.

A difference between these last two examples is that in Example 5.15 the group are discussing changes, but are not problem-solving. Another difference is that in Example 5.15 the person who has disagreed does not pursue the disagreement further and the discussion moves on.

> Disagreement can be expressed weakly or strongly. In examining examples from backstage settings it is important to consider the purpose of an interaction, as well as the norms of the community of practice from which the data has come.

What does disagreement look like in frontstage settings?

Disagreement in frontstage settings can look very similar to disagreements in many backstage settings. Compare Example 5.16 for instance, which comes from a meeting between a company and a subcontractor, with Example 5.15, which came from an internal meeting.

Example 5.16

Context: Meeting between a multinational company team and a subcontractor, Garry. The company is based in Europe.

SAM:	we are here with Paul right to resolve some of the issues right
	I know you have several complaints right
	about the amounts right [financial details omitted]
	for example I know there is an issue right
	about the [deadline details] //right\
GARRY:	/that\\ was=
SAM:	=wait and listen to me right
	for example for the wood planks in the stack right
	in the contract right it states that it is your responsibility
	right [details] it's in the con//tract\
GARRY:	/no it's\\ //not\
KEVIN:	/it is\\ in the contract
PHIL:	it's in the con//tract\
SAM:	/it\\ is in the contract
	but I can understand right the loss in [details]
	so I'm //willing to pay an amount\
GARRY:	/what about the amount\\ the [details] is a lot of money

Reprinted from *Journal of Pragmatics 44*, Angouri, Jo, Managing disagreement in problem solving meeting talk, p. 1570, © 2012, with permission from Elsevier.

Garry overlaps Sam and begins to disagree. As in Example 5.15, the speaker who has the floor, in this case Sam, insists that he be allowed to finish outlining the issue. After listening for a bit longer, Garry again overlaps and this time clearly disagrees, 'no it's not'.

The disagreement in both Examples 5.15 and 5.16 is expressed and responded to very forcefully; it is expressed strongly and looks potentially conflictual. Angouri (2012: 1571) notes that Example 5.16 was not perceived as conflictual by the participants. In this case, a long history of working together meant that Sam and Garry expressed their disagreement very strongly and this was not seen as a problem. The interaction continued and a satisfactory resolution was found to the problem.

Both Examples 5.15 and 5.16 also involve other participants siding with the first speaker who was holding the floor before the disagreement was expressed. As in Example 5.15, the people agreeing in Example 5.16 echo each other's words.

Other frontstage settings where participants may have ongoing relationships although they do not interact on a daily basis include healthcare contexts. Example 5.17 for instance is from a session between a therapist and a patient.

Example 5.17

Context: Counselling session. Recorded in Finland.

PATIENT:	[inhales] niinku et jos ne on	*like if they are*
	tommossia niinku suurin osa aamista	*like kind of most mornings*
	niinku maanatai ja tiista oli	*like Monday and Tuesday were*
	ni en mää en mä semmosta jaksa et ei	*then I can't I can't handle it*

	[slowly]: ei: niinku [inhales] +	[slowly]: no: like [inhales]
	se että niinku kokis mielekkääks sen että	that you'd feel like
		it would be meaningful
	mm mitä tekee	mm what you do?
	ja se että niinku olis mielekästä	and that it would be meaningful
	en mä usko että	I don't believe that
	kyl nyt varmasti jokasel on	I'm sure that everyone has
	niitä että ei huvita huvittais nyt tänä aamuna	those [days] that they don't feel like
		wouldn't feel like
	//lähtee\ nousta mut että	//getting\ up in the morning but that
THERAPIST:	/mm\\	/mm\\
PATIENT:	//mut et nn\	//but that nn\
THERAPIST:	/[inhales] Maanatai aamuna voi	/[inhales] on Monday morning
	olla aika yleistä siinä bussissa	that kind of feeling can be quite
	semmonen tunne [laughs]	common on the bus [laughs]\
PATIENT:	/niih [laughs] nii [inhales]\	/yes [laughs] yes [inhales]\
	nii mut et se se on niin semmonen s-	yes but that it it is so kind of s-
	ku mä en usko et se on niin voimakas	but I don't believe it's so strong
	se tunne että se on nn	that feeling that it's nn

In this case the client is describing how awful she felt on the bus on her way to work. She realises other people feel like this but feels that it is worse for her. The therapist agrees with her client about the feeling and that other people feel this way too. She disagrees however with the client's assessment of her own feelings as necessarily being worse than other people's. Part of a therapist's role is to challenge a client's negative feelings and to help them shift their thinking, so disagreement is therefore an important part of this. In expressing her disagreement, the therapist hedges with 'kind of' and 'quite' but she overlaps the patient. In disagreeing with the therapist, the patient speaks faster and uses 'yes but' so the disagreements here combine features of weak and strong disagreement.

Because call centres often deal with complaints there is always the potential for disagreement and this is another frontstage context where disagreement is expected. Call-takers have training on how to deal with callers who are complaining and whose views may disagree with or question a company's policies. In Example 5.9 for instance, we saw the caller disagreeing with the agent's claim that she was responsible for her problem with the accommodation because she 'had had the opportunity to see it'. In disagreeing, the caller said 'no no no no we didn't see it', using a repeated disagreement token and an opposition format.

Face-to-face interactions in frontstage settings where disagreement is expected include broadcast interviews and discussions. These are public contexts where the disagreement is being expressed in front of an audience. In Example 5.18, the interviewer asks questions of different people who have been invited along because they represent different viewpoints.

Example 5.18

Context: News panel interview with politicians. Recorded in the UK.

INTERVIEWER:	John Mackintosh an Autumn election
	or a Spring election next year?
JOHN:	oh I think an Autumn election
	but for quite different reason
	I think the budget does not-
	it's not an electioneering budget
	it's a steady sensible budget
	and the case for an Autumn election
	is [slowly]: the: difficult position of the government
	in Parliament and I would have thought
	that the government would want to go
	for a proper majority in October
INTERVIEWER:	Teddy Taylor do you see an Autumn election?
TEDDY:	actually I don't see an Autumn election
	because I think we're going to have a lot of trouble
	by the Autumn # I think the government will stagger on
	until the last possible [slowly]: time:

Reprinted from Greatbatch, David, On the management of disagreement between news interviewees. In *Talk at work: Interaction in institutional settings*, p. 279, © 1992 Cambridge University Press. Reproduced with permission of Cambridge University Press through PLSclear.

The interviewees in this case wait their turn and respond when directly asked. They follow the rules of interaction for interviews. In disagreeing with John's view, once given the floor, Teddy promptly replies and is direct and straightforward in the way he puts his opposing view on the topic. In analysing this extract, Greatbatch (1992) argues that because the interviewer is a third party in examples like this, and the interviewer has directly elicited what will presumably be a disagreement, the circumstances mean the disagreement is automatically mitigated. The

© Jacynta Scurfield 2019

situation is one where the disagreement is by the nature of the context weaker than if John and Teddy were responding directly to each other. Of course interviewees in panel shows do not always behave in the way that is expected and may at times express strong disagreement using overlapping speech and other disruptive features as noted above.

In legal discourse there are also rules concerning who can contribute and in what way. In a police interview for instance, like other types of interviews, the interviewer's role is to ask questions and to manage the interaction. The interviewee's role is to answer questions. At certain times in court proceedings there is a similar pattern with lawyers questioning defendants and witnesses. Example 5.19 comes from the cross-examination of a witness in court in the O. J. Simpson civil trial. The witness has testified before in the criminal trial, where Simpson had been acquitted. The families of the victims then filed a civil suit. The lawyer is asking the witness about the colour of the vehicle the witness said he saw.

Example 5.19

Context: Cross-examination from O. J. Simpson civil trial. Recorded in the USA.

LAWYER: now one other thing you testified did you not
         that the colour was light or white?
WITNESS: no it was definitely white sir
LAWYER: let me just get your …
         [reads criminal trial testimony transcript from the witness –
         section omitted]
         [reading question]: what colour was the colour?
         [reading answer]: very light colour white or light:
         [reading question]: white or light?:
         [reading answer]: it was white or something:
         does that refresh your recollection sir?
WITNESS: it was white definitely white
LAWYER: so it wasn't white or light?
WITNESS: no it was white
LAWYER: it wasn't white or light?
WITNESS: it was white
LAWYER: thank you nothing further

Reprinted from Cotterill (2002: 155)

The lawyer's first question here relates not to the colour of the car but to the content of the previous testimony given by the witness. In disagreeing, however, the witness refutes the assertion that the car was 'light or white'. The lawyer then reads the testimony transcript from the earlier trial and asks the witness if the transcript 'refreshes' his mind. Since there is a discrepancy the witness has a choice here of either disagreeing with his own testimony or with what he has just said. With the next question, the witness is expected to agree or disagree. Because the question is prefaced with 'so', there is a preference for agreement. So-prefaced questions have been seen to be challenging and part of the challenge here is that the witness has changed his testimony. Preferred agreement in this example also seeks to get the witness to accept that he does not have a reliable memory of the event. One of the roles of the lawyer in this context is to present a clear outline of the story the witness has to tell so challenging questions and disagreement are strategies that lawyers use to clarify aspects of the narrative. This can be particularly pertinent when the lawyer, as in this case, is trying to discredit or raise doubt about a witness.

> In examining examples from frontstage settings, norms and expectations for interaction in different settings are important. In some frontstage settings there are rules which allow disagreement to be carefully managed. This is particularly true for public frontstage settings in which there is typically an audience.

Features of Disagreement

So what are features of disagreement?

Disagreements can be expressed in either a weak or a strong way. Weak disagreements tend to have:

- delays in responding
- agreement tokens such as *yes, yeah, right*
- hedging.

Disagreement can also be weakened because of the context in which it occurs, as in the case of broadcast interviews.

Strong disagreements tend to have:

- overlapping speech or latching
- louder speech
- faster speech
- lack of hedging
- opposition formats
- preference reversal.

Another common feature of disagreement is that speakers use a subjective stance, i.e., they express things from their own point of view (Koester 2006: 129–35). We can see these types of elements in the speech of several of the people in the examples of disagreement above; for instance, 'I think' occurs frequently: see Examples 5.11 and 5.18.

Disagreement, Power and Identity

How do power relationships influence the ways disagreement is expressed and responded to?

Disagreeing is a way of exercising power. When we view power as something that is reinforced, contested, and negotiated in interaction then the expression of disagreement, along with the way disagreement is responded to, can show how people both assert and contest power.

Someone in a powerful position can assert their right to make decisions, as Jocelyn did in Example 5.1. In the meeting that Example 5.12 comes from, the manager Leila encourages further discussion until she has everyone, including Zoe, agreeing with her solution to the problem. In Example 5.15, Stephen sides with Jason. Stephen is the managing director of the company so this is strong support for Jason's position and Rob does not pursue his disagreement.

In settings where the culture of the workplace means that workplace hierarchies are acknowledged and directly reinforced in the way people communicate, a higher status person is institutionally sanctioned to express disagreement strongly, or alternatively silence or divert disagreement from people in lower status positions. When the sergeant reprimands the recruits in Example 5.5 he expects them to accept his criticism in silence and not to disagree, and they comply with this expectation.

In frontstage contexts, the institutional representatives are the ones who tend to hold the power. This is particularly relevant in high-stakes interactions where the person with less power has the most to lose. Those with less power however can use disagreement to contest power asymmetries. In Example 5.20, a member of the public who has rung an emergency call centre challenges the call-taker when it is suggested that she should have rung earlier.

Example 5.20

Context: Call to an Italian emergency call centre. The call-taker is trying to diagnose the problem.

CALL-TAKER:	adesso fa fatica a respirare?	*now does he have (any) difficulties breathing?*
CALLER:	fa fatica a //respirare\	*he has difficulties breathing*
CALL-TAKER:	/molto?\\	*a lot?*
CALLER:	(mah) abbastanza //( )\	*well quite ( )*
CALL-TAKER:	/da quanto\\ tempo?	*how long for?*
CALLER:	ah ha detto da un po' ieri sera un pochino poi sta notte [inhales] [slowly]: e:	*er he said since a bit last night a little bit then in the night [slowly]: er:*
CALL-TAKER:	ma non avete chiamato per niente ma//da-\	*but haven't you (guys) called at all?*
CALLER:	/[loudly]: ah\\ ue' io cioe non- me me l'ha detto solo: stamattina sono andata di là adesso ho visto messo cosi non mi han dieto niente! io stamattina sono andata a lavorare non sapevo niente!	*/[loudly]: er\\ c'mon I I mean not he told me just: this morning I went there now I've seen him like this they haven't told me anything I this morning I went to work I didn't know anything*
CALL-TAKER:	[tut] ho capito	*I see [right]*

Reprinted from *Journal of Pragmatics 41*, Monzoni, Chiara M., Direct complaints in (Italian) calls to the ambulance: The use of negatively framed questions, pp. 2470–1, © 2009, with permission from Elsevier.

The call-taker's question highlights what she considers a failure on the part of the caller. It is clear in the caller's response that she has interpreted the question as a complaint about her behaviour. She justifies her position, contesting the call-taker's accusation and rejecting any responsibility for the problem. She asserts that she did not seek help earlier as she was not aware of the problem, so she shifts the blame away from herself.

How is the expression of disagreement related to the enactment of identity?

The way that people express disagreement is influenced by the way they want to be perceived by others. For lower or equal status individuals the expression of disagreement may be avoided in some cases. When it is important to disagree, the expression of weak disagreement helps people enact their identity in a way that helps them manage workplace relationships, and that presents them as individuals who do not disagree in a direct and aggressive manner. At other times, strong disagreement can help someone demonstrate their expertise and assert their identity as a skilled and knowledgeable worker.

Responding to disagreement in backstage settings in constructive rather than aggressive ways enables participants to demonstrate that they are focused on transactional goals. This is important for leaders, subordinates and equals when wanting to enact a professional and competent workplace identity.

Disagreement is a problematic aspect of work talk, but avoiding disagreement when in a leadership position can create more problems. Dealing with it in an indirect or mitigated way allows rapport to be maintained while enacting a non-authoritarian leadership style that acknowledges the importance of team relationships. Being able to solve disagreements and negotiate consensus are skills that good leaders are expected to possess. There are also situations when it may be important for leaders to strongly express a different opinion or idea.

Mitigation, negotiation and indirectness are strategies for managing interaction which are associated with feminine interaction styles. Masculine interaction styles are perceived as being more direct. Both women and men however may use features of weak disagreement, because these features can also be associated with appropriate ways to enact professional identity in many contexts.

Cultural considerations are also always relevant. In many cultures and contexts, acceptable ways of expressing and responding to disagreement require mitigation and negotiation, particularly if a person is interacting with someone who has power over them in some way. In other cultures it is acceptable to be more direct, particularly when in a leadership position. Norms and expectations at a number of levels are important.

Factors Influencing the Way Disagreement Is Expressed and Responded To

So what factors affect the way disagreement is expressed and responded to?

The examples above highlight a number of contextual factors which affect the way disagreement is expressed (or not) and how it is responded to. As with complaints, when examining disagreement we need to consider a range of questions:

- do the participants have ongoing relationships?
- how well do they know each other?
- what are the participants' roles? (e.g., a manager disagreeing with a worker, or vice versa);
- are they interacting face-to-face or not?
- are other people present?
- what is the current purpose of the interaction?
- how important is it to disagree?
- what are the norms for the workplace setting or within the community of practice?
- how might cultural values be important?
- what about factors related to the enactment of gender or other aspects of a person's identity?

Another important feature of disagreement illustrated above is the way participants respond. The person (or people) someone is disagreeing with will react in such a way that either the differing point of view is accepted (so the disagreement is not sustained) or in ways that extend the disagreement. Often when rejecting a differing point of view a speaker will provide justification and further reasons to support their position, as in Example 5.11.

> Depending on the context, the expression of disagreement may have an effect on relationships. Disagreement is therefore often softened and expressed and responded to in ways that minimise threats to rapport. This does depend on the community of practice and/or the cultural norms and expectations that underlie interaction in different workplaces and settings. As with complaints, when disagreement is handled in ways that pay attention to the addressee's face needs, i.e., to relational aspects, then they are less likely to result in prolonged and sustained disagreement.

Conflict Talk

Definition of *Conflict Talk*

When complaints are made, there is always the potential for the recipient of the complaint to reject the complaint and disagree. There is also the potential for complaints and disagreement to turn to conflict talk.

What is conflict talk and where do we find conflict talk at work?

Conflict talk has been defined as sustained disagreement that is not resolved and that impacts negatively on rapport: see Figure 5.2.

Figure 5.2
The relationship of
disagreement to
conflict talk.

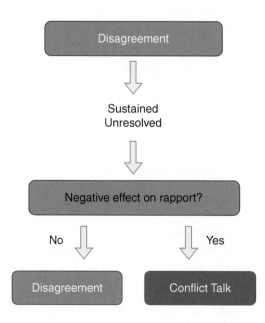

For an exchange to be seen as conflictual, negatively marked disagreement must involve at least two participants and extend over a number of turns. While disagreement or a complaint can involve single utterances, conflict talk unfolds across a disagreement sequence.

The target of disagreement is another aspect that has been used to distinguish between conflictual and non-conflictual disagreements: when disagreements are aimed at a task (content-oriented) they are less likely to be conflictual than when they are aimed at a participant (relationally oriented).

Complaints and disagreement can lead to conflict. Impolite behaviour can also lead to conflict. 'Impoliteness' has been defined as inappropriate and negatively evaluated talk or behaviour. In exploring impoliteness, Locher and Watts (2008: 79) note that people 'respond quite forcefully when the level of relational work does not match their expectations'. The interpretation of something as impolite depends on the intentions and perceptions of the participants in an interaction. Determining someone's intentions is difficult, but people's perceptions can often be clear from the way they react and if something is perceived as impolite, even if not intended to be, then conflict can arise.

In all cases, it is important to take into account speaker relationships. How long the participants have known each other and how well can be important, as well as whether the relationship is friendly or not. These factors affect the tolerance of disagreement and impoliteness and the likelihood that they will turn into conflict talk.

Conflict talk can look like strong disagreement. In Examples 5.15 and 5.16, we saw direct and unhedged disagreement. This was strong disagreement where there was no partial agreement, as seen in some of the other examples above. In Example 5.15, Rob did not further challenge

Jason and although the two speakers overlap neither raises his voice. The discussion moved on and conflict talk did not develop. With Example 5.16, the disagreement continued, but Angouri (2012) notes that the participants told her that they did not perceive the disagreement here as conflictual. This example does however provide an example of what conflict talk looks like. If the participants did not have long-term relationships that affected how they perceived this interaction then this could well have been an example of conflict talk. Talk that is acceptable and non-conflictual in one setting can be conflictual when it occurs in another context.

Conflict talk can potentially be found in any workplace setting. Anywhere that complaints or disagreement can be found is a potential place for conflict. Since conflict talk impacts negatively on relationships, people in many backstage settings will try to avoid direct conflict.

In frontstage settings, workplace representatives are encouraged to avoid conflict in interacting with the public. This means that when conflict arises, for instance when someone is becoming aggressive in complaining to a telephone call centre, the conflict tends to be one-sided. Agents are expected to keep calm and remain polite. The linguistic and interactive resources to 'do conflict' reside with callers, and therefore conflict talk does not usually occur.

Expressing and Responding in Conflict Talk

What does conflict talk look like in backstage interaction?

Koester (2018: 276–7) provides some examples of conflict talk from a meeting that looks similar to Example 5.16. In interviewing the participants she found that both felt there had been conflict. One of these examples is presented in Example 5.21.

Example 5.21

Context: An office manager, Val, and her boss, Sid, discuss a problem with a customer. The customer has a complaint and does not want to pay. Recorded in the UK.

VAL: well she said she had conversations with you //her<u>self</u>\
SID: /no she didn't\\
VAL: and so did <u>Patricia</u>=
SID: =no she didn't //if\ that's the case why didn't she (   )
VAL: /so-\\
VAL: she didn't- because it all went to [slowly]: the: i- it was all according to the
       <u>art</u>work she said it went down through to NPL

In Example 5.21, Val tells Sid what the customer has said to her on the telephone. Sid immediately disagrees with the factual content of what the customer has said. His disagreement is expressed strongly and like Rob and Garry in Examples 5.15 and 5.16 he overlaps his speech with the person he is disagreeing with. His next turn then latches to Val's turn as he reinforces his disagreement by repeating what he has just said. This example also includes the use of an 'opposition format': as the two argue, 'she didn't' is repeated several times. The disagreement continues in this interaction for some time, and a resolution is not found.

As discussed earlier, talk like this is not always perceived as conflictual by the participants. It can also be the case that talk that appears harmonious can be conflictual. In the next example one of the speakers uses mock politeness in a conflictual way. The conflict develops further as the women in this meeting make fun of the man who is chairing the meeting.

Example 5.22

Context: Meeting in a manufacturing company. David is detailing how certain product codes are calculated. The meeting has already gone over time and he had been asked to wind it up, but has started on a new topic. Recorded in the UK.

DAVID:	there are you know thirty forty different [type] codes
	depending whether it's colour red non-colour
	red charcoal um you know whatever it might be
	//er\
CAROL:	/mm\\
	[laughter from all women managers]
DAVID:	I realise //I'm\
BECKY:	/sorry\\ David we'll all stop //laughing\
DAVID:	/I realise\\
BECKY:	[laughs]
DAVID:	I'm boring you but the scary
	//there is an important point to all this\
CAROL:	/[laughs] yes yes come on then\\
DAVID:	//there's a scary\ scary footnote to all of this um
KATE:	/[laughs]\\
DAVID:	having looked at the
	//export side of things\
BECKY:	/[bangs cup on the table repeatedly]\\
DAVID:	stop hassling me
BECKY:	I wasn't I was giving you a drum roll
	[laughter from all women managers]
DAVID:	oh right
JULIE:	important //exciting bit\
BECKY:	/important\\
	[Becky and Sharon bang cups again in the sound of a drum roll]

From Mullany, Louise, 'Stop hassling me!' Impoliteness, power and gender identity in the professional workplace, p. 243. In *Impoliteness in language: Studies on its interplay with power in theory and practice*, © 2008 Mouton de Gruyter.

Carol's response to David's description of codes here results in laughter from the other women present. Becky apologises to David, and says they'll all stop laughing, but laughs herself after saying this. Her mock politeness here is impolite and conflictual. Other women in the meeting also join in with Becky, making fun of David. The women managers here are being strategically impolite to David and the performance of face-threatening impoliteness over a stretch of talk like this is conflict-laden.

What can conflict talk look like in frontstage settings?

Conflict talk in frontstage settings can look like conflictual talk in backstage settings. Example 5.23, for instance, is from a meeting where the participants are strongly disagreeing with each other, as Val and Sid did in Example 5.21. The meeting here is between the operations director of a pub chain, Patrick, and the estates manager of a multinational brewer, Luke. Patrick is attempting to resist the conditions of the brewer's contract with the pub chain requiring them to buy beer from Luke's company. This is the first time Patrick and Luke have met.

Example 5.23

Context: Meeting between two company representatives. Recorded in the UK.

PATRICK:	and the rent's + stupid so
LUKE:	not as stupid as I was trying to make it
PATRICK:	it's ridiculous already the the the amount you were trying
	to make it was absolutely um + beyond any
	business sense whatsoever

Reprinted under STM guidelines from *Text & Talk 30*, Handford, Michael and Koester, Almut, 'It's not rocket science': Metaphors and idioms in conflictual business meetings, p. 31, © 2010. Reprinted with permission of the authors and the administrators of the Cambridge CANBEC corpus.

Clearly Example 5.23 illustrates strong disagreement. The two men dispute each other's claims and use opposition formats and there is also strong vocabulary (*ridiculous, stupid*) and intensifiers (*absolutely*). While it is the rent that is characterised as 'stupid', the use of the pronoun 'you' makes this sound like a personal insult.

When the police interact with members of the public who are committing an offence of some kind there is always the potential for conflict. In Example 5.24 two male police officers have chased a motorcyclist into the countryside and have finally managed to stop him. They have demanded that he takes a breathalyser test. The motorcyclist has co-operated with this request, but resists when the police officers want to take him to the police station and leave his motorcycle unattended. The motorcyclist tries to move his motorcycle to a nearby hedge.

Example 5.24

Context: Interaction between a police officer and a motorcyclist. Recorded for a German TV documentary.

POLICE OFFICER:	ne	*nope*
	das Ding bleibt jetzt hier stehen=	*the thing stays here now=*
MOTORCYCLIST:	=ne ich schieb ihn bloβ //zur Hecke\	*no I'm just going to move it //to the hedge*
POLICE OFFICER:	/ne das Ding\\	*/nope the*
	bleibt hier	*thing\\ stays here*
	[slowly]: ne:=	*[slowly]: nope:=*
MOTORCYCLIST:	=wo die Hecke ist=	*=where the hedge is=*

POLICE OFFICER:	=[slowly]: ne:	=[slowly]: no:
	das Ding bleibt //jetzt hier stehen\	the thing stays //here now\
MOTORCYCLIST:	/ich kann ihn doch	/I can't leave him (it) out\\
	nicht so\\ in Gelände stehen lassen=	in the open like that=
POLICE OFFICER:	=das steht das bleibt jetzt /so stehen\	=it remains it's not going anywhere ...
	[the motorcyclist continues to insist that he move his motorcycle	
	to the hedge while the police officer continues to insist he leave it where it is]	
POLICE OFFICER:	[loudly]: sie bocken das jetzt hier	[loudly]: you put that here on its stand now
	sofort hier öf oder ich werd richtig	or I'll get really unpleasant:
	ungemütlich	

From Limberg, Holger, Threats in conflict talk: Impoliteness and manipulation, pp. 170–2. In *Impoliteness in language: Studies on its interplay with power in theory and practice*, © 2008 Mouton de Gruyter.

The motorcyclist is resisting the police order to come immediately with them to the station, while the police officer is refusing to allow the motorcyclist to move his bike. The officer insists repeatedly that the motorcyclist leave his bike where it is. He is obviously frustrated with the man and is not giving in to the man's requests to be allowed to move his bike. Neither participant in Example 5.24 is willing to compromise so the conflict escalates. Eventually the police officer loses patience and threatens the man. Again, we see overlapping speech, latching, and both men repeatedly use the same phrases.

© Jacynta Scurfield 2019

Examples 5.23 and 5.24 come from face-to-face frontstage interactions. Example 5.25 comes from an airline telephone helpline. As noted above, this is a context where the conflict is typically one-sided since company representatives are supposed to remain calm and not react in an aggressive manner towards angry clients. The call-taker in this interaction has previously told the caller that they should have asked for the contact number for the call centre when the problem arose at the airport as it is too late now to get compensation.

Example 5.25

Context: Call to an offshore airline helpline. The caller is British, but the call-taker is Polish and is based in Poland. They are speaking English.

CALLER:	why doesn't [company name] say that there is a phone number there ( ) why doesn't [company name] do that?
CALL-TAKER:	why didn't you ask for it?
CALLER:	[loudly]: because it's [company name] to offer it:
CALL-TAKER:	[loudly]: hold on:
CALLER:	[loudly]: stop:
CALL-TAKER:	the discussion now is very hard to manage … if you ask for this information you would be given
CALLER:	[loudly]: why should I ask for information it's [company name] who should be giving this information:
CALL-TAKER:	okay
CALLER:	[loudly]: [company name] should have given us information it is your job we are flying with your airlines: +
CALL-TAKER:	could you calm down please mister [name] I'm not giving you an option to a refund and I believe you are not willing to accept

Reprinted from *Journal of Pragmatics 76*, Archer, Dawn and Jagodziński, Piotr, Call centre interaction: A case of sanctioned face attack?, p. 63, © 2015, with permission from Elsevier.

The call-taker has turned the responsibility for asking for the contact number back onto the caller and this makes an angry caller even more angry. Both engage aggressively with each other, directly questioning each other as to 'why' and raising their voices, before the call-taker tries to calm the caller down. The caller continues to complain loudly, repeatedly insisting that the airline 'should' have given the customer the information, stressing a failure to meet their obligations on the part of the company.

Features of Conflict Talk
What are some features of conflictual talk?

In examining disagreement, we saw a number of features which are often used when disagreeing. Since conflict talk often involves disagreement these features can also be features of conflict talk.

Conflict talk therefore can have:

- overlapping speech or latching
- louder speech

- faster speech
- lack of hedging
- opposition formats
- markers of subjective stance, e.g., use of 'I think'.

Speakers may also use strong vocabulary and intensifiers as the disagreement escalates into conflict talk. They often also speak more loudly and in an aggressive manner. Because it can also arise from impoliteness, conflict talk can involve speakers making fun of others or responding in socially inappropriate and unacceptable ways that negatively impact rapport.

Conflict Talk, Power and Identity

How do power relationships influence conflict talk?

In settings where the culture of the workplace means that workplace hierarchies are acknowledged and directly reinforced in the way people communicate, a higher status person is institutionally sanctioned to express disagreement strongly. Lower status individuals in these situations are expected to accept this. Disagreement and conflict talk are therefore typically suppressed in these situations as in Example 5.20. If power relations are resisted or challenged, however, this can result in conflict. In Example 5.21 conflict talk resulted after the lower status participant, Val, continued the disagreement. Koester notes that the long-standing working relationship enabled her to disagree strongly with her boss, although in this case conflict arose because the participants were unable to find a resolution to the problem and both later described the interaction as conflictual.

Being able to solve disagreements and negotiate consensus are skills that good leaders are expected to possess. Leaders may negotiate through conflict, or assert their authority to end any conflict. In frontstage contexts, the institutional representatives are the ones who tend to hold the power. In Example 5.24, the police officer asserted his authority and power over the motorcyclist, although the man resisted this for quite some time. The imposing of authority in this way is particularly problematic for a member of the public in a high stake interaction like this where they have more to lose.

How is conflict talk related to the enactment of identity?

Since people generally want to be perceived in a positive way by others, especially when interacting with colleagues, conflict talk tends to be avoided in backstage settings. There may be times where a situation requires strong disagreement from someone in authority or someone who has expert power (i.e., power because of skills and knowledge). The imposing of a decision or point of view can result in conflict talk if this is not accepted by the addressee. Responding to disagreement in backstage settings in constructive rather than aggressive ways and by not reacting in a strongly emotional way, however, enables a participant to enact a professional and competent workplace identity.

In frontstage settings, some institutional representatives feel it is important to assert their authority and position and to engage in conflict. The police officer in Example 5.24 could have allowed the man to move his motorcycle as there would have been no harm in this, but instead insisted on enacting power over the man, presenting a forceful institutional identity.

Women have been noted to be less likely to engage in conflict talk, while also being more likely to perceive strong disagreement as having a negative effect on relationships, and therefore as being conflictual. Men in many cultures tend to view disagreement differently from how women perceive it, with strong and frequent disagreement being more acceptable, particularly when interacting with other men. The women in Example 5.22 however were seen to interact in a conflictual way towards the man chairing the meeting. Mullany (2008) notes that they did this in order to enact power over him.

As with complaints and disagreement, cultural considerations are also always important. In some cultures speakers will tend to avoid direct conflict wherever possible so as soon as an interaction begins to become conflictual they seek to defuse or divert the developing conflict. In other cultures speakers are less inclined to shy away from conflict. When speakers from backgrounds with different norms interact this can cause difficulties.

Factors Influencing the Way Conflict Talk Unfolds

So what factors affect the way conflict talk unfolds in workplace interaction?

In examining complaints and disagreement, a number of contextual factors were identified as affecting the way these are expressed (or not) and how they are responded to. A range of questions needed to be considered and these are also relevant when exploring conflict talk:

- do the participants have ongoing relationships?
- how well do they know each other?
- what are the participants' roles? (e.g., a manager disagreeing with a worker, or vice versa);
- are they interacting face-to-face or not?
- are other people present?
- what is the current purpose of the interaction?
- how important is the issue?
- what are the norms for the workplace setting or within the community of practice?
- how might cultural values be important?
- what about factors related to the enactment of gender or other aspects of a person's identity?

People manage conflict in complex and varied ways. Direct confrontation is not common in backstage workplace contexts. However, conflict talk can also appear fine on the surface and superficially polite contributions might convey a contestive or subversive message, and thus be negatively marked. If participants have a pre-existing relationship that is antagonistic this is one way it may be expressed.

Chapter Summary

This chapter has explored how people may manage both transactional and relational goals, with a focus on complaints, disagreement and conflict talk. Complaints, disagreement, and conflict talk are all potentially problematic aspects of workplace talk. Because of this, complaints and disagreement are often softened or expressed indirectly although there are some settings and contexts where norms mean that they are expressed and responded to explicitly. In examining examples from backstage settings it is important to consider the purpose of an interaction, as well as the community of practice from which the data has come. Because conflict talk is negatively marked and affects relationships, it is likely to be avoided in backstage contexts. In examining examples from frontstage settings, norms and expectations for interaction in different settings are important. In some frontstage settings, institutional representatives are encouraged to avoid conflict, while in others conflict talk is used as a way of asserting institutional authority.

Exercises

Exercise 5.1

Consider the excerpt below and then answer the questions.

Excerpt 5.A (Source: LWP)
Context: Interaction recorded in an eldercare facility in New Zealand.

NANCY: someone's taken my place at the at that table
with Vera and that
where I've //been sitting\ yeah I've been sitting there
ALEC: /have they?\\
NANCY: I went down at lunchtime and the
Rodney was bringing the thing down with the food
and he'd put mine on the tray
so I said oh I'd take it and have it in the lounge
cos I was all ready you know
so I picked the tray and I went in the lounge
and there was another woman in my seat
an old lady I didn't see her properly
I just looked away and came out
cos I felt embarrassed
so I had it down here #
gonna have all my meals in here in future I've decided
//if they're gonna put someone in my seat\
ALEC: /[voc] + s- I'm\\ I'm sure it's just the new lady
she's just trying to find a spot …
we can find another spot for you
we can find another spot for her

NANCY: what?
ALEC: if you want that spot we can give it to you …
NANCY: I'll come down and see about the sitting
ALEC: alright that's good I'll find you a spot
NANCY: yeah but I don't want to l- sit anywhere else

1. What do you think is going on in this excerpt?
2. Who is Nancy? What role do you think Alec has?
3. How does Nancy present her message? What features are there in her speech that soften the message or make it stronger?
4. How does Alec respond? What features of his speech mitigate his response?

Exercise 5.2
Consider the excerpt below and then answer the questions.

Excerpt 5.B (Source: LWP)
Context: Problem-solving meeting in a New Zealand commercial organisation. They are discussing the draft of a report, including the wording, although some members of the group do not think this is important.

LINDY: so that word research
            I don't know how people felt about it
            but there's a separate research function
            and so whether the word research
            is the appropriate word for that stage in the process …
JACOB: we tossed out some other words
            we tossed out words like modelling
            cos //you could\ also say that's what //you're\ doing …
LINDY: /yeah\\   /yep\\
CALLUM?:   it's too narrow though
BARRY?:   it's too narrow
DUDLEY: //yeah\
JACOB: /but\\ it is a little bit too narrow …
BARRY: it's something we can work on //later like let's not get hung up on\ about it now
LINDY: /yeah (   )\\
LINDY: no
CALLUM: oh i- when I read it it enabled me to dis- to differentiate between those
            um the people that were doing sort of low powered
            //assessment\
DUDLEY: /assessment\\
CALLUM: which is what you used
DUDLEY: yeah
CALLUM: which which I previously would have been used low powered analysis …
BARRY: can people get past you know their today's hang ups //on what that word means?\
DUDLEY: /oh yeah [laughs]: yeah:\\
BARRY: [laughs]

1. What do you think is going on in this excerpt?
2. Are all the speakers in agreement?
3. What features are there that soften the message throughout the excerpt?
4. What features strengthen it?
5. What factors would you want to consider in order to decide if this interaction is conflictual or not?

....

Further Reading

Stubbe et al. (2003) is a useful paper that explores a complaint using different approaches to analysis, while the articles in the 2012 Special Issue of the *Journal of Pragmatics* on complaints explore data from a range of settings. There is also a 2012 special issue of the *Journal of Pragmatics* which explores disagreement in relation to conflict and (im)politeness and includes contributions on workplace discourse. Greatbatch (1992) is a helpful resource in relation to disagreement, while Koester (2018) provides an excellent introduction to conflict talk.

What about Identity and the Way This Is Enacted in the Workplace?

III. What about
Identity and
the Way This
is Enacted in
the Workplace?

6 The Language of Leadership

CHAPTER PREVIEW

This chapter provides a brief introduction to the language of leadership, including:

- a brief definition of **leadership**;
- consideration of the importance of language in leadership;
- illustration of leaders achieving transactional goals;
- illustration of leaders achieving relational goals;
- exploration of different styles of leadership; and
- exploration of different models of leadership.

Leadership is important when exploring interaction in many workplace settings. In any situation where people with different status interact, leadership may be enacted. People may also enact leadership even when they do not have a formal leadership role.

Leadership and Language: Introduction

Being a leader is an aspect of someone's identity that will be evident in the way they interact. Consider Example 6.1:

Example 6.1 (Source: LWP)

Context: Meeting of all staff recorded in a private organisation in New Zealand.

YVONNE: so for the last month or so
           business support has been minus a manager …
           I think it is a credit April and um Briar
           who have managed to sort of keep everything going er relatively easily …
           we had a [subject] workshop in Māori
           that was taken by Sheree and Pat that was amazing …
           all credit to them they were just fantastic I thought

Yvonne is the managing director of the company and this excerpt is from a meeting of all the organisation's staff, where she is providing updates on various areas and also calling at times on her managers to report on issues related to the sections they manage. In this small excerpt from the staff meeting, Yvonne updates staff on a couple of things, keeping them informed on what has been happening. She also compliments staff on their performance. The content of her utterances here clearly shows that she is someone in a position of authority, that she is a leader.

In this chapter, the ways that people can enact leadership are explored, along with issues of importance when considering leadership in a range of workplace settings. This includes a basic definition of leadership, as well as exploring how leadership is evident in the strategies people choose and the ways people interact at work. Different styles of leadership are outlined and illustrated, as well as different models of leadership.

Definition of *Leadership*

What is *leadership*?

This is a rather complex question and there are many different definitions of leadership. A simple definition is that leadership is something people *do* to provide direction to others. It involves the enactment of authority in interaction.

Leadership has been talked about in terms of innate traits or learnable behaviours. This approach, however, reflects an essentialist view. When considering leadership from a social constructionist perspective we instead examine how people *enact* or *do* leadership and how this is negotiated and constructed in interaction with others, acknowledging the crucial role that language plays in leadership.

© Jacynta Scurfield 2019

Researching leadership while acknowledging the crucial role of language in the leadership process has been referred to as a **discursive leadership** approach (Fairhurst 2007). This is in contrast to **leadership psychology** which is concerned with the perceptions and self-reflections of leaders.

Researchers taking a **discursive leadership** approach utilise analytical approaches such as those outlined in Chapter 2, for instance, CA or interactional sociolinguistics. They therefore aim to provide insights into how leadership is *actually* done by examining authentic workplace talk.

What about formal and informal leadership?

Yvonne from Example 6.1 is a **formal leader**. **Formal leaders** are appointed or elected to direct and control the activities of subordinates. In Yvonne's case, she is the managing director of a company which she set up and she has a formal role as company director.

Informal leaders can also often be found in workplace settings. In many situations there are people who command respect and who others feel they can approach for help or guidance, even if these people are not officially and formally recognised as leaders. They may have expertise, knowledge and/or experience that others recognise and acknowledge.

If someone has expertise in an area they may also be expected to step up and lead when an issue is in their area of expertise, depending on the norms for the group. Different groups may also come together for different projects or sub-projects and may have different leaders for each one.

Anyone, however, may at times potentially enact leadership. In Chapter 2, Example 2.1 for instance, Tina, a registered nurse was seen to speak up in a way that showed her constructing herself as a leader among the group of nurses.

Leadership, and the way it is enacted, is important in many different workplace contexts, from offices to hospitals to schools to factories. In many situations, people need to work as part of a team, so will often have a leader or manager who is responsible for making sure goals are achieved. Even when someone does not officially have this role, one or more people may step up as informal leaders to make sure things go smoothly, and as noted above, anyone may enact leadership depending on the demands of a particular situation.

Leadership Behaviours

What are some leadership behaviours that leaders need to enact?

When people think of leaders they often think of charismatic politicians making inspirational speeches. And sometimes leaders do need to make motivational speeches, as in Example 6.2.

Example 6.2 (Source: LWP)

Context: Management team meeting in a private organisation. Recorded in New Zealand.

STEPHEN: you guys are managing all areas which are gonna be affected ...
you've got to own your own areas and the change within them
promoting and embracing the change within our teams ...
the ones that want to do well
the ones that want to embrace the change
they'll be jumping out of their skins to be part of it ...
and the last part of what I've got to say
and polarise everything I've just said about this er
consequences of any individual not coping
or not wanting to or not just not doing it that
that sometimes will happen
we will need to find people that can
and I put that expectation on you guys
and you need to put that with your guys
nothing's gonna hold us back here
and if er if it does we're gonna remove it
we can't get somewhere great
without having everyone on board
everyone doing their best
and without removing obstacles

Reproduced from Holmes, Janet, Marra, Meredith and Vine, Bernadette, *Leadership, discourse, and ethnicity*, p. 114, © 2011 Oxford University Press. Reproduced with permission from Oxford Publishing Limited through PLSclear.

In Example 6.2, Stephen, the managing director of a company, is talking about some changes that will be made in the company in the near future. Stephen uses strong, persuasive language here. He directly appeals to the team, 'you've got to own your own areas', and talks about 'promoting' and 'embracing' change. He is highly motivated to succeed and has high expectations of his management staff.

Leaders do need to inspire and motivate their staff on a daily basis, but this does not often mean making speeches like this. Motivation can be more subtle, for instance, giving positive feedback to staff, listening to them or having them see you achieving objectives.

The two key behaviours a leader needs to demonstrate relate to the achievement of:

- transactional goals; and
- relational goals.

Transactional behaviours aimed at achieving workplace goals and outcomes are indispensable for effective leaders in workplace contexts, but they also need to balance this with relational behaviours aimed at enhancing interpersonal relationships and creating a positive working environment. Both types of behaviours are needed to keep staff motivated.

Both behaviours are therefore equally important aspects of leadership and they are often closely intertwined with each other. In the small section of the staff meeting shown in Example 6.1, for instance, Yvonne orients to transactional goals in terms of updating her staff and keeping them informed on what has been happening. She also orients to relational goals in the way she compliments members of her staff on their performance.

Achieving Transactional Goals

What are some transactional goals leaders need to achieve?

Transactional leadership goals (or functions) leaders need to achieve include:

- initiating action/giving directives;
- managing disagreement/conflict/complaints;
- setting goals;
- organising;
- co-ordinating/guiding to achieve goals;
- decision-making;
- managing meetings.

Since these behaviours are typically associated with the notions of power, authority and influence, by performing them, people enact leadership. We have seen examples throughout this book which show leaders achieving transactional goals. In Chapter 3, for instance, there were many cases of leaders directing staff to complete tasks and in Chapter 5, we saw leaders complaining or dealing with complaints and disagreement. Example 6.3 shows a further example of a leader complaining and also issuing a directive.

Example 6.3

Context: Section chief/supervisor complaining to staff at a foreign language school. She is talking to fourteen subordinates at a regular faculty meeting. Recorded in Japan.

SUPERVISOR:	dakara ano	*so um*
	orijinaru wa	*the originals*
	moo nani ga attemo	*no matter what happens*
	modoshite kudasai ne	***please return them***
	... orijinaru nai to hora	*... without the originals look*
	kopii dekinai desho	*we can't make copies can we?*
	are ga nai to yappari	*without those*
	sugoku komatchau node	*we are really in big trouble so*

The polite Japanese imperative form 'verb root+*te kudasai*' is used here by the supervisor to the teachers to give a directive that relates to actions that take place in another time and place. She also supports her directive by providing reasons for it. She issues the directive because people have not been returning the original teaching materials after using them for their classes. Takano (2005) notes that the polite way she does this enables her to construct an appropriate leadership identity.

Leaders often need to issue directives, and studies on leadership which have explored team meetings have also highlighted the crucial role of leaders in setting goals and guiding staff to achieve these. In Example 6.4, Karen, the board director of Human Resources (HR) for an organisation, outlines goals and guides the team in what she wants them to do in relation to these goals.

Example 6.4

Context: Meeting of regional HR directors of an organisation. Major restructuring is occurring in the organisation and Karen has been outlining the implications of this for the HR directors and how she wants them to manage this process. Lily is Karen's personal assistant. Recorded in the UK.

KAREN: ... so er Lily you've obviously captured that point
but I've captured all of the others that you've been sending me in
... and it's great
please continue to do so
Gail had a another one late last night
er and you know in some ways they seem quite small
but er with the modernisation programme
our part time recruitment form isn't fit for purpose ++
I know some of you are sitting there saying recruitment?
recruitment? ... we're doing the opposite
but there are some regions that are having to change their mix
and are clearly needing to do some part time recruitment
so there's some effects like that and they're coming thick and fast
so please continue with them

um then I will do a session in January
where we go through those answers
and ideally bring group HR lead team in to bring their bit as well

Karen wants the group of HR directors to accept her guidance here about how the restructuring process will be managed. She had already started talking about the feedback process she has put in place and here she continues her explanation of this process, offering a justification of its value and encouraging the team members to contribute.

One of the things that leaders are expected to do is make decisions. Looking at decision-making in meetings is therefore an interesting place to explore the enactment of leadership. Do leaders impose their decisions on others or do they consult and involve other people in the decision-making process? In Example 6.5, the chairwoman of a women's co-operative strongly influences the decision that is made, but does this in a way that presents her opinion as one that will save the group from problems. The women are discussing a trip to buy material.

Example 6.5

Context: Meeting of a women's co-operative. Recorded in Zanzibar.

CHAIRWOMAN:	mkutano wetu wa leo kuhusu safari	*our meeting today is on our trip*
	yetu ya kwenda kuchukua kanga	*to get kangas*
	mpaka hivi hasa pesa zinakuweko si nyingi	*until now there is not enough money*
	kwa kuchukua nguo na matenge hazitutoshi	*to get cloth [kanga] and fabrics*
	kwa ninavyoona mimi bora mwezi huu	*as I see it it is better if we cancel our trip*
	tusitishe kwenda chukua	*so what do you say my friends? ++*
	sasa nyini wenzangu mnasema vipi hapa? ++	
	[she talks about the problem with people not paying in the past	
	which means they do not have money for the trip] ...	
CHAIRWOMAN:	sasa pesa hizo hatujazipata	*now we haven't got this money yet*
	mwezi ishirini tutafanva vipi?	*what will we do on the twentieth of the month?*
MEMBER:	tutakwenda kopa	*we will borrow*
	[Laughter from group members]	
CHAIRWOMAN:	[laughs] kwa fikiria zangu # ee #	*[laughs] in my opinion yes*
	nilikuwa naona huko nyuma kama tulikuwa	*I thought as we had problems*
	na wasiwasi kuhusu pesa na huku nyuma tuna	*concerning money before*
	deni basi bora sasa naona tu tusimame	*and even from earlier we have debts*
	tulilipe lile deni kwanza halafu wakati	*well now it would be better*
	ule mwisho wa mwezi ule ukafika	*if we stopped we should pay that debt*
	tutakuja kupata pesa kwa urahisi zaidi	*first and then at the end of the month*
	za kukopa kuliko kwenda kuja kwa madeni	*it will be easier to get the borrowed*
	ya mara mbili ...	*money instead of incurring double debts*

The chairwoman of the group introduces the topic for discussion. Hanak (1998: 41) notes that her switch from the initial *we*, 'mkutano wetu' (*our meeting*) to *me*, 'ninavyoona mimi' (*as I see it*) is a hedge as she knows that her proposal is not yet shared by all members. Lack of money will prevent the group from carrying out the trip as planned as many customers have not paid. The chairwoman uses her authority to put the lack of money on the agenda before stating her personal opinion. There is no immediate response by other group members when she invites contributions from other participants, so she continues by summing up a previous decision of the group to stimulate the discussion. She then asks the group again what they should do. When someone suggests they borrow money, the group responds with laughter. The chairwoman continues to explain her suggestion and there then follows a long and lively discussion on the problem of incurring debts. Consensus is finally reached that there will be no trip until former debts have been paid, with the chairwoman persuading members to a common strategy. In the lively atmosphere of a heated discussion, the chairwoman takes control and makes the others listen to her explanations and strongly influences the final decision.

The manager of a group often takes the role of chair, being in charge of opening and closing the meeting, introducing the agenda, keeping the discussion on track, and summarising progress. Example 6.6 shows the beginning of an informal meeting in an Italian company. The chair, who is also the most senior of the three people present, introduces here the topic for discussion at the meeting.

Example 6.6

Context: Meeting of three people in the Quality Assurance section of a company. Recorded in Italy.

CHAIR: allora nell ambito di quella discussione   *now then last time from that*
        la volta scorsa e venuta fuori er   *discussion* a proposal *came*
        una proposta che poi e stata   *out agreed on by nearly everyone*
        condivisa un po da tutti me compreso   *myself included and last night*
        e ieri sera anche dal capo che er   *also by the boss which would*
        vedrebbe er una responsabilitia   *envisage global responsibility*
        globale dell'assicurazione qualita   *by Quality Assurance in the*
        nella quality review di   *marketing quality review*
        commercializzazione

Reprinted with permission from Bargiela-Chiappini, Francesca and Harris, Sandra, *Managing language: The discourse of corporate meetings*, pp. 70–1, © 1997, John Benjamins Publishing.

The most senior participant in Example 6.6 acts as chair. The role of chair is a leadership role which is not always performed by the leader of a team. Some work groups have a system where they use a revolving chair, sharing this role from one meeting to the next between different members of the team. In some situations a person may be brought in to chair a meeting because they do not have a vested interest in the outcomes. Whoever chairs needs to enact leadership in order to facilitate a successful meeting.

Examples 6.7 and 6.8 are from meetings where a member of the group, Caleb, is chairing for the first time. A system of a revolving chair has recently been introduced to the work team by Daniel, the chief executive officer (CEO) of the organisation. Caleb has chaired other groups before, but not this one. He is not the most senior person present and the CEO prompts him to start, and also gives him feedback at the end on how he should allocate the role of chair for the next meeting.

Example 6.7 (Source: LWP)

Context: Opening of a management team meeting in a government organisation. Recorded in New Zealand.

DANIEL: way you go Caleb
CALEB: oh okay kia ora anō tātou katoa   *[hello again everyone]*

Reprinted under STM guidelines from the *Journal of Cross-Cultural Psychology*, Vine, Bernadette, 2019. Context matters: Exploring the influence of norms, values and context on a Māori male manager, p. 1189.

Example 6.8 (Source: LWP)

Context: Closing of a management team meeting in a government organisation. Recorded in New Zealand.

CALEB: nothing else?
          thank you very much
          who's chairing next week? +
DANIEL: you get to pick them Caleb
CALEB: oh do you I thought it was just a +
          oh because it's your first week of ( ) do you want to chair Hari?

Reprinted under STM guidelines from the *Journal of Cross-Cultural Psychology*, Vine, Bernadette, 2019. Context matters: Exploring the influence of norms, values and context on a Māori male manager, p. 1190.

Caleb has had the role of chair in this meeting so opens and closes the meeting, introduces the agenda and keeps the meeting on track. Because this is the first time he has done this, Daniel, the group's leader, directs Caleb, making clear his own position in the group.

Leaders often dominate the talking time and manage and control the contributions of others in meetings. Although Caleb facilitates the meeting in Examples 6.7 and 6.8 by introducing the agenda, summarising and keeping the meeting moving through the agenda items, he does not talk much when issues that are within other people's areas of expertise and responsibility are being discussed. Daniel guides Caleb by prompting him to start the meeting and also takes a more active role in managing the talk once Caleb has introduced each agenda item. In Example 6.9, from the same meeting, we see how Daniel directs Frank, another member of the team, to provide feedback on an issue.

Example 6.9 (Source: LWP)

Context: Management team meeting in a government organisation. Recorded in New Zealand.

DANIEL:	how do you wanna deal with it Frank? +
FRANK:	er my initial reaction was to ask him
	well to go back and find out what his [tribe name]
	what's the arrangement he's got with [tribe name]
	what are they wanting
DANIEL:	mm
FRANK:	if he's not working in with his iwi *[tribe]*
	I don't really see that we should be
	//necessarily\ providing sort of support to him
DANIEL:	/yeah\\
CALEB?:	yep
FRANK:	one individual even though the sort of mahi *[work]*
	is sort of more important at one level
DANIEL:	yeah

Daniel's identity as a leader is evident here as he seeks Frank's input on an issue. He asks him to speak and listens as Frank, who has a great deal of experience and knowledge about the issue, gives his view. He involves Frank in the decision-making process on this issue, and in the end endorses the solution that Frank proposes here.

> There are a range of transactional leadership goals (or functions) that leaders need to achieve. This includes issuing directives, setting goals, organising, decision-making and managing meetings. Performing these types of behaviours is how people enact leadership.

Achieving Relational Goals

What are some relational goals leaders need to achieve?

Relational leadership goals (or functions) leaders need to achieve include:

- building/maintaining rapport within teams;
- building confidence in followers.

Again, there are many examples of leaders orienting to relational goals in the earlier chapters of this book. In Chapter 4, for instance, we saw how leaders used social talk and humour to build and maintain rapport with members of their teams.

In Example 6.10, a leader uses humour to help defuse tension when meeting participants have been struggling to reach agreement on something. She uses direct strategies, expressing her leadership position quite strongly, but balances this with more mitigated strategies which orient to maintaining a good relationship within the group.

Example 6.10

Context: Meeting of people from different groups discussing where different company logos need to go on a backdrop for a conference. Badria is the chair and Dr Sara is from another organisation (UOD). Recorded in Bahrain.

Dr Sara:	what happens is that usually the main people are er on the top
	and the ones who're supporting or something come at the base
Badria:	we don't accept this
Amal:	//no\
Omar:	/no\\
Dr Sara:	//wha-\
Badria:	/for\\ example in the opening of the Centre
	it was always SATCO56 then Bahrainco
	but that was an event between Bah-in Bahrainco
Amal:	GPC it happened before so we ar- I know we know
	//similar to this case\
Omar:	/usually we put all\\ of them on the bottom
Amal:	at the bottom
Dr Sara:	we can put UOD on top and
	//we can\
Badria:	/no no\\
	[everyone laughs]
	do you want these guys to lose their jobs?
	[everyone laughs]

From Baxter, Judith and Al A'ali, Haleema, *Speaking as women leaders: Meetings in Middle Eastern and Western contexts,* p. 54, published 2016 Palgrave Macmillan. Reproduced with permission of SNCSC.

There has been a long heated discussion about this issue, with Dr Sara disagreeing with the other meeting participants. At the beginning of this excerpt she attempts to convince people by offering her expert knowledge on what normally happens. Badria responds by explicitly disagreeing, 'we don't accept this'. Amal and Omar also reinforce Badria's position and Badria explains the reason behind her disagreement, recounting the case of a previous event. Her justification here softens her disagreement as she explains to Dr Sara what they have had to do in the past, which is different from the norms Dr Sara has been referring to. Again, Amal and Omar support Badria's position. Dr Sara has been outnumbered throughout the discussion and at this point tries to ease the tension by suggesting that UOD's logo should be on top. Al A'ali notes that this is obviously a joke, and everybody laughs (Baxter and Al A'ali 2016: 56). Badria maintains the humorous tone at this point, commenting 'do you want these guys to lose their jobs?' Badria has utilised assertive language strategies here, but balances this with facilitative language strategies which orient to relational goals.

As noted above, leaders will often orient to both transactional and relational goals. Example 6.11 also shows a manager skilfully achieving transactional and relational goals.

Example 6.11

Context: A school principal is making her report to a school forum. Recorded in Austria.

PRINCIPAL: we were all very happy with every class …
we've still got <u>a few</u> problems
a few worries with the first year classes …
they've still got a few problems with the discipline
but I think we're hoping that soon enough
it'll be alright and we'll soon have them
just like in the other classes
and that's also something
that I would like to point out very positively
you notice here that all the teachers chime in together …
I think that has a really good effect on the atmosphere here

Reprinted with permission from Wodak, Ruth, 'I know, we won't revolutionize the world with it, but…': Styles of female leadership in institutions, p. 364. In *Communicating gender in context*, © 1997, John Benjamins Publishing.

Wodak (1997: 366) observed that the school leader here skilfully disguised her criticism with praise and avoided conflict by creating a general consensus while emphasising co-operation. The principal highlighted a problem with the first year classes at the school, but in identifying with the teachers and saying 'we'll soon have them just like in the other classes' she is not blaming the teachers and creates a sense of solidarity among the

© Jacynta Scurfield 2019

people at the forum. The criticism is also surrounded by positive comments, 'we were all very happy with every class' and 'that's also something that I would like to point out very positively', which soften it.

Complimenting is one strategy leaders can use to build confidence in their followers. Other strategies they can use include encouraging subordinates to take on tasks that help develop their skills. In Example 6.12, Daniel asks one of his team to take on a task that he could have easily undertaken himself.

Example 6.12 (Source: LWP)

Context: Closing of a meeting of all staff in a government organisation. Recorded in New Zealand.

DANIEL: we started with a karakia *[prayer]*
        we'll finish with one eh um … Hari ++
HARI: kia ora mai tātou …   *hello/thank you everyone*

Daniel nominates the youngest member of his management team to lead the final prayer to close the meeting. This is an important cultural component of the meeting and assigning this role to Hari recognises Hari's status within the group, as well as allowing Hari to build confidence in taking on roles of this type.

This type of mentoring behaviour from Daniel is a way that leaders can build confidence while enacting leadership. Giving advice rather than directives is another strategy that a leader can use to do this. In Example 6.13, a company president gives advice to his sales manager.

Example 6.13

Context: Meeting between Chris, the company president, and Joe, the sales manager. Joe has compiled a list of ways the sales representatives should *not* begin conversations with prospective customers. This will be used for training purposes. Chris has looked at the list. Recorded in the USA.

CHRIS: er I got a suggestion by the way with this
JOE: okay
CHRIS: two things … I was thinking this also
        the I was wondering approach [laughs] //[laughs\
JOE: /yeah I was\\ wondering
        [laughs] yeah I like that okay

This is the last of a list of topics which the two have discussed in this meeting. Chris is clear at the beginning of this discussion to signal that what he is about to say is advice and not a directive. He is the advice-giver so this is a role that he can take on quite legitimately as boss, but he is also empowering Joe because he deals with this as advice, rather than issuing directives. Joe has the option of accepting or rejecting the advice, although here he does seem to accept the advice, which given the power differences between the two might be expected. The framing of this as advice by Chris though supports Joe as someone who Chris trusts to make good decisions and who does not need to be explicitly told how to deal with the issue.

> Leaders need to achieve relational as well as transactional goals, building and maintaining rapport and building confidence in team members. They may use a range of strategies to do this, including humour, complimenting and mentoring behaviours.

The Joint Construction of Leadership

How is leadership jointly constructed?

An important consideration when approaching leadership from a social constructionist perspective is the idea that it is jointly constructed. Leadership behaviours are not just performed by an individual but are collaboratively enacted among various members of a team. Followers play a crucial role in leadership, and not just because without followers there would be no-one to lead.

In the meeting Example 6.1 comes from, Yvonne's staff help her to enact her identity as a leader. They listen and do not challenge or question her about her assessments of how the company and its staff are performing.

Helping a leader to enact leadership may also be as simple as answering their questions, speaking when directed, and agreeing to plans that leaders propose. In Example 6.10, Amal and Omar both support Badria's disagreement with Dr Sara, providing support when she challenges Dr Sara about norms. Their behaviour helps Badria enact her leadership identity.

Others can also help construct a person's identity as a leader in a more active way, for instance, by asking the leader for advice or guidance. In Example 6.14, two members of a leader's team seek clarification and direction from her in a team meeting.

Example 6.14 (Source: LWP)

Context: Team meeting in a government organisation. Recorded in New Zealand.

a. JARED: Angelina what was the trigger for the um reports
            being sent to the review panel in the first place?

b. CANDICE: so Angelina does this matter call for
            some immediate response from the commission
            or do we have to do something?

Reproduced from Holmes, Janet, Marra, Meredith and Vine, Bernadette, *Leadership, discourse, and ethnicity*, p. 109, © 2011 Oxford University Press. Reproduced with permission from Oxford Publishing Limited through PLSclear.

Followers can also construct a leader when the person is not present. They may refer to decisions the leader has made in relation to issues or to directives or advice they have been given by the leader, or which they need to seek from the leader. In Example 6.6, the chair introduced the topic of the meeting and then referred to the agreement of the boss to the proposal they were going to discuss. He is the leader in the context of the meeting he is opening, but clearly marks his place as a link in the chain of command.

Example 6.15 demonstrates how one of Yvonne's senior managers, Quentin, constructs Yvonne as a leader because she needed to be consulted about the appointment of a new member of staff. He had met with the potential employee along with Joseph, another manager from the organisation. He tells a senior member of his team about this.

Example 6.15 (Source: LWP)

Context: Meeting between a manager, Quentin, and a member of his team, Paula. Recorded in a private organisation in New Zealand.

QUENTIN: she brought Hana along
           her //um\ e- employee representative
PAULA: /oh okay\\
QUENTIN: //so\ they we had a good discussion
PAULA: /[laughs]\\
QUENTIN: we had a good meeting yesterday
           and so we've just got some things that um
           Joseph and I met with them
           and cos they had some additional things
           that they wanted to be considered
           so and we had to talk with Yvonne this morning

Quentin and Joseph have met with the potential new employee, but it is clear here that they will not make a decision on the interviewee's additional conditions regarding employment without consulting Yvonne, the company director. This positions her as the head of the organisation and the person with the authority to make the required decision.

Rather than supporting leaders in enacting leadership, followers may also challenge leaders. This can put a leader in a position where they need to assert their leadership identity more forcefully and/or manage disagreement and challenges to their authority, as in Example 6.16.

Example 6.16 (translated from Danish)

Context: Meeting involving three men and one woman, Natalie. Natalie is the leader and chair. Recorded in Denmark.

PETER: *but [slowly]: er: what are we [slowly]: er:*
           what are we supposed to talk about sort of?
NATALIE: *well I've been //sort of thinking what might*
PETER: */what are we what are we (   )*
           is there an agenda? or do we just er or how do we

NATALIE: *well you know I've sort of been thinking*
           that we might perhaps [slowly]: er:
           there's no agenda but if you wanted to discuss something
           [slowly]: er: a particular problem
           then perhaps we might do that you know
ALL: *okay*

Peter here challenges his boss, Natalie, about the purpose for the
meeting. His criticism is hedged through the hesitant way he is speaking
and his use of 'sort of', but it is still clear that he is criticising the way
Natalie is chairing the meeting. He is questioning Natalie's authority, and
her competence as a leader, and is enacting power by suggesting she is
not managing things appropriately.

Natalie replies to this in a similarly hedged manner, which has the
effect of suggesting that she does not have a clear agenda. However,
Ladegaard (2011a: 14) notes that in subsequent turns, she says that she
intended these meetings for 'free discussions of ad hoc problems', which
reflects her collaborative, person/process-oriented approach to leadership.
The meeting continues for another forty minutes, demonstrating that
there were plenty of issues that needed to be discussed, even without a
formal agenda.

Natalie is the leader of the team. Sometimes when someone enacts
leadership when their official role is as a peer, others may feel a legitimate
need to challenge them, as in Example 6.17.

Example 6.17

Context: Meeting of the editorial board of a corporate magazine. The editor, Clas,
introduces a new topic, a column called 'Inventing people'. The company was
created when a Swedish company and a Finnish company merged. The working
language is English.

CLAS: [slowly]: so: what about inventing people ++
        one page Finland one page Sweden one page=
LIISA: =one page each=
CLAS: =Germany //mm\
LIISA: /ja [yes]\\ ++
KARL: I think we should ++ three examples should be enough
CLAS: //yeah\ [nods]
MATS: /mm\
LIISA: /ja [yes]\\ [nods]
VESA: it's enough +++
CLAS: and we- someone of you needs to write an an ingress about it as well ++
MATS: [tut] [leans back in chair] [pause]
        [discussion about labelling of documents] ...
MATS: bu- but er I think that it's [slowly]: a: good idea to let
        Germany [holds open hand towards Vesa]
        //er (   ) take\ the first //er\ step here

CLAS: /exactly as I was\\   /yes\\
       [Mats taps fingers on the table]
CLAS: I think so too
MATS: mm …
       so you- [slowly]: so: you are going to write the intro
       and so on [gazing at Vesa]
VESA: really?

Reprinted from *Journal of Pragmatics 78*, Svennevig, Jan and Djordjilovic, Olga, Accounting for the right to assign a task in meeting interaction, pp. 107–8, © 2015, with permission from Elsevier.

Clas, the editor has introduced the new topic of a column which will have a page on each of three countries. The team members have responsibility for different countries so they know who will be involved. Clas also comments that an 'ingress' or introduction will be needed, so this is a task that one of the three needs to undertake, although he does not nominate anyone to take this on. After a discussion of a related issue, Mats returns to the issue of who will write the introduction, proposing that this task falls to Vesa (who has responsibility for writing the Germany page). It is not Mats's role to assign this task and Vesa questions this. When someone enacts leadership when they do not have clear authority to do so they place themselves in a position where they may be challenged.

> Leaders cannot lead without followers. Followers play an important role in helping leaders enact leadership. This can involve the way team members accept a leader's enactment of their leadership identity by supporting them, either passively or actively. People can also challenge a person's enactment of leadership.

Leadership Styles

What about different styles of leadership?

There are many different ways of doing leadership. As well as being male, the stereotypical leader is authoritative and direct when interacting with subordinates. Acknowledgement of the important role of relational behaviours as well as transactional behaviours in leadership means that this stereotype does not even begin to adequately portray how many effective leaders enact leadership.

In leadership psychology, there has been a great deal of discussion of different types of leaders and leadership styles, and different labels have been used to refer to these. For instance, four main types that have been identified are:

1. *The Charismatic Leader*
   This type of leader has an infectious energy and a passionate personality. They are said to be highly effective at motivating teams to act and

to solve problems. Examples 6.1 and 6.2 showed Yvonne and Stephen, the managing directors of their companies, behaving in this way.

2. *The Democratic Leader*

The democratic leader makes all team members feel valuable and acknowledges individual input as part of the wider team. They create dedicated work teams by giving them ownership of goals. This type of leadership style has also been referred to as **consultative**. When Daniel asks Frank what he wants to do in Example 6.9, he is enacting this type of leadership style. In Example 6.18, Harry, the chair of the meeting, demonstrates this style, consulting the group about adding a new item to the meeting agenda.

Example 6.18 (Source: *Corporation: After Mr. Sam* documentary)

Context: Management meeting from a private company. Recorded in Canada.

IRVING:	alright so I say to start it off
	why don't we give
	why don't we take the barriers as Oscar just suggested …
	I would like to suggest that we do this
	I think we should just bring out and let the people say <u>why</u>
	they feel these things were suggested
	and I think we're gonna learn more about what's wrong
	than we would in any other manner
	[several people talk at once]
?:	(I think that was) a good suggestion actually
?:	that that we look at barriers
	to //( )\
HARRY:	/[to the group]: how\\ do you feel
	about barriers? you want to go into barriers?:
?:	yes I would
?:	I think it's a good suggestion
?:	( )
?:	absolutely
HARRY:	( ) we're on barriers now

Having heard Irving's suggestion and at least one person endorsing this, Harry then turns to the group and asks them if they want to discuss this issue. Several people agree and Harry then confirms that this is a topic that they will cover. As chair, Harry could have adopted or rejected the suggestion. Instead, he involves the group in this decision, and allows the topic to be added to the agenda.

3. *The Commanding Leader*

This type of leader has a forceful personality which can cause conflict with the wider team. They do not consult and issue forceful directives. This **authoritarian** style of leadership is said to be vital in times of business crisis. In Example 6.19, the section head of a unit in a bank can be seen to enact this style.

Example 6.19

Context: Unit meeting from a bank in Hong Kong.

Section Head:	gaam ni yeung ye ngo mm maan	*I'm not going to ask you*
	lei yaumou maantaai laak	*whether you have any questions*
	yui jou mou yaumou maantaai	*about this one # you must do it!*
	gaak laak	*there's no question about it*

Reprinted under STM guidelines from *Discourse & Society 9*, Yeung, Lorrita N. T., 1998. Linguistic forms of consultative management discourse, p. 85.

Yeung (1998: 85) notes that the supervisor was forced into a position where he felt he needed to exercise power in this way because his subordinates had repeatedly failed to comply with regulations.

This type of leadership is also appropriate in contexts where work is time-sensitive and/or high-stakes. The surgeon in Chapter 3, Example 3.4, was shown giving explicit directives using imperatives in a context where the success of the operation, and potentially the life of a patient, does not allow for consultation and negotiation of when and how actions are carried out.

4. *The 'Laissez Faire' Leader*

The fourth type of leader takes a 'hands-off' approach to leadership, giving little guidance to teams and allowing them to make most of the decisions. This type of leadership is successful in mature teams, but can be very unhelpful if a team needs clear direction and has less experience. In Example 6.20, Greg demonstrates this type of leadership. He generally has a more consultative, democratic leadership style, but here he takes an even more hands-off approach. He is the CEO of this company and is interacting with his senior management team, who are all very experienced senior managers. The issue they are discussing at this point of the meeting is one that relates most to Theo's team.

Example 6.20 (Source: LWP)

Context: Management team meeting in a government organisation. Greg is the CEO. Recorded in New Zealand.

GREG:	so what are we gonna do then?
THEO:	I guess I guess I should have the first say
	seeing (he's) my staff member and I would support it
MARAMA:	mm
AROHA:	I think it's a good idea too +

Different leadership styles have a place and a time when they are the most effective way to lead. Leaders may need to demonstrate elements of each style in different contexts to be effective, responding to differing work demands and situations.

GREG: yep + Kendra?
KENDRA: mm
BLAKE: Susie's looking sad there //why (   ) [laughs]\
SUSIE: /no not at all I'm just\\
          I just I don't feel I've got a um particular opinion on it
          I haven't got a handle on it really about what
          I mean I d- I don't see any reason why not
          although I just wondered about it becoming quite a big committee
          that was all
GREG: [reassuring tone]: it's just //the same size:\
AROHA: /it's quite small\\
BLAKE: it's still quite small
SUSIE: oh well that's alright then
BLAKE: it's um one two three four five six

From Holmes and Vine (forthcoming)

Greg asks the team what they should do and makes sure everyone has input. He is quite happy to let Theo take the lead on this issue, and for Blake to also step in and garner the opinions of others at the meeting.

What about leadership in different types of activities?

Meetings are an activity type where leadership has often been studied. Leadership may be enacted, however, whenever and wherever interaction takes place. Research on leaders interacting in different situations has shown differences in how leaders lead depending on the context. In research in a Hong Kong workplace for instance, Schnurr and Mak (2011) found that the woman manager they followed used different styles depending on whether she was in a large meeting, interacting one-to-one or via email (see Chapter 7, Example 7.14).

In Chapter 5, Example 5.2, Ginette used humour to complain to a worker on the packing line, doing leadership in her role as the team co-ordinator. She had also used humour when making a complaint about this issue in a team meeting (Chapter 4, Example 4.11), but had then issued a much more explicit and forceful directive. Both these situations highlight the fact that in one-to-one interactions as opposed to larger meetings there is often more emphasis on relational aspects.

Context is important and a leadership style that works well in one situation may not work well in another. Sometimes different parts of the same meeting may require a leader to switch the way they are interacting. The informal style of one of the leaders in the LWP database, Daniel, was noted in Chapter 4. One point where we see him being more formal than usual is when he is discussing a case of fraud. The serious nature of this discussion is reflected in his shift in style (see Vine and Marsden 2016: 394).

Four styles of leadership are when a leader leads in a charismatic way, democratically, in a commanding way or as a laissez-faire leader. Each approach to leadership has been seen to be effective in different situations. This includes consideration of different contextual factors, such as the level of experience of team members or the activity participants are engaged in. Different styles may also be needed in different parts of the same interaction as a leader responds to different issues.

Models of Leadership

Also of relevance when considering how people enact leadership is the model of leadership that is implemented within an organisation. The traditional model of leadership says that there is an assigned leader and others answer to this person. This hierarchical understanding of leadership is one where relationships, roles and responsibilities are clear: see Figure 6.1.

Research on organisations has found that things are not always so clear-cut and that leadership relationships are much more dynamic, either by design or by practice. For instance, in some companies there are leadership partnerships between managers that are not simply a matter of someone having expertise or responsibility for, say, general management or management of the accounting side of a company. Co-leadership partnerships are quite common in terms of the relational and transactional sides of leadership. A co-leadership partnership will look more like Figure 6.2.

We saw above how effective leaders need to enact both transactional and relational behaviours. A manager who does not look to the relational side of management is felt to be lacking as a leader, and one who only worries about the relational side will be failing to make sure workplace goals are met. Although someone may not completely neglect one side, there are often situations where one senior manager will focus more on relational aspects while another takes care of the transactional side. This is what tends to happen within the organisation where Daniel and Frank work (from Example 6.9). Frank is in charge of the day-to-day implementation of transactional goals and the practical side of implementing company policy decisions. Daniel takes on main responsibility for relational

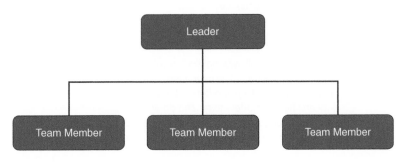

Figure 6.1
Traditional leadership model.

Figure 6.2
Co-leadership
partnership.

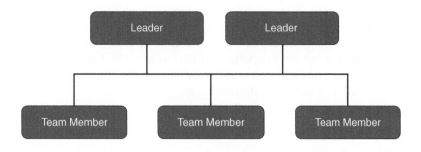

aspects of leadership, developing and managing collegiality, particularly within his executive management team, although he also manages the overall goals and objectives for the company.

In other situations, one leader may be the charismatic figurehead, while another is involved in more day-to-day management in terms of both transactional and relational goals. In the company in which Yvonne works, Yvonne has a positive and inspirational leadership style. She leaves the practical aspects of leadership, however, to Quentin, her number two. He is involved in the day-to-day running of the company, making sure that transactional goals are achieved. He does this in a way though that also supports and nurtures staff, creating team and looking after relational aspects. Example 6.21 shows Quentin chatting with his team before he starts a team meeting.

Example 6.21 (Source: LWP)

Context: Team meeting in a private organisation. Recorded in New Zealand.

PAULA:	good exercise walking up that hill
QUENTIN:	I love walking up it you know
	I really look forward to walking //up it\
??:	/it's a challenge [laughs]\\
QUENTIN:	I mean I'm now cos cos now that [wife's name]'s not in town
	I mean I'm I'm walking more and I really enjoy just
	//to walk up hill\
RANGI:	/yeah yeah hill\\
PAULA:	has she got a new job?
QUENTIN:	no she's not working at all //( )\
IRIHAPETI:	/oh [slowly]: cool:\\
RANGI:	way to go that's (the) life
PAULA:	now you see are you into polygamy?
	I'll be another wife if I can
	[laughter]
PAULA:	actually I don't really wanna give up work but
QUENTIN:	no well she she's just having a break now
	and she's just looking at different things
	I mean she's had offers to go and do work
	but I said well you know the good thing about it
	you can just decide whether you wanna do it (or not)

The team are talking before the meeting about personal aspects of Quentin's life: the fact that he walks up a steep hill to get home from work, which leads to a discussion of what Quentin's wife is now doing. It is obvious that they all know where he lives and that his wife had given up her previous job. Quentin is quite happy about sharing personal information and this helps build rapport with the team. The friendly relationship is also apparent in the way that Paula feels she can joke about becoming his second wife since she suggests that she likes the idea of not working.

Co-leader partnerships still mean a small number of individuals are the ones who have the power, influence and responsibility in an organisation, even when these are shared.

Flatter structures of leadership also exist in many organisations. Another model of leadership that contrasts with the one shown in Figure 6.1, for instance, is **distributed leadership**. This approach places the emphasis on team processes rather than an individual leader who is in control. Clifton (2017), for instance, demonstrates how members of a group can all contribute in decision-making and how each person's turns can help manage meaning and influence the final decision. Consider Example 6.22:

Example 6.22

Context: Decision-making episode from a meeting in a training organisation. They are discussing the need for continuing professional training of staff. Recorded in France.

NIGEL:	ce qu'il nous manque	*what we are missing*
	c'est une formation sur les	*is a training on*
	//micro compétences se	*micro-skills presenting*
	présenter devant un\	*oneself in front of a*
BETH:	/[gestures, nods, looks at Nigel]\\	
NIGEL:	tableau et ecrire pas n'importe	*blackboard and not writing*
	où mais d'une façon structurée	*anywhere but in a structured*
	par exemple er présenter	*way for example er present*
	un point de //grammaire	*a point of grammar*
	présenter un du vocabulaire\	*present one of vocabulary*
BETH:	/oui [gestures	*yes*
	in Nigel's direction, looking at Nigel]\\	

Nigel does not hold the most senior position at the meeting from which this excerpt is taken. Here, however, he suggests what is missing in the training and is the first person to do this. Clifton (2017: 51) points out that in being first to provide an assessment he presents himself as a leader since this allows him to control how the issue is discussed. Beth supports him in this in the way she responds. In the subsequent discussion (not shown here) both Beth and Alice align with him at different times, but also challenge and modify the suggested solution, influencing the final decision. Each of their moves to do this can also be seen as them enacting at times followership, but at other times leadership. Decision-making episodes like this provide rich data for exploring the way leadership can be distributed throughout a group.

Another case where we saw this was in Chapter 5, Example 5.14, from Choi and Schnurr (2014). The members of the group in this example all disagree and it is part of the norms of the group that everyone be allowed to do this, before the problem is smoothly solved. The group does not have a formal leader and each person therefore can at times behave in a way that shows them as enacting leadership, as the group find the best solution to problems.

> The traditional model of leadership has one assigned leader leading a group. Co-leadership partnerships may frequently be found, however, where leaders share aspects of leadership. There are also situations where there are no clear leaders, or leadership is enacted dynamically by members of a team.

Gender, Culture and Leadership

What about gender, culture and leadership?

The examples in this chapter show both women and men enacting leadership and are drawn from studies of leadership from around the world. Research on leadership and gender has explored stereotypes about women and men leaders, and how specific leadership behaviours are seen as gendered. Gender and leadership are explored in Chapter 7.

As with men and women there are also stereotypes about the impact of culture on leadership. Presupposing gender and culture-specific leadership styles, however, overlooks the way leadership is enacted dynamically in different contexts. The socio-cultural context is important, but is not the only important factor to consider. Research has illustrated that there is not only one way of doing leadership, and this is true of men and women, as well as people interacting in different cultures and countries. Culture and leadership are explored in Chapter 8.

Chapter Summary

The focus of this chapter has been the language of leadership. Language plays a crucial role in leadership, with leadership being evident in the ways people interact at work. This includes people who have formal leadership roles, as well as the enactment of informal leadership. Leadership goals include both transactional and relational aspects, with the achievement of both types of goals often being intertwined. This chapter has also explored the important role of team members in the enactment of leadership.

There is not only one way of leading and some of the styles of leadership that people may adopt have been considered, along with models of leadership. The traditional model of leadership has an assigned leader and others answer to this person. Leadership relationships are often much more dynamic, either by design or by practice, and different leadership styles and constellations may be adopted in different workplaces and contexts.

Exercises

Read the excerpts below and then answer the questions.

Excerpt 6.A (Source: LWP)
Context: Project meeting in a private organisation in New Zealand.

CLARA:	okay well we might just start without Seth
	he can come in and can review the minutes from last week
RENEE:	are you taking the minutes this week?
CLARA:	no I'm just trying to chair the meeting
	who would like to take the minutes this week?
RENEE:	who hasn't taken the minutes yet?
BENNY:	I (have not) I will
CLARA:	thank you Benny

Excerpt 6.B (Source: LWP)
Context: Management team meeting in a New Zealand government organisation.

CT:	do we need to hold a meeting next week? +
	the only thing that's really it's just on th- the agenda
	for the next week would be to make certain that the board papers
	the monthly board report is on track
FA:	well we can do that given that we were telling everybody
	that they've got to have it done by Thursday the fourteenth
	by Maureen sending us a message
CT:	yep okay so we won't have a meeting next week?
AC:	no
CT:	okay if there's anything that comes //up\
AC:	/we\\
	//could have one at we could h- we could have\ one
MD:	/let me let me know if yous do\\
AC:	at ten o'clock on Friday the fifteenth
	[there is something else on at this time
	that AC would be happy to avoid.
	They have discussed this earlier]
	that would probably be quite a good time [laughs]
	//[general laughter]\

CT: /for two hours\\ ++ okay alright so there's no meeting next week?
FA: no
MD: no
AC: unless an issue comes up
       //( ) but I think there's no point in us all ( ) together\
CT: /yep yep ++ yep\\
DR: well there's two away and it'll only be us three
CT: okay thanks guys
AC: yeah I may not be away but I might as well (be)
CT: okay
AC: thank you

1. Who do you think are the formal leaders in the meetings the excerpts are taken from? What evidence can you provide?
2. Who else can be seen to be enacting leadership in each case?
3. Do other team members support this? If yes, how?

Further Reading

Jackson and Parry (2011) is a general introduction on the topic of leadership from the perspective of business studies, while Fairhurst (2007) provides a discussion of discursive leadership. Clifton (2006) demonstrates the benefits of approaching leadership using conversation analysis. The chapters in Ilie and Schnurr (2017) highlight and challenge leadership stereotypes.

7 Gender and Language at Work

CHAPTER PREVIEW

This chapter provides a brief introduction to issues related to gender and language at work. This includes:

- language features that have been linked to gender;
- how gender has been viewed in research on gender and language;
- how women and men talk at work;
- a range of factors that may influence how they do this;
- issues of importance when considering gender and leadership.

Gender is another aspect of identity that is important when exploring language in the workplace. It has been argued that gender is always relevant at some level when people interact.

Gender and Language at Work: Introduction

Throughout this book examples have been provided of both women and men interacting at work. In this chapter the focus is on whether women and men speak differently, and how they might signal gender identity through language. Consider Example 7.1:

Example 7.1 (Source: LWP)

Context: Opening of a meeting of two male managers in a private organisation. Recorded in New Zealand.

ROB: I broke it down [clears throat]
         what I what I figured was what I thought was the most logical
JASON: what happened to the small talk?
ROB: [laughs] [laughs]: just I love the colour:
         of what you're doing with your hair
         //there [laughs]\
JASON: /[laughs]\\
         oh you're just I mean
         you're so //straight into it you know like [laughs]\
ROB: /[laughs]\\
         um when we talked about [sighs] the style of operation
         o- of the type of buyer …

Reproduced from Holmes, Janet, Marra, Meredith and Vine, Bernadette, *Leadership, discourse, and ethnicity*, p. 64, © 2011 Oxford University Press. Reproduced with permission from Oxford Publishing Limited through PLSclear.

Jason stops Rob because he has launched straight into discussing business issues without any small talk. Jason's interactions do typically start with small talk, so Rob has violated this norm. In response to this Rob introduces a topic for small talk that is stereotypically female, marking the use of small talk as something he views as a female trait. He makes fun of this and of Jason. While Rob suggests he does not value small talk, the humorous way he does this shows he does value humour. When Rob next speaks he has returned to the business topic.

Small talk and humour are two features of interaction which people believe differentiate the talk of women and men, the stereotype being that women engage in small talk more and men in humour. The discussion below begins by considering some features that have been suggested as characteristic of women's talk as opposed to men's and highlights some early research which explored gender differences in language at work. The way gender was viewed in early approaches to gender and language is then considered, followed by more recent perspectives. Patterns of interaction in masculinised, mixed-gender and feminised workplaces and professions are then explored. A topic that has received a great deal of attention in gender and language research in workplace contexts is leadership, and issues that have been highlighted in this area are examined in the last section of this chapter.

Early Work on Gender and Language

What are some aspects of talk that have been seen as characteristic of women's talk?

A range of speech features were proposed by Lakoff (1973, 1975) as being associated more with women's speech rather than men's. They included use of:

- hedges and intensifiers;
- rising intonation on declaratives and tag questions;
- 'empty' adjectives; and
- indirect requests and polite forms.

Lakoff suggested these features based on her own observations rather than on empirical research. The publications on her impressions prompted numerous studies comparing women's and men's speech with the aim of uncovering the differences between how women and men talk.

Further factors investigated in this early work included exploring features of turn-taking:

- do women or men talk more?
- who interrupts more?
- who provides more minimal feedback?

Some early studies did find differences, while others did not. Example 7.2 comes from an early study that examined the features identified by Lakoff in a workplace setting.

Example 7.2

Context: A witness is giving testimony in court. Recorded in the USA.

LAWYER: ... you observed what?
WITNESS: well after I heard I can't really I can't definitely state
whether the brakes or the lights came first
but I rotated my head slightly to the right ...
and er very very very instantaneously after that
I heard a very very loud explosion ...
and er it was it was terrifically loud

The male witness here uses 'very' five times, and other modifiers, 'really', 'definitely', 'slightly', 'terrifically'. O'Barr and Atkins (1980) therefore challenged Lakoff's proposition that these types of linguistic features differentiate the speech of women and men. They found them in the speech of both women and men, and in particular in the speech of people in powerless positions, such as inexperienced witnesses. This highlighted the need to look at other contextual factors, such as the roles people hold in different settings, and to explore more fully the functions of language features.

Lakoff had suggested certain 'feminine' features express uncertainty – such as a frequent use of hedges, tag questions and indirect requests. The association of these language features just with uncertainty however is problematic given the range of other functions they might have. They can help speakers pay attention to interpersonal relationships, allowing them to establish and maintain rapport. They can also help people enact a polite and reasonable professional identity, or to persuade someone to do something.

Relational aspects of language have been associated more with women, but as noted in Chapter 4, relational skills are important for both women and men. In Chapter 3, it was also evident that using indirect requests and directives to achieve transactional goals not only allowed people to manage relationships and enact their professional identity but also to take account of a range of relevant contextual factors.

Example 7.3 provides an example from an early study that investigated turn-taking patterns of women and men in university committee meetings.

Example 7.3

Context: University committee meeting about programme and scheduling issues. There are seven women and four men on the committee. Recorded in the USA.

CF: [counting student papers]
L: [low voice]: commit to memory if you will these elements of style
       read this [word]:
CF: so out of twenty five there's eight in that group
S: [whispers]: oh my gosh:
CF: //and there's one two [counts papers]\
L: /[low voice]: said thirty percent:\\
S: yeah two out of eighteen is about thirty percent [laughs] isn't it?
L: well I said thirty percent of the ones I know that have reading problems
       and I assume they have writing problems also
       [long pause – CF still checking papers]
CF: I don't know what my division was on this

From *Language in Society 10*, Edelsky, Carole, Who's got the floor?, pp. 406–7, © 1981 Cambridge University Press.

Edelsky (1981) concluded that turn-taking and considering who has the floor is actually a very complex question. In this example, the floor belongs to speaker CF, and even when she does not talk she can be seen to still hold the floor because the others do not attempt to take it from her, offering only quiet comments while she is counting student papers, or remaining silent while she finishes this task. At other times, speakers would share the floor, creating what Edelsky termed jointly developed floors.

Overall Edelsky found that when the floor was singly developed rather than jointly developed, men did not take more turns but did take longer turns. In jointly developed floors, they were less active, although again their turns were longer on average in this context. She also concluded that overlapping talk is not always appropriately classified as 'interruption', since it may often be a collaborative feature of interaction.

> Gender differences were found in some early studies on gender and language, but the importance of context was also highlighted. The association of certain language features with uncertainty overlooks the range of other functions they may have and the importance for both women and men of managing interpersonal relationships.

How did this early research on gender and language view gender?

Early research on gender and language viewed gender as a fixed, static category. Women and men were perceived as separate, homogeneous groups.

There were two broad theoretical perspectives in early research on gender and language:

- difference; and
- dominance.

The **difference** perspective considers that women and men have grown up in differently gendered subcultures. The male subculture means men are more transactional or goal-orientated. The female subculture sees women as more relationally oriented. These gendered orientations are then reflected in the use of different language, with unchanging and incontestable norms.

When considering workplace interaction from a **difference** perspective, male styles of language mean that men are direct, assertive, competitive and task-focused. In contrast, female styles of language mean women are less direct, less assertive, more consultative and that they are more relationship-focused.

The **dominance** model is based on a perception of men as the more powerful sex and suggests that men's use of language dominates weaker women. This is due to their higher position in the social hierarchy and either consciously or subconsciously men use language to exert power and maintain their dominance. Again, the norms are seen as unchanging and incontestable.

This perspective views workplace communication in many settings as primarily a masculine construct because men have dominated most professions in the past. Their behaviours are therefore seen as the norm, while women's are marked as exceptions in many contexts.

More Recent Approaches to Gender and Language

What approach does more recent research take?

More recent research on gender and language in the workplace has taken social constructionist and discursive approaches which challenge the essentialist notion of differently gendered ways of speaking. A social-constructionist perspective sees gender as dynamic and fluid, and as something enacted and worked out within interaction.

A theoretical development often integrated into the social constructionist approach when investigating gender and language is Ochs's (1992, 1996) notion of **indexicality**. Elinor Ochs proposed the **Indexicality Principle** (Ochs 1996: 411) to account for the way that language becomes associated with different groups, such as women and men. In this approach very few linguistic features directly index gender. More commonly, gender is indirectly indexed through speech features and styles that are associated with either women or men through regular use. These gendered expectations of female and male speech patterns determine our language choices and affect how we are assessed.

An important part of Ochs's model is the idea of **stance**. Through using a different linguistic feature a speaker can invoke different **stances**, or qualities. As illustration, the table below shows the stances that Ochs identified for the Japanese sentence final particles *ze* and *wa*.

Because women tend to use the particle that denotes a delicate intensity, this has become associated with women. Similarly, the tendency of men to use the particle which denotes coarse intensity means this has become associated with men. This aligns with the societal expectations of how women and men should talk. Men can still of course use the particle that denotes delicate intensity, just as women can use *ze*. Such choices however lead to more complex interpretations.

> At times people may explicitly mark gender. In Chapter 4, Example 4.10, a small group of women made fun of status symbols associated with male power and wealth. In distancing themselves from these symbols they reinforced their common identity as women who do not value the same things as men. Rob also highlighted gender in Example 7.1 when he made fun of Jason's reference to small talk, introducing a 'feminine' topic.

Table 7.1 Stances associated with Japanese sentence final particles

Particle	*ze*	*wa*
Stance	coarse intensity	delicate intensity

Adapted from Ochs, Elinor, 1992. Indexing gender, p. 342. In Alessandro Duranti, Charles Goodwin and Stephen C. Levinson (eds.), *Rethinking context: Language as an interactive phenomenon*, © 1992 Cambridge University Press. Reproduced with permission of Cambridge University Press through PLSclear.

Table 7.2 Stances stereotypically associated with women and men	
Women	Men
facilitative	competitive
conciliatory	confrontational
collaborative	autonomous
affective	referential
relational	transactional
consultative	authoritative
formal/strict	informal/easy-going

Stances that are associated with different genders in many societies include those highlighted in Table 7.2.

If women are associated with relationally focused talk, we can say that strategies used for this purpose, such as small talk, denote an affective or relational stance. Looking at some of the functions associated with social talk that were identified in Chapter 4, social talk is used to:

- build and enhance rapport; and
- create bonds.

Because women are stereotypically more focused on these aspects of communication than men, with affective and relational stances denoted by its use, then social talk has become associated with women's speech and therefore indirectly indexes a feminine identity. Transactional behaviours on the other hand, such as those that aim to get things done and solve problems, and which therefore denote a referential or transactional stance, are stereotypically coded as masculine and index a masculine identity.

Of course men use social talk too and they also need to pay attention to the relational side of interaction and to building and enhancing rapport. Other stances that can be indexed through the use of social talk which are valued by men legitimise its use when they do this, for instance, the fact that social talk also denotes an informal and easy-going stance. As highlighted in Example 9.1, there are also topics that are more common in small talk among one gender as opposed to another. Jason frequently engages in small talk, talking about issues that he values, like sport or family.

Women may achieve transactional goals using strategies that denote facilitative, collaborative and consultative stances rather than competitive, autonomous and authoritative ones. Lakoff (1973, 1975) would predict that they will use indirect ways of doing this and it may well be that they often do. As we saw in Chapter 3, however, the use of indirect requests and directives is affected by a range of contextual factors and both women and men produce both indirect and direct requests and directives for a range of reasons.

So what contextual factors can influence how women and men talk at work?

In Chapter 3 the focus was on directives and requests, providing insight on strategies used by both women and men to achieve transactional goals. A range of ways of doing this were illustrated and the use of different forms was affected by a range of contextual factors. This included factors relating to:

- the speaker and addressee;
- the physical setting;
- the type of speech event;
- what else is going on;
- the action required.

The first four of these factors are also important in accounting for the ways other transactional goals are achieved, as well as influencing how someone achieves relational goals. A whole range of aspects related to each of these factors may be important. When considering the participants, the gender of the speaker and the hearer(s) both influence how people interact.

> Both women and men in the workplace need to achieve both transactional and relational goals. Women may do this in ways that denote stances they value, while men may use strategies that allow them to take other stances. How both women and men do this will be influenced by norms at different levels, including societal norms relating to how women and men are expected to behave. A range of factors related to context are also always relevant.

How are the speaker's and addressee's gender important?

In Chapter 6, Example 6.20, there was an example from a mixed gender team, which is repeated below as Example 7.4. Examples of how men from this team interact when the women are not present are shown in Example 7.5.

Example 7.4 (Source: LWP)

Context: Management team meeting in a government organisation. Five women and three men are present. Greg is the CEO. Recorded in New Zealand.

GREG: so what are we gonna do then?
THEO: I guess I guess I should have the first say
          seeing (he's) my staff member and I would support it
MARAMA: mm
AROHA: I think it's a good idea too +
GREG: yep + Kendra?
KENDRA: mm

BLAKE:	Susie's looking sad there //why ( ) [laughs]\
SUSIE:	/no not at all I'm just\\
	I just I don't feel I've got a um particular opinion on it
	I haven't got a handle on it really about what
	I mean I d- I don't see any reason why not
	although I just wondered about it becoming quite a big committee
	that was all
GREG:	[reassuring tone]: it's just //the same size:\
AROHA:	/it's quite small\\
BLAKE:	it's still quite small
SUSIE:	oh well that's alright then

From Holmes and Vine (forthcoming).

The group have been discussing the formation of a committee to deal with a particular issue. The section of talk here begins with Greg asking 'so what are we gonna do then?'. Theo responds, but hedges his nomination of himself as the first to speak with 'I guess'. Marama and Aroha agree with Theo's assessment of the situation and Greg then directly elicits a response from Kendra. Blake then steps in and in what could be interpreted as a facilitative move elicits Susie's response. Greg, Aroha and Blake then all reassure Susie about the issue she has raised, with Aroha and Blake both qualifying the size of the group as 'quite small'. Both the women and the men here use language that is associated with feminine styles of speech. The men take consultative stances and both women and men use hedges and pay attention to interpersonal aspects.

When interacting one-to-one with Greg, both Theo and Blake are quite direct in the way they talk: Examples 7.5a and 7.5b.

Example 7.5 (Source: LWP)

Context: One-to-one meetings with Greg, CEO. Recorded in a New Zealand government organisation.

a. GREG: and what do I have to do?
      do I have to sign this off do I?
   THEO: no don't sign that no …
      I'll do it I'll do a er summary for the minister …

b. BLAKE: I looked very closely at the leave and sick leave …
      I do look at the hours of work indicators because ++
      that's what battered it batters us every negotiation + …
      the collective says thirty seven and a half hours a week
      and we're working forty three forty four forty five forty
      it's not good enough

Both Theo and Blake speak directly to their boss with little hedging or softening devices, both using a style more associated with masculine speech. This contrasts with the way they interacted in Example 7.4.

When only women are present there tends to be indexing of stances that women value. Similarly, when only men are present, stances that men value

> The gender mix of a group may be one relevant contextual factor that influences the way people interact. Exploring the influence of gender in one-to-one white collar interactions and the use of the hedge *just*, Vine (2018a) found differences between interactions based on both the gender of speakers and their addressees. Both women and men used *just* more when speaking to a woman than when speaking to a man.

are more likely to be indexed. Saito (2013) commented that in Japanese society men need to prove their masculinity to other men. She found the use of direct forms associated with male speech in situations characterised by other factors that are seen as more feminine, as in Example 7.6.

Example 7.6

Context: Sasaki, the company president, interacts with Murata and Abe, non-titled employees from the manufacturing department of a company that produces dental products. Abe is going to Hawai'i soon for his honeymoon. Recorded in Japan.

SASAKI:	[slowly]: ano:	*you know*
ABE:	hai	*yes*
SASAKI:	Keiichi	*Keiichi*
MURATA:	hai	*yes*
SASAKI:	Abe hawai iku tte yuu	*Abe said that he will be going to Hawai'i*
	kara ikutsuka motashite	*so have him carry some with him*
		[synthetic replacements, e.g., dentures and crowns]
ABE:	a //nan desu ka\	*oh what is it?*
SASAKI:	/mukoo iku\\ kara	*since he is going over there*
	kookuubin de na	*[sending synthetic replacements should be] by air*
MURATA:	sabishii deshoo kara	*because Abe will miss them [while in Hawai'i]*
SASAKI:	un	*yeah*
ABE:	[laughs]	
SASAKI:	[laughs] **junbi shitoke yo**	***prepare [some synthetic replacements] in advance!***
	[laughs]	
ABE:	//[laughs]\	
SASAKI:	/[laughs]\\	

Reprinted with permission from *Gender and Language 7*, Saito, Junko, Gender and facework: Linguistic practices by Japanese male superiors in the workplace, pp. 247–8, © 2013 Equinox Publishing Ltd.

Sasaki jokes here with his subordinates, focusing on relational goals. He creates a fantasy scenario where Abe will take some of the products he makes with him when he goes on his honeymoon, so that he does not miss them. Because a relational focus is associated with a feminine style, when Sasaki gives a directive as part of this fantasy scenario he uses a direct masculine form to do this. Saito (2013) notes that his use of rough language allows him to prove his masculinity to the other men present.

Research has found that humour in all-male groups tends to be competitive, minimally collaborative or involve contestive conjoint humour. Example 7.7 illustrates contestive humour from an all-male meeting.

Example 7.7 (Source: LWP)

Context: Regular meeting of a project team in a large commercial organisation. There are six men present. Callum has failed to update a header in a document leading Barry to think he's got the wrong version. Recorded in New Zealand.

ERIC:	didn't update the er header probably didn't that'll be Callum probably
BARRY:	okay so this is actually one point four
CALLUM:	yeah it's definitely the one I definitely sent you the right version

ERIC: Callum did fail his office management word processing lessons
CALLUM: I find it really hard being perfect at everything
          [general laughter]

Eric identifies the mistake as Callum's fault and then makes Callum the target of a jocular insult. Callum responds to this with his own humorous quip, claiming it is difficult for him to be 'perfect at everything'. This type of humour has also been found in mixed-gender groups in which men predominate (Holmes 2006b). Again, this indexes stances men value, such as a competitive stance. When men interact with women and when women interact with other women there is generally more orientation to stances valued by women.

Gender Composition of Workplaces

So what about interaction in masculinised workplaces?

Some workplaces and professions are dominated by one gender, meaning that either masculine or feminine norms tend to predominate. This relates to norms for achieving both transactional and relational goals.

Research in masculinised workplaces has found more competitive and direct styles; for instance, in Chapter 3, Example 3.28, directives in an army context were found to be explicit and lacking in mitigation. Women in these types of workplaces tend to interact using more stereotypically masculine language. McElhinny (1992, 2003) found that in a profession previously dominated by men, women police officers felt obliged to adopt particular masculine ways of speaking simply to appear to be doing their job effectively.

Example 7.8 shows a woman interacting in a masculinised workplace and profession. The team here work in an engineering company and are discussing a report that needs to be sent to an external company. They have decided that it would be useful for one of their own employees to translate the report so that they can provide this with the finished report. Peter has suggested that one of the junior staff members, either Mary or Paul, can do this. As the discussion progresses it is clear that he thinks Mary should complete the task. Chloe challenges this.

Example 7.8

Context: Routine team meeting in a multinational engineering company. Recorded in Europe.

CHLOE: but they need [details] and it's not their job=
FIL: =yes you are very right here I'm afraid
PETER: okay tomorrow I will discuss with Mary to
          and see if she can translate er …
CHLOE: hang on why Mary? Mary or Paul or both
          that's a lot of extra work for //Mary\

PETER:	/it's okay\\
	it's easy to translate but it needs time
	some days to translate all these
GABRIEL:	um yes and what about …
	[he refers to a project part of which has been assigned to Mary]
CHLOE:	how long is this going to //take because\
PETER:	/I don't know [number]\\ days
	let's give Mary [number] days
	and Paul can take on [Mary's normal duties]
	and we will take it from there
GABRIEL:	sounds okay //to me\
CHLOE:	/no\\ that's not good
	[refers to project] this is Mary's
	I want her to learn
	keep Paul out of this
GABRIEL:	okay Chloe your wish is my command
	[general laughter]
CHLOE:	[soft voice]: thanks Gab:

Chloe's challenge of Peter's proposal and of Gabriel's agreement with the proposal is very explicit and direct. She reacts forcefully and does not internally soften her disagreement at any point, although she does provide explanations for her overt disagreement. She can also be seen to orient to others' needs and concerns, a normatively feminine interaction strategy, when she defends Mary's and Paul's rights saying 'it's not their job' and 'that's a lot of extra work for Mary'. Gabriel resolves the potential conflict, accepting Chloe's suggestion and joking that her 'wish is my command'.

Angouri (2011) notes that this is a tightly knit community of practice and their unmarked style is fairly collaborative, while being overall normatively masculine. Throughout the interaction Chloe shifts from a more aggressive and masculine interactional style to a style that could index femininity. The industry is still perceived and constructed, however, as a masculine domain.

In Example 7.1, we saw Rob's reaction to Jason's attempt to engage in small talk at the beginning of a one-to-one meeting. He does use humour, a potentially relational-oriented strategy in dealing with this, but then continues on with addressing transactional goals. Humour is one strategy for relational work that has been associated with men, and of course it has other functions too as discussed in Chapter 4. Humour is generally valued by men, denoting an easy-going and informal stance, although as in male only interactions, in male dominated workplaces humour is often competitive and may involve jocular abuse, as in Example 7.7. Social talk is also a useful strategy to use for relational purposes and in male dominated workplaces this tends to be about topics that men value, such as sport (see Chapter 4, Example 4.7). Example 7.9 was recorded in a factory, where male norms predominate, and shows the team coordinator, Ginette, making small talk with a male worker while doing her rounds to make sure everything is going well.

Example 7.9 (Source: LWP)

Context: Ginette, team leader, stops to talk to Lesia, one of the workers on the packing line in a factory. Lesia keeps on working throughout the interaction, moving back and forth between a stack of empty boxes and the bench where he is packing. Recorded in New Zealand.

GINETTE: get up to anything funny over the weekend?
LESIA: [shakes head]
GINETTE: did you go to church bro?
LESIA: no no no no
        well we went to our game on Saturday afternoon + practice
GINETTE: you didn't go to church bro?
LESIA: no
GINETTE: [smiling, mock serious tone]: very sad bro:
        [emphatically]: how many times have I told you
        go to church every Sunday:
LESIA: [smiling] oh yeah [turns away]
GINETTE: [teasingly] you just didn't want to put any money
        in the offering bowl eh bro
LESIA: [smiles and keeps moving back and forth with boxes]
GINETTE: you're broke eh bro

Reprinted from Stubbe and Brown (2002: 40)

Ginette begins by asking Lesia about his weekend. He did not do anything noteworthy so she teases him about not going to church. She wants to engage in relational work here, and teasing allows her to do this after Lesia has failed to provide the requested funny story. Teasing is a strategy which can create a sense of solidarity and belonging. Because teasing makes the addressee the target of humour it has stereotypically been seen as a more masculine strategy.

What about interaction in workplaces with more of a gender mix?

One type of humour found in contexts where both women and men are present is high energy conjoint humour (Holmes 2006b). This type of humour involves a highly collaborative shared floor, typified by frequent turn overlapping and strong ties between contributions, as in Example 7.10.

Example 7.10 (Source: LWP)

Context: Mixed-gender project meeting in a private company. The team are discussing the setting up of a customer call centre. Vita is talking about the music that will play when callers have to wait for a customer representative to talk to them. Recorded in New Zealand.

VITA: yeah but it also depends on what music
      I mean everyone's got different musical taste
      //haven't\ they?
SANDY: /yeah\\

PEG: well we //maybe we can have a selection of\
VITA: /(party)\\
PEG: //country and western country and western two for modern pop\
TESSA: /press one to listen to country and western pick two\\
PEG: three for [laughs]
VITA: [laughs] //[laughs]\
SANDY: /(   )\\
ROBERT: now what's wrong with that sentence?
            country and western //would be on the\
VITA: /one for Spice Girls\\
            two for Spice Girls and three for Spice Girls
DAISY: oh yeah
PEG: and if you want to see the movie
            [general laughter]

Vita, Tessa and Robert all join in here as they elaborate on Peg's humorous comment about the type of music they will play while callers are waiting. She suggests callers should be able to select different types of music to listen to. The first type of music she suggests is country and western, and Tessa repeats this. Robert questions whether country and western should be an option and Vita responds by suggesting they play music from the Spice Girls (and nothing else). Unlike Examples 7.7 and 7.9 the humour here is collaborative.

So what about interaction in feminised workplaces?

Research in all-women teams has identified collaborative styles of interaction, although again other contextual factors are important. When considering examples of directives and requests in Chapter 3 we saw women interacting together on a number of occasions. Sonia, who featured in Examples 3.1, 3.17, 3.25 and 3.26, used a range of forms to express her directives. These were not always indirect and did not always involve discussion and negotiation of what needed to be done.

Humour in all-women teams is often collaborative, as seen in Example 5.10. Holmes (2006b) noted that there was a tendency for humour to involve a highly collaborative shared floor in groups that included a number of women, and not just in all-women teams.

Research on men in feminised workplaces has mainly considered interview data and has not examined authentic interaction. The findings of these studies suggest that men in these types of workplaces may emphasise their masculinity. McDowell (2015), however, found that in a profession dominated by women, nurses who were men adopted ways of speaking typically associated with women in order to interact in a way appropriate for their job, just as the women in McElhinny's research had adopted masculine styles. Examples 7.11 and Example 7.12 show men interacting in feminised workplaces.

Example 7.11

Context: Two male nurses, Joe and Mike, and one female nurse, Amy, are talking about a patient who needs extra treatment. Recorded in a hospital in Northern Ireland.

JOE: surely the community nurses have to provide the pressurising mattress wouldn't they?

AMY: yeah
MIKE: the district nurses (   ) have they nothing better to do
          than ring us up asking us when was the last time we had seen the patient?
          I rang them back on the phone and says we are enquiring
          //and\ (   ) will need a a mattress when goes home from //here\
JOE: /aye\\   /I know\\
          if someone went home with me they would soon ring //us\
MIKE: /oh\\ definitely
JOE: wouldn't they? why did this patient why weren't we informed?
AMY: but I suppose then maybe they wouldn't know if it was there or
          not would they ...
MIKE: cos then the family weren't letting them into the house for while //either\
AMY: /were they not?\\
MIKE: no
JOE: that would make it very difficult like you know

The hospital nurses here are criticising the district nurses. They use
intensifiers such as 'surely' and 'definitely' and tag questions, features
Lakoff identified as typical of women's talk. Collaborative agreement
is also apparent in the nurses' use of overlapping turns, showing their
agreement and support for one another's comments.

Example 7.12 (Source: LWP)

Context: A male carer in a residential care home, Harold, is helping a resident,
Florence, get dressed after aiding her shower. Recorded in New Zealand.

FLORENCE: did the staff go in and buy the rolls and soup + on Thursday?
HAROLD: yeah it's very popular
FLORENCE: is it?
HAROLD: but the rolls they get I don't know where she gets them from
            but they're lovely
FLORENCE: good
HAROLD: I'll bring a couple in next time + you be the judge +
            next thing you'll be having that for lunch as well [laughs]
            nah they're //really\
FLORENCE: /(you)'re\\ very well fed + I think
HAROLD: [laughs]

Here, the caregiver and the resident chat while Harold helps Florence
dress. Florence introduces the topic of social talk on this occasion, but the
two always engage in small talk at times like this with both participants
providing topics. Harold here also uses what Lakoff (1973, 1975) would
refer to as an 'empty' adjective, describing the rolls as 'lovely'. Both these
examples show men in feminised workplaces using features that have
been identified as aspects of women's talk. Given the workplaces in which
they work these features are part of enacting an appropriate professional

identity and communicating in a way that is suitable for the situations in which they work.

© Jacynta Scurfield 2019

Some workplaces and professions are dominated by one gender meaning that either masculine or feminine norms predominate. This relates to norms for achieving both transactional and relational goals. The same way of speaking can signal both a professional identity and a gendered identity, and these are difficult to separate. The particular context in which someone is interacting also has a vital impact on influencing how someone will interact and how they will enact their identity. Effective communicators, both women and men, are able to draw expertly on a repertoire of linguistic strategies stereotypically coded feminine and masculine in response to contextual factors.

Gender and Leadership

Intersectionality

Gender is only one aspect of a person's social identity: individuals have multiple and complex identities that are only partially defined by gender. They move between different discursively constructed identities as they interact. Integrating a consideration of gender with other variables is therefore important. The interplay between facets of someone's identity is referred to as **intersectionality**.

An aspect of identity that was examined in Chapter 6 was leadership. The discussion below explores how people manage the **intersection** of two aspects of identity: gender and leadership.

Gender and leadership has been a major focus of research on gender and language in the workplace. Women leaders are a reasonably recent

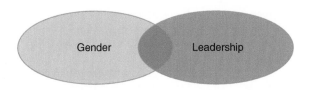

Figure 7.1
Intersectionality of gender and leadership identities.

phenomenon, particularly in some countries and cultures, so have drawn the attention of researchers. A central theme in sociolinguistic research on gender and leadership is the language that women and men use to enact leadership.

Traditionally, an effective leader was perceived as someone authoritative and focused on transactional goals, characteristics that are indexed for masculinity. Relational practices were undervalued and had a strong association with a more feminine style. Nowadays, these stereotypical feminine speech styles are recognised as part of a range of discourse strategies that leaders are expected to acquire in order to be effective.

In Chapter 6, Examples 6.3 to 6.5 all showed female leaders achieving transactional goals, while Examples 6.6 to 6.9 involved male leaders doing this. Nothing in particular about the language in these examples marked them as produced by women or men. There are plenty of examples in the literature of women leaders achieving transactional goals in a forceful way, using a stereotypical masculine style. In Example 7.13, Clara is very direct and assertive when Sandy suggests that the group should vote on the wording of the message for their new customer call centre.

Example 7.13 (Source: LWP)

Context: Project team meeting in a private company. The team are discussing the setting up of a customer call centre. Recorded in New Zealand.

SANDY: are we going to have a vote on whether
           it's um welcome or is it kia ora?
CLARA: oh it's welcome
VITA: yeah
SANDY: you sure?
CLARA: yes

Clara does not hedge her opinion here and when Sandy seems a little surprised at her response and questions her about this, she simply replies 'yes', reasserting her opinion.

Example 7.14 also illustrates a female leader taking control of a situation where a decision is needed.

Example 7.14

Context: Internal weekly staff meeting at a public company. Participants are discussing the new layout of the office. Recorded in Hong Kong.

SABITHA: … okay I think what we're required
           I tell you the third stage is get rid of
           [slowly]: all: the publications okay

just keep few hundreds of each okay
I think the only exception to that is maybe um +
[name of publication] yeah actually is two for everything

??:   you know when I //(   )\
SABITHA: /and what\\ I would like to recommend
if possible is to try and store it [slowly]: in boxes:
do we have boxes or no?
[several people answer]

SABITHA: so for a start I think let's get rid of
[slowly]: all the + all the: publications

??:   mm
SABITHA: so if you can do that by next Monday
??:   yeah
SABITHA: okay that's the preference the second step I would say is ...

Sabitha uses direct strategies here and takes control of the decision-making process. She does balance this with some use of hedging and embedding, for example when she says 'so if you can do that by next Monday', but has clearly taken the lead in deciding what needs to happen.

Example 7.4 illustrates Greg, the organisation's CEO, being consultative and eliciting his team's views. Example 7.15 and 7.16 show other male leaders taking similar approaches.

Example 7.15 (Source: LWP)

Context: Team meeting in a government organisation. Len is the manager. Recorded in New Zealand.

LEN: how do we can we capture some of these things that we want to um?
BELINDA: do you want me to write them down?
LEN: can you? I mean I just think where we've we've identified
//something we want\ to carry that through
CELIA: /yeah + yeah\\
LEN: cos later on we may want to come back to it
BELINDA: mm okay
LEN: um
CELIA: do we need the whiteboard?
BELINDA: no it's all right I'll just write it here
LEN: see how we go just //with\ that for a minute and see
CELIA: /mm\\

In a long problem-solving meeting, Len highlights the need to keep track of points that are being raised. He asks for input on how to do this and Belinda makes a suggestion, which Len agrees with. Len has consulted the group here and provides reasons for having a strategy to keep track of issues. He also uses the hedge *just* twice.

Example 7.16

Context: Meeting between company president, Chris, and the circulation manager, Mike, in a postcard advertising company. Recorded in the USA.

CHRIS: and it's and it's kind of a- you know
         you don't have to like write down the minute that you- got the request
         and the minute that you got- it done and you just say
         well that took me about four hours to deliver it (   ) four
MIKE: so what if the request comes er by email at the end of a day on Monday
         and I don't even see it until?
CHRIS: I don't know # how were you- how were you gonna keep this before?
MIKE: er that's a good point okay so I'll
         so I'll just- ignore time between me leaving and- [laughs] and me coming
         in +++ okay

Reprinted with permission from the author. From Koester, Almut, *Investigating workplace discourse*, pp. 44–5, © 2006 Almut Koester, published by Routledge.

Chris explains to Mike how to manage requests to the company. When Mike asks how he should deal with requests that come in late in the day, Chris asks him how he has managed this aspect in the past. This strategy prompts Mike to think about a solution rather than Chris just telling him what to do. Like Len, Chris elicits input from his addressee(s). Both examples therefore show men adopting consultative strategies and language features stereotypically associated with women.

Chapter 6, Examples 6.10 and 6.11 illustrated female leaders achieving relational goals, while Examples 6.12 and 6.13 involved male leaders. A range of strategies were used including humour, complimenting and emphasising co-operation, mentoring behaviours and giving advice rather than directives. Again, the examples could have come from leaders of any gender. Example 7.17 provides a further instance where a male leader uses a strategy that is often found in the speech of both male and female leaders, but that is stereotypically associated with a feminine speech style.

Example 7.17

Context: Meeting in a retail company. Recorded in the UK.

STEVE: thank you very much for looking after the ship while I've been away
         especially to Sue thank you very much er
         it was great coming back
         you know no issues or anything
         and that's all down to you and the team
         so thank you very much okay?

Reprinted from Mullany (2007: 104)

Steve has been away and here thanks his team for looking after everything in his absence. He compliments them, particularly Sue. Mullany (2007: 104) notes that this helps him strengthen feelings of collegiality in his team as he recognises and shows appreciation for their contributions to achieving goals.

Generalisations about the language use of women and men leaders, or of women and men more generally in the workplace, need to consider other aspects of the context that may affect how people interact. Schnurr and Mak (2011) also examined the interaction patterns of the woman leader from Example 7.14 in one-to-one interaction and in internal emails. They found that she used different language in the three interactional contexts they examined: in her emails she adopted a stereotypically masculine leadership style; in one-to-one interactions she used a more feminine style; and in larger meetings her speech contained a combination of both masculine and feminine features. The specific interactional context in which leadership was enacted was important.

> The myth that men and women leaders use different speech styles at work has been refuted by research, which highlights the importance of context on identity construction. Men and women leaders skilfully switch between normatively masculine and feminine discourse strategies, depending on the context, and adaptable leaders make use of a wide verbal repertoire.

Important Issues for Women Leaders

What issues are important for women leaders?

There are two issues that have often been highlighted as problems for women in leadership:

- the glass ceiling; and
- the double-bind.

The glass ceiling is an unacknowledged barrier to advancement in a profession. This is especially likely to affect women and members of minorities.

Researchers have focused on how leadership is constructed through the linguistic choices that are made (see Chapter 6). A leader's language is always bound up with power and with others' perceptions of how they exercise their authority. Women have a particularly challenging task in negotiating power relationships as there are often gendered expectations of leadership. Research has shown that women leaders have a more difficult job than men:

- to be listened to;
- to be included in key decisions;
- to be taken seriously; and
- in influencing the views of others (Baxter 2014; Holmes 2006a).

This can make it difficult for them to secure higher level positions.

In Chapter 6, Example 6.16, we saw a male team member challenging his female boss. In the following example a senior woman leader's concerns on an issue are listened to but then disregarded.

Example 7.18 (Source: LWP)

Context: Meeting in a government organisation. Henry is the CEO and is chairing the meeting. Selene is a senior manager. Henry is checking through the items on the agenda and a topic Selene has been involved with has just come up. Recorded in New Zealand.

SELENE: can I make a comment on it? …
           I've only been away for ten days um
           I didn't come back till last night
           I didn't come in and look at papers
           I had thought through the fact that I wouldn't get any major papers
           unless they'd been out for consultation
           so there couldn't be anything I didn't expect today
           I had discussed with strategic HR who undertook
           that the [topic] paper wouldn't be up
           until (they) had consulted with me
           and I find today an unconsulted paper on approving new capital bids
           and a [topic] paper for decision
           and I have skimmed them not read them
           and I don't feel very + well prepared to participate
           particularly in the [topic] one where I have been very strongly involved
           so I feel I don't I'm not at the stage
           that the papers not be handled today
           but I don't feel very comfortable about participating in the decision
           I hadn't finished reading the [topic] paper
           I had commitments and catch ups this morning
           and I wasn't anticipating unconsulted papers
HENRY: yeah okay Selene what what as I understand
           you're registering your concern about that
           but not asking for us not to consider the paper is that right
SELENE: [slowly]: no: but I mean um ++
           yeah you you've summed it up correctly that I'm uncomfortable
HENRY: okay + well let let's um er if during the course of that discussion
           you you continue to be uncomfortable
           let's um discuss it at the time
SELENE: right

From Holmes (forthcoming).

Here, Selene expresses her concerns at some length, making use of many strategies associated with a normatively feminine style of interaction. She is indirect, polite, and apologetic, instead of explicitly insisting on the discussion being deferred until she has had time to catch up. In response to this, Henry succinctly sums up Selene's concerns and says she can bring these up later when they get to the topic. Holmes (forthcoming) comments that later in the meeting when the topic comes up, decisions are made and Selene's concerns are ignored.

A **double-bind** involves a situation in which a person is confronted with two irreconcilable demands or a choice between two undesirable courses of action. In leadership studies it has been used to refer to the situation where women leaders are judged negatively for how they speak. If they speak in an authoritative manner, this is judged as being in conflict with

© Jacynta Scurfield 2019

their identity as women, but they are also judged to be less competent if they display linguistic characteristics that are deemed too feminine.

Women and men are also assessed unequally for using the same strategies. Men are commended for their use of more feminine communicative strategies and admired or at least tolerated if they speak in an authoritative manner, whereas women are not.

Women often have to work twice as hard as men to gain the same respect as leaders, especially in masculine workplaces and industries. Baxter (2008: 217) notes that women leaders often utilise a range of strategies to avoid being stereotyped or negatively evaluated. This includes making use of:

- rigorous preparation;
- warmth of manner;
- humour;
- an acceptance of being teased;
- mitigated commands; and
- forms of politeness such as apology.

Another way women may deal with this problem is to draw on strategies associated with acceptable feminine leadership roles, such as mother. In Chapter 4, Example 4.16 (from Baxter and Al A'ali 2016: 65), Fatima, a woman manager, enacted a motherly style, asking her team if they would like her to bring them back anything from a business trip to Japan. Baxter and Al A'ali (2016) see Fatima as empowered by the co-construction of her as a mother figure to the group.

Another acceptable way for women to enact leadership is by behaving like a queen. Clara, who featured in the Exercise Excerpt 6.1 from Chapter 6 (see Exercise Excerpt 7.2 below) and in Example 7.13, enacts leadership in this way. This is regularly acknowledged by the team. At another point in the meeting from which Example 7.13 comes, for instance, Clara again makes an explicit and unhedged decision. Example 7.19 shows her team's responses to this.

Example 7.19 (Source: LWP)

Context: Project team meeting in a private company. Sandy is in charge of the project, but Clara is his manager. Recorded in New Zealand.

HARRY: look's like there's been actually a request for screen dumps
             I know it was outside of the scope but people will be pretty worried
             about it
CLARA: no screen dumps
MATT: we-
CLARA: no screen dumps
PEG: [sarcastically]: thank you Clara:
CLARA: //no screen dumps\
MATT: /we know\\ we know you didn't want them
             and we um er //we've\
CLARA: /that does not\\ meet the criteria
             [several reasons provided why screen dumps should be allowed]
CLARA: thanks for looking at that though
SANDY: so that's a clear well maybe no?
CLARA: it's a no
SANDY: it's a no a royal no

Reprinted from Holmes (2008: 11)

Clara issues a directive that there is to be no printing of screen dumps. This is unhedged and she repeats this several times, despite the team arguing to be allowed to do this. At the end of the extract Sandy clarifies her decision and asserts that this is 'a royal no'. He is making an overt reference to Clara as a queen as he defuses the tension caused by her directness. Clara has drawn on the authoritative aspects of her queenly role and her team accept this. However, the fact that the team use humour to lighten the mood when Clara behaves in this way highlights the fact that they feel a need to hedge her language, even when she does not.

> Many women leaders face barriers at work and they may be excluded and find it difficult to advance to higher levels of management. However, analysis of authentic interaction has also shown how some women skilfully manoeuvre their way through challenging leadership situations by adapting their interaction patterns and through adopting acceptable female leadership personas.

What about other aspects of someone's identity?

In this chapter gender and leadership have been considered. Other aspects of a person's identity are also important, such as race, ethnicity, and religion. Identity is dynamic and fluid and also multidimensional. Different social identities can be conveyed indirectly via an array of stances indexed by linguistic and discursive features, or more directly through, for instance, topics of small talk. Gender is just one of many factors that may shape the ongoing construction of identities. In Chapter 8, culture and language is explored.

Chapter Summary

The focus of this chapter has been gender and language, including a brief exploration of early work in this area. Gender differences were found in some early studies, but the importance of context was also highlighted. Early work tended to view gender from a difference or dominance perspective, although more recent approaches see gender as dynamic and fluid, and as something enacted within interaction.

Some workplaces and professions are dominated by one gender meaning that either masculine or feminine norms predominate. The same way of speaking can signal both a professional identity and a gendered identity. Effective communicators, both women and men, tend to draw on a repertoire of linguistic strategies stereotypically coded feminine and masculine in response to contextual factors.

As there are ways of talking that can index gender, there are also ways which index leadership. Certain linguistic features that index leadership are associated with particular stances (e.g., authoritative, consultative) which are associated with masculinity or femininity. Transactional leadership behaviours are stereotypically coded as masculine, whereas more relationally oriented leadership behaviours are traditionally seen as feminine. Skilled leaders use a wide range of discourse styles.

Exercises

Exercise 7.1
Consider the data excerpt and then answer the questions that follow.

Excerpt 7.A (Source: LWP)
Context: Social talk in a government department. The Crusaders are a local rugby team, while the All Blacks are the national New Zealand rugby team. Graham Henry coached the All Blacks for several years. Recorded in New Zealand.

TAI: but Saturday ... I was very discouraged
ABI: and Crusaders won?
TAI: um do we have to talk about their win? [laughs]
      [laughs]: yes yes they won: they won
      I think the ref was on their side
      I think he was paid a large amount of money
ABI: bribed
TAI: yes ...

VANHI: well you know All Blacks didn't want to have him
TAI: [coughs] sorry?
VANHI: All Blacks didn't want to have //([name])\
TAI: /and with re-\\ with re-
         with good //reason\
VANHI: /except\\ for Graham Henry
TAI: Graham Henry's awesome
VANHI: Graham Henry is a teacher
TAI: sorry? yes yes those are the best coaches
VANHI: (teacher)
TAI: teachers
VANHI: [laughs]
TAI: that's what makes this nation strong
         Vanhi are you paying attention to me?

1. What assumptions might you make about the gender of the speakers
    and why?
2. What other factors may be important here?

Exercise 7.2
Consider the data excerpt and then answer the questions that follow.

Excerpt 7.B (Source: LWP; repeated from Chapter 6, Exercises)
Context: Project meeting in a private organisation in New Zealand.

CLARA: okay well we might just start without Seth
         he can come in and can review the minutes from last week
RENEE: are you taking the minutes this week?
CLARA: no I'm just trying to chair the meeting
         who would like to take the minutes this week?
RENEE: who hasn't taken the minutes yet?
BENNY: I (have not) I will
CLARA: thank you Benny

1. Are the speakers interacting in a way you would expect given their
    gender and your expectations about gendered behaviour?
2. What features of their speech can you identify that might align with or
    challenge stereotypes about how women and men interact?
3. Clara was noted in the discussion above to enact a 'queenly' leadership
    style. Can you see evidence of this in Excerpt 7.B?

....

Further Reading

Holmes (2006a) and Mullany (2007) explore how women and men construct
their gender and professional identities. Ford (2008) provides an interesting
examination of women in a range of professions, while Cameron (2007) explores
myths about how women and men speak. The 2011 issue of the journal *Gender
and Language* includes a number of papers on gender, language and leadership
from around the world.

8 Culture and Language at Work

CHAPTER PREVIEW

This chapter provides a brief introduction to issues related to culture and language in the workplace. This includes:

- providing a brief definition of **culture**;
- exploring how people may enact their cultural/ethnic identity when interacting at work;
- defining cross-cultural and intercultural communication;
- exploring different cultural norms and expectations;
- examining how leadership, gender and cultural identity can intersect.

Another aspect of identity that is important in workplace interaction is cultural identity. Like gender, culture is always relevant when people interact.

Culture and Language at Work: Introduction

People may enact their cultural identity when they interact at work either consciously or unconsciously. A person's cultural identity can be evident both in interaction with other people who share this aspect of their identity, as well as in interaction with those who do not. Consider Example 8.1:

Example 8.1 (Source: LWP)

Context: Management team meeting in a Māori organisation. The team have been discussing deadlines for reports that need to be lodged by outside groups. Frank has visited one of these groups and is recounting what happened when he did. Recorded in New Zealand.

FRANK: [recounting what the group said]: what are you doing here?:
         [recounting what he said]: well I'm part of the kaumātua council:
         [recounting what the group then said]: what's that one made for then?:
CALEB: so what did they say about you?
         what are you here for? [laughs]
DARCY: just say just say I'm a *whangai* [adoptee]
         [laughter]

This example is interesting for a number of reasons. It comes from a Māori workplace where Māori norms predominate, although the organisation is operating within a society where Māori is not the dominant culture. Māori is not the language of business in this organisation either, because although the majority of the employees in this company are Māori, many do not have high proficiency in the language. It is common though for them to use Māori words and phrases and this is one way they can mark their identity. Others who are not Māori also use Māori words and phrases, in this case showing their affiliation and alignment with their Māori colleagues and with the Māori context.

The participants at this meeting are mainly Māori, but Frank is not. He has worked for the organisation for many years and is an experienced and knowledgeable member of the team. Here he talks about attending a meeting of a Māori group who need to send in a report to the organisation, and how the group seemed to be unclear about what was going on. In this context, Frank is an outsider and he does highlight this himself when he recounts how people asked him what he was there for. He also recounts what he told them, referring to his role on 'the kaumātua council', a place he holds because of his professional role. Caleb then draws attention to Frank personally and the fact that he is an outsider in another way because he is not Māori. This marks Frank as an *outsider* in terms of cultural identity, and shows the way that others can also be involved in the way someone's identity is constructed.

Darcy joins in at this point and jokes that Frank can tell them that he is a 'whangai'. While identifying Frank as non-Māori, this still gives him status as being a legitimate part of the group. *Whangai* is a form of adoption in Māori culture where a child is adopted within the extended family.

In Example 8.1, Frank's cultural identity has been consciously and explicitly marked by others in the team, and this is one way cultural identity can be evident. More commonly, interactional norms at a (generally) unconscious level reflect someone's cultural background. In this chapter, issues related to culture, cultural identity and language use in the workplace are explored, and examples of both salient and less obvious markers of cultural identity and affiliation are shown. As noted in Chapters 6 and 7, individuals have multiple and complex identities so cultural identity is just one facet of someone's identity that is relevant when they interact. Taking a social constructionist approach, it is also important to acknowledge the way identity is negotiated, and how language use reflects social norms and expectations, including cultural norms. To begin, a definition of culture is provided.

Definition of *Culture*

What is *culture*?

Culture is a complex concept and has been defined in many different ways. Spencer-Oatey defines **culture** as:

> a fuzzy set of basic assumptions and values, orientations to life, beliefs, policies, procedures and behavioural conventions that are shared by a group of people, and that influence (but do not determine) each member's behaviour and his/her interpretations of the 'meaning' of other people's behaviour. (Spencer-Oatey 2008b: 3)

This is a useful definition when considering the role of language and the way that people may signal their membership of different groups. It acknowledges the assumptions and values that underlie behaviour, while also recognising that someone's behaviour may or may not represent the practices of a cultural group nor reflect the assumptions and values of relevant groups to which they belong.

We can add to this definition the notion that it is through interaction that culture is constructed, and that people negotiate and enact their cultural identity, responding to a range of contextual factors, such as who they are interacting with, where they are and the purpose of the interaction.

Culture has been used to refer to a group who share a common heritage, as well as to an organisation or team that has developed practices over a shorter period. We can talk about the culture of Western or Eastern society, of particular countries, of particular ethnic groups within those countries, of religious groups, of workplaces and of work-place teams.

The focus in this chapter is on national and ethnic culture, with a focus on how someone's cultural membership may be constructed in interaction. This may be conscious, with explicit marking of cultural identity, as in Example 8.1, or may involve interacting in a way that reflects often unconscious cultural norms.

It has been argued that as with gender we can never separate communication from culture. Culture is always an important aspect of the context in which communication takes place. It may be invisible to participants when outsiders are not present, but may become salient when people of different cultures interact, where it may or may not cause communication difficulties.

Explicit Marking of Cultural Identity

What about explicit marking of cultural identity?

In Example 8.1 others highlight Frank's cultural identity. Example 8.2 comes from a meeting of a group of Māori women, and illustrates how Ripeka, a member of the group, identifies as she talks about an outsider who is not present.

Example 8.2 (Source: LWP)

Context: Team meeting in a government organisation. Ripeka is telling the group how she discovered that the person she was speaking to on the phone was South African. Recorded in New Zealand.

RIPEKA: Hera gave me contacts over in in [Māori organisation]
            and I finally got a South African guy
HERA: [laughs] //[laughs]\
RIPEKA: /[clears throat]
            (I don't know whether he's) the same colour but he's South African\\
            a South African chap in [Māori organisation]
ELLA: for what?
RIPEKA: to to to talk with about [topic] …..
            Brad Theron I said oh *kia ora* [hello] I know some Therons
            he says //(   )\ I'm from South Africa I said oh
ELLA: /[laughs]\\
            [laughter]
RIPEKA: I'll just say are you the right colour but the wrong tribe?
            but I didn't say that
ELLA: [laughs]

Reprinted with permission from Vine, Bernadette, Kell, Susan, Marra, Meredith and Holmes, Janet, Boundary marking humour: Institutional, gender and ethnic demarcation, p. 134. In *Humor in interaction*, © 2009, John Benjamins Publishing.

Ripeka recounts how she contacted someone in a Māori organisation, greeted him in Māori, and then told him that she knew some people with the same surname as his. This is a standard Māori greeting style, namely a greeting followed by an attempt to establish links. She says she was surprised when he tells her he is South African. She then goes on to report what she thought in response to this information, 'are you the right colour but the wrong tribe?'.

The humour here results from Ripeka paying the South African man the compliment of including him in her in-group, since she thinks he may be non-white, 'the same colour', and subsequently 'the right colour'. The man is however 'the wrong tribe', i.e., he is not Māori, unlike Ripeka and the other members of the group she is currently interacting with. Ripeka's boundary-marking humour enables her to create bonds with her group, who all share this aspect of identity with her.

Humour and social talk may also signal culture because of the topics discussed in a less explicit way. Example 8.2 also involves indirect indexing of cultural values because of the importance of family links. Another example would be social talk about sport. Sport is a common topic of small talk in many cultures, but to talk about particular sports or particular teams or players is a way to mark identity. To support a particular team that comes from an area where the speaker either resides or used to reside, for instance, whether Fijian, Brazilian, Welsh, Dutch, South African, or Indian, may be a way to signal membership of a culture that the team is associated with.

What about the use of different languages?

Another way to mark cultural in-group or out-group status is the use of different languages. It has already been noted that people may use words and phrases from a language other than the dominant language in a situation to enact their cultural identity, or to align themselves with others. But how does multilingualism and the use of different languages relate to a person's cultural identity?

If a person speaks two languages, a common way to refer to them is to say that they are **bilingual**. Research in this area has produced a number of other terms to describe individuals who speak more than one language and the use of more than one language when communicating. **Plurilingualism** is used to refer to the way someone can switch between languages.

hello bonjour **ciao** guten tag

shalom **ПРИВЇТ** **aloha** hej

The choice of language, especially when it is not the main one used in a workplace, or when its use may be unexpected in some way, is a powerful way of enacting identity. In Example 8.3, Sheree switches the language of the meeting from English to Māori. The meeting had been a mix of English and Māori, but for several minutes prior to Sheree's turn here the team had been speaking mainly English. All meeting participants are fluent in both languages.

Example 8.3 (Source: LWP)

Context: Team meeting in a private organisation. Three members identify as Māori and two as Pākehā. Recorded in New Zealand.

SHEREE:	ā kei te rapu tonu au	*er I'm still looking for*
	i ētehi kāri	*some cards*
	i i tono mai	*Ana and Irene ([name])*
	a Ana rāua ko Irene ([name])	*Airini Tuhiwai sent in some*
	Airini Tuhiwai i ētehi	
	ā yep engari kei te rapu tonu	*er yep but I'm still looking*
	[laughs]	*[laughs]*
QUENTIN:	ā okay	*er okay*
SHEREE:	kei reira ngā whakaaro	*the ideas are there*
	tērā pea	*perhaps*
	ka mahi tahi māua	*Ana and I will work together to*
	ko ko Ana kia	
QUENTIN:	whakanikoniko?	*enhance them?*
SHEREE:	āe	*yes*

English is the dominant language of this workplace, but does not need to be for this particular team since all are fluent in both English and Māori. They do often converse in English, but Sheree knows that in shifting the language no one will be excluded. Quentin's first response after Sheree shifts the language still includes English, but his next comment is in Māori, and the discussion after this point continues in Māori (with the odd word in English). The next person to switch to a full utterance in English over a minute later is Sheree, although after her brief comment in English another team member again continues the discussion in Māori. As with Ripeka's use of boundary-marking humour in Example 8.2, language choice here contributes to creating and reinforcing bonds within the group, and signals the members' cultural identity and affiliation for non-Māori team members.

If not all participants in an interaction understand a particular language, the choice of language has the potential to exclude people, and can therefore be a way of enacting power. Being plurilingual means having some freedom of choice about which language to speak. However, people may also find themselves in a situation where they have to use a non-preferred language or one they do not know well. This requires closer attention and increased cognitive processing, so can make people feel ill at ease or discriminated against. Speakers may also choose strategies that reduce discrimination, for instance by switching to a language that they know others speak confidently. Doing this can help speakers support others, enacting a considerate, professional identity, supporting both relational and transactional goals. Language choice is an explicit way people can mark aspects of their identity, including, but not restricted to, their cultural identity. This issue is discussed more below.

Culture is always relevant when people interact. It may be invisible when outsiders are not present, but can become salient when people from different cultures interact, especially when there are communication difficulties. People may also consciously orient to culture and explicitly mark commonalities or differences.

Culture and Language Norms

Different cultures can have different language norms. This can affect a range of aspects of interaction, such as turn-taking rules, the level of directness appropriate in different contexts, the topics and times for social talk, humour and narrative, and the ways problematic talk is handled.

Interactional norms are something that are often taken for granted. Only when these are violated by someone from another group do people even consider that there might be different norms (and often even then they do not).

Research has often looked at cultural differences in discourse norms and has taken what is referred to as either a cross-cultural or an intercultural approach.

Cross-cultural Research
What does cross-cultural research focus on?

Cross-cultural communication can be defined as the communicative practices of different cultural groups. Research taking this approach examines distinct groups. For instance, Murata (2011) analysed meetings recorded by a Japanese company in Japan who employed only Japanese people, and compared these to meetings recorded in a New Zealand organisation. One salient difference she noted was an absence of pre-meeting small talk in the Japanese meetings compared with the New Zealand meetings, where pre-meeting small talk was always present and everyone joined in.

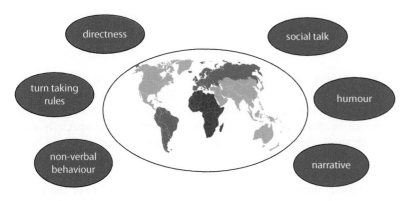

Figure 8.1
Culture and language:
Some interactional
norms that can differ.

Cross-cultural research aims to highlight similarities and differences. Consider Examples 8.4 and 8.5:

Example 8.4

Context: Opening of a senior leadership meeting. There has been small talk between members of the meeting for around five minutes before this.

CHAIR: I think er it's time to start and er everybody
        [eye contact with all the participants to signal the beginning of the meeting]
        er I did the er follow up in the progress er meeting
        in our er last meeting we left with er certain action items
        and I think the designs is one of them
        er have you looked at it from the PR side?
M: yeah we have a few comments
CHAIR: can we see them from
        //er?\
M: /you\\ have comments on the er drawings?
CHAIR: yes …

From Baxter, Judith and Al A'ali, Haleema, *Speaking as women leaders. Meetings in Middle Eastern and Western contexts*, p. 2, published 2016 Palgrave Macmillan reproduced with permission of SNCSC.

Example 8.5

Context: Opening of a senior leadership meeting. There has been small talk between members of the meeting for around five minutes before this.

CHAIR: okay shall we start? um let's at the end of each session
        do what we said in terms of saying what communications
        are out to the rest of the company
        in terms of through the line what goes into the newsletter
        anything else we said? what was the third one? newsletter? through the line?
A: team meetings wasn't it?
CHAIR: yeah that's through the line
B: through the line
CHAIR: I thought there was a third? ++ I can't remember
        we'll see as we go anyway …

From Baxter, Judith and Al A'ali, Haleema, *Speaking as women leaders. Meetings in Middle Eastern and Western contexts*, p. 2, published 2016 Palgrave Macmillan reproduced with permission of SNCSC.

One of these meetings was recorded in the UK and the other was recorded in Bahrain. Baxter and Al A'ali (2016) comment that senior meetings in international companies increasingly follow generic patterns so it can be difficult to tell which is recorded where, especially since in both the language of the meeting is English. Both meetings begin with the chair signalling to the team that they want to get started. In Example 8.4, the Bahraini leader comments 'I think it's time to start and er everybody' and makes eye contact with the members of the group, signalling the opening of the meeting. The leader then supplies some information about the purpose of the meeting. In Example 8.5, the UK leader uses the discourse marker *okay* and follows this with a question to gain people's attention, 'shall we start?'. This leader then talks about what the team needs to achieve. Having set the scene, both leaders then ask questions to elicit responses from team members. In both examples, the leader manages the interaction but the discussion is open, democratic and focused.

Understanding the similarities in meeting openings can make it easier for people to know what is expected when going to another country for business purposes or when others visit them. Identification of differences in cross-cultural studies may also help people communicate more effectively in intercultural contexts and to understand communication differences and why problems may arise. Of course there are also many other contextual factors that are also important and that may affect how people interact. And understanding that different teams can have different interactional norms even within the same organisation in the same cultural context can also help communication go smoothly if expectations based on knowledge from cross-cultural research are challenged.

Intercultural Research

What does intercultural research focus on?

Intercultural communication focuses on interaction *between* people from two (or more) distinct cultural groups. Gumperz' research on interviews shown in Chapter 2, Examples 2.4 and 2.5, for instance, examines interaction between a South Asian applicant and British interviewers, so is intercultural research. Example 8.1 above also shows an intercultural interaction, with Frank, a Pākehā New Zealander, involved in a meeting with mainly Māori participants.

Intercultural research often aims to highlight communication problems and the differences that can cause these. However, there are a growing number of studies which focus on successful intercultural communication, as in Example 8.6.

Example 8.6

Context: Opening of a sales call recorded in a British publishing house. A senior sales executive is calling a German company.

RICHNER: Richner
PETER: er hello good morning Mister Rikner?
RICHNER: yes
PETER: hello it's Peter Sikes speaking
RICHNER: //yes\
PETER: /you\\ recall me?
            how are you?
RICHNER: yes thank you I'm fine
PETER: that's //nice\
RICHNER: /how\\ are you?
PETER: I'm er hot [exhales]

RICHNER: ha ha ha hot [laughs]
PETER: [laughs] we have er we are enjoying very nice weather here
RICHNER: yes we had it er recent days er ago er very hot season
            but er
PETER: //yes\
RICHNER: /at the\\ present moment it's- it's just er
            the temperature is going down
PETER: er it t- t- there's not too cold I hope though
RICHNER: no no no it has been it's quite nice now
PETER: er that's that's that's reasonable [laughs]
RICHNER: all right
PETER: um very quickly er well not so quickly if it doesn't have to be
            er but last time we've been er spoken …

Reprinted with permission from Bubel, Claudia, 'How are you?' 'I'm hot':
An interactive analysis of small talk sequences in British-German telephone
sales, p. 250. In *Beyond misunderstanding: Linguistic analyses of intercultural
communication*, © 2006, John Benjamins Publishing.

The conversation starts off here with greetings and a recognition/
identification sequence. This is accomplished smoothly, as is the
accommodation to English by Richner. Peter then enquires after Richner's
health and after saying he is fine Richner asks Peter how he is. Bubel
(2006: 252) notes that Peter's response at this point, 'I'm er hot' is not a
typical expected response to this question, but it does introduce the topic
of the weather, a topic which is a common topic of small talk in Britain.
The men then both orient to the topic and discuss the weather in each
country before Peter turns to the business topic that he has rung about.
The people interacting in Example 8.6 come from different cultures with
different norms relating to small talk, but successfully negotiate this
sequence, with both contributing, before Peter turns to business.

Cultural Differences That May Impact Language Use

**What are some cultural differences that might affect how people
communicate?**

There have been a number of different approaches that have aimed to
capture the differences between cultures. Two distinctions that have
been made between cultures are whether they are:

- individualistic or collectivist;
- low-context or high-context.

What about the individualistic/collectivist distinction?

Different cultures have different ways of viewing the world which impact
on the way people communicate. One distinction that has been made
is between **individualist** and **collectivist** cultures. In individualist
cultures the needs of the individual are stressed over the needs of the
group. In this type of culture, individuals strive to be strong, self-reliant,
assertive, and independent. Cultures in North America and Western
Europe tend to be individualistic.

In **collectivist** cultures the needs of the group are stressed over the needs of the individual. In this type of culture, individuals strive to be dependable, selfless, generous, and helpful to others. Relationships with other members of the group and the interconnectedness between people are very important in collectivist cultures. Cultures in the Pacific, Asia, Africa and Central and South America tend to be more collectivistic.

Cultures may show more or less of an **individualist** or **collectivist** orientation, and of course not all individuals can be defined by cultural stereotypes, but this distinction has been seen as a useful way to understand differences between cultures.

An individualist or collectivist orientation can be evident in the way people talk. In Example 8.7, a professor in the USA tells a narrative during a lecture. In this he establishes his superior status when he relates how people come to him for advice and help. Speaking in this way is appropriate and acceptable in an individualist culture.

> The individualistic/collectivist distinction is one of the dimensions of cultural difference that Hofstede used to compare cultures (e.g., Hofstede 1980). His other dimensions include masculine–feminine, power–distance and uncertainty avoidance.

Example 8.7

Context: Engineering lecture at a university. Recorded in the USA.

PROFESSOR: … I was <u>um</u> ++ appointed er by the
by the er state chapter of the Sierra Club
to manage their annual er canoe lottery
and I was <u>told</u> though in the beginning
alright now be be be sure you you gotta gotta buy that canoe for us
don't buy a canoe with any mahogany or teak trim on
eh? well that's not politically <u>correct</u> these days that that that's jungle
or whaddya call it rain forest wood harvested by oppressed
elephants and what not
we don't want wanna be associated with <u>that</u>
if it's if it's <u>pine</u> or er maple or something okay
well I I I settled that matter by not getting
getting a canoe without any trim at all
but I thought how about this <u>bal</u>sa wood
this guy doesn't know about the <u>bal</u>sa wood
all these fibre glass boats lot of other fibre glass thing
any any fairly big structure that that is made of fibre glass
probably has a balsa core inside
Sierra Club hadn't found out about that

Reprinted under STM guidelines from *Discourse Studies 2*, Dyer, Judy and Keller-Cohen, Deborah, 2000. The discursive construction of professional self through narratives of personal experience, p. 290.

By portraying himself as the manager of the Sierra Club's canoe lottery, the professor shows his students that his knowledge is valued outside the university context and has practical applications. Dyer and Keller-Cohen (2000: 289) note that this is highly desirable for an engineer and allows him to affirm his professional expertise. The Sierra Club asked him, an expert, for help. The club did direct the way he should carry out the role they gave him though, stipulating that he had to avoid buying a canoe with certain types of wood. This challenges his professional identity, but he then exposes their ignorance regarding boat building materials, criticising them and highlighting his own superior knowledge on this issue.

The professor in Example 8.7 is operating in an individualistic culture where it is important for him to establish his professional expertise. He draws attention to himself, his status, expertise and knowledge. Example 8.8 comes from a culture with a collectivist rather than individualistic orientation. This means that modesty is valued and individuals do not explicitly state their own professional status and achievements; it is their role to endorse others instead.

Example 8.8 (Source: LWP)

Context: Meeting of all staff. Sheree is reporting on an awards evening she attended. The organisation has won an award for a film on which she was the main producer. Recorded in a Māori organisation in New Zealand.

SHEREE:	… but it was a lovely evening
	and the judges they read out um little excerpts
	from the from the judges' reports
	and what they said about [production name]
	was just fantastic
DAVID:	yeah //yeah\
SHEREE:	/so\\ they're going to send a report down
	//they had a\
QUENTIN:	/fantastic is that\\ all they said just fantastic [laughs]
SHEREE:	whole spiel about [production name]
	… it was really //good\
DAVID:	/what\\ she's trying to say is
	it's a real tribute to the producer
QUENTIN:	yes it is … [in Māori]: ka pai: [*well done*]
SHEREE:	no it's a tribute to the director …
	for the the record
	seeing as we've got records going
	I hardly did any producing on this film
	[general laughter]
SHEREE:	//so\ it was um it
DAVID:	/oh\\
SHEREE:	//was really good\
YVONNE:	/(yeah) that's good\\
GRETEL:	well well done that's fantastic
RANGI:	very good
QUENTIN:	(ka pai [*good*])

Reprinted under STM guidelines from *Text & Talk 28*, Marra, Meredith and Holmes, Janet, 2008. Constructing ethnicity in New Zealand workplace stories, p. 409.

Sheree describes the positive response of the judges to the organisation's award-winning production. Quentin is aware of Sheree's role as producer, so prompts her to elicit more positive comment, behaviour consistent with a collectivist cultural norm of encouraging others. Sheree responds with information about the judges' report. Nowhere has she stated her own involvement in the production. At this point, David teases Sheree that the film won an award because of her contribution, and Quentin joins in with an explicit compliment. Sheree laughingly refutes this, and others add humorous comments (not shown here). Sheree follows up with an even more self-deprecatory comment, saying she hardly did any producing on the film. While this elicits further laughter, it is also quite clear that she is behaving in an appropriate way in terms of Māori collectivist values where modesty is important.

Norms may also vary in terms of who can engage in talk, including social talk and humour, in different cultures. In individualistic cultures people are generally expected to contribute to discussions, particularly if they have expertise in an area. In collectivist cultures on the other hand, people tend to wait until invited to contribute, especially when they are of lower status. In collectivist high-power distance cultures where hierarchy is important, only higher status individuals may be able to initiate talk of certain types, as illustrated in Example 8.9.

Example 8.9

Context: Meeting in a Japanese company. A sales staff member, Chida, is completing a report to the group about a company product demonstration he made to an outside group. Another person affiliated with a rival company was at the demonstration. Komeda is the CEO. Recorded in Japan

CHIDA:	watashi wa moo kocchi toka kocchi to iu [company O] kara kiteru kedo mo [company O's product's name] o osu toka simasen //akumademo\	*[the man from company O said] though I'm from some company which is affiliated with company O I don't mean to push [company O's product's name] really*
KOMEDA:	/[humorous tone]: sorya iu wa\\ sorya: [laughter]	*[humorous tone]: he's sure to say so: [laughter]*
ASHIZAWA:	ore demo iu [laughs]	*if I were he I would definitely say so [laughs]*
YOSHIOKA:	sorya soo desu	*that's right*
MANABE:	ware ware demo ii masu	*we're sure to say so*
TANIMOTO:	iuyo iuyo [laughter]	*sure to say sure to say [laughter]*
ASHIZAWA:	sooka (4)	*I see (4)*
CHIDA:	watashi no tantoo bun wa ijoo desu ++	*that's all from me ++*

Reprinted from *Journal of Pragmatics 60*, Murata, Kazuyo, An empirical cross-cultural study of humour in business meetings in New Zealand and Japan, pp. 258–9, © 2014, with permission from Elsevier.

Chida has been reporting on the demonstration he did of the company's product to an outside group. Another person present at this demonstration was a man affiliated with a company that makes a rival product. Chida reports how this man said that he acknowledged his association with the rival company but did not 'mean to push' the rival product. Komeda, the CEO, humorously notes that the man is sure to say this. This is followed by laughter and then one after another the other meeting participants develop the humour. The humour here is initiated by the CEO and then responded to and built on by the others. Murata (2014: 259) comments that the use of humour in this way could be seen to contribute to the status relationships and to affirm the CEO's superior position, particularly since all the conjoint humour in the Japanese meeting was initiated by the CEO.

What about the low-context/high-context distinction?

Another perspective on cultural differences has been to differentiate between **low-context** and **high-context** cultures (Hall 1976). This distinction relates specifically to how people communicate. **Low-context** cultures rely on explicit verbal communication. Typically a **low-context** culture will be individualist. Because members are not as close and so do not necessarily have the same degree of shared understanding, more explicit communication is needed. Cultures in North America and Western Europe tend to be more low-context.

High-context cultures are those that communicate in ways that are implicit and rely heavily on context. Typically a **high-context** culture will be collectivist with a high value placed on interpersonal relationships and group membership, and with members being close. Cultures in the Pacific, Asia, Africa and Central and South America tend to be more high-context.

Cultures are not completely **high-context** or **low-context**, and of course, once again, individuals cannot all be defined by cultural stereotypes, but this distinction has been seen as a useful way to understand differences between cultures when considering communication patterns. It highlights the fact that different cultures do have different language norms.

Communication in low-context cultures tends to be more explicit and direct. In Example 8.6, we saw the way that Richner, a German, answered the phone by just saying his surname. This is an efficient, direct communication strategy which is the norm in low-context German culture. The person ringing immediately knows who has answered the phone, and in this case there was not even a 'hello'.

Communication in high-context cultures tends to be more implicit and indirect. In Example 8.10, Salvador, a Filipino migrant in New Zealand, refuses an offer.

Example 8.10 (Source: LWP)

Context: An occupational health officer, Ann, is concerned about the height of Salvador's desk. She offers to change it for him. Recorded in New Zealand.

ANN:	sorry about that
SALVADOR:	oh it's no problem
ANN:	I can do it now if you like [laughs]
SALVADOR:	[laughs] actually tomorrow is my last day so [laughs]
ANN:	[slowly]: aw:
SALVADOR:	and besides I'm also was comfortable

Reprinted from *System 48*, Riddiford, Nicky and Holmes, Janet, Assisting the development of sociopragmatic skills: Negotiating refusals at work, p. 138, © 2015, with permission from Elsevier.

Rather than directly saying 'no' here, Salvador refuses by telling the occupational health officer that the next day is his last day of work.

Implied in this is the fact that she does not need to make the changes. His laughter before and after he tells her this, along with his follow-up comment reassuring her that he was comfortable, implying that the desk height was not a problem, soften his speech further. Salvador comes from a high-context culture so his indirect strategy for refusing here reflects his cultural norms.

What about cultural values?

Underlying cultural language norms and orientation are a culture's value system. These are the commonly held 'principles or standards of behaviour … judgement of what is important in life' (https://en.oxforddictionaries.com/definition/value). They determine what people see as acceptable, important, right or appropriate and are reflected in the way people interact.

There are some values that are more overt and which people are more aware of, and some that are more unconscious. In talking about cultural orientation above, some of the values of individualist and collectivist cultures were mentioned. Individualist (and typically low-context) cultures adopt open, explicit communication styles, and often minimise status differences because equality and independence are valued. Collectivist (and typically high-context) cultures tend to value modesty and indirectness, and often have hierarchical structures with people being very aware of where they fit into these and of their responsibilities towards others.

Are cultural differences always important in intercultural contexts?

Although it has been argued that culture is always relevant in interaction, it cannot then be assumed that cultural *differences* will always cause problems when individuals from different cultures interact. Sometimes differences do not cause problems because the resulting language behaviour is compatible with values held by each group. This is evident in New Zealand society where both Pākehā and Māori tend to value humility and disapprove of self-promotion. For Pākehā this stems from the importance of egalitarianism, while for Māori this tends to be a reflection of a collectivist orientation. It is not generally appropriate for Pākehā New Zealanders to behave like the American professor did in Example 8.7, but to behave more like Sheree did in Example 8.8, and not draw attention to their own achievements.

If people come from different cultures with different expectations and norms then there is potential for misunderstandings and even for conflict talk when they interact. Understanding another group's norms can help smooth the way to successful interaction, as seen in Example 8.6. The norm in German culture is not to have small talk at the start of interactions like this, but Richner accommodates to what he knows to be the British norm.

In Example 8.11, American and Japanese factory workers use a range of resources to effectively communicate even though Sunaoshi (2005) notes that they have severely limited knowledge of the other group's language and sociolinguistic norms.

Example 8.11

Context: Rob brings up the topic of ordering grind wheels. He is holding one. Recorded in the USA.

ROB: grind wheels? [looks at grind wheel in his hand then back to Hashida]
HASHIDA: [looks at the grind wheel] yeah
              [both continue to look at the wheel and then at each other throughout
                 the next section]
ROB: [slowly]: er: Glen ordered two hundred
HASHIDA: two hundred?
ROB: [nods]: yesterday: [nods]
HASHIDA: [slowly]: er: yesterday?
ROB: [nods]: yesterday: [nods]
              today maybe Okano order [Hashida nods] also
HASHIDA: [nods] er four four hundred?
ROB: I don't know I'll talk to Okano san [*Mister*] ...

From *Language in Society 34*, Sunaoshi, Yukako, Historical context and intercultural communication: Interactions between Japanese and American factory workers in the American south, p. 196, © 2005 Cambridge University Press.

The men here effectively negotiate meaning, using not only spoken language but nonverbal aspects. Rob has brought a sample of the item he wants to discuss with Hashida and uses this to help convey his message. Both men use gaze and nod to show understanding.

The harmony that does seem to exist in many intercultural situations generally results because people work at building and maintaining rapport. It is not until breakdown occurs that cultural differences are regarded as having significance.

When people are interacting with members of their own culture, problems may also occur, although when they do they tend to be blamed on personal rather than cultural differences. Just because people share the same cultural background at a broad level, this does not mean that they share all the same norms. As we have seen in other chapters, norms may develop within a particular work team or community of practice, and newcomers, whatever their cultural background, need to learn these norms to interact effectively and appropriately.

Workplaces in many countries are increasingly diverse, employing people from many different countries and ethnic groups. This enriches workplace interaction linguistically and culturally, although it can also provide challenges, especially when there is no understanding of differences from one or more sides. Members of minority groups are generally much more sensitive to areas of difference between their norms and those of other groups. Powerful groups take their norms for granted and this is true of language as well as customs, values and beliefs.

Differences can cause problems when people make assumptions about language behaviour, or when they have different expectations and norms. As noted in Chapter 4, research by Spencer-Oatey and Xing (2003) showed how different expectations and norms surrounding the use and functions of small talk left both British and Chinese feeling unhappy with the outcomes of intercultural interactions. This type of discontent can impact the achievement of transactional goals for businesses when different groups interact. And the interview between a South Asian applicant and British interviewers from Gumperz' research in Chapter 2, Examples 2.4 and 2.5, demonstrates the ramifications of a lack of understanding of differences when the applicant is unsuccessful in securing a position.

© Jacynta Scurfield 2019

Training placement and job interviews are a high-stakes genre for the applicant. Other high-stakes situations include police, court and medical contexts. Work by Eades in Australian legal contexts demonstrates the potentially serious consequences when minority culture discourse patterns are not understood. Eades (1996), for instance, provides an account of the case of an Aboriginal woman who was convicted of murder without any understanding by anyone involved on the legal side that she acted in self defence.

People may also shift their interaction patterns when interacting with someone with a different cultural background. This can have ramifications that may not be immediately obvious. Hudak and Maynard (2011), for instance, investigated doctor/patient interactions which included intercultural as well as same culture interactions. In Example 8.12, a white surgeon is interacting with an African American patient. They engage here in social talk.

Example 8.12

Context: Surgeon/patient consultation. The surgeon is showing the patient a photo of his twin granddaughters. The patient has twin daughters. Recorded in the USA.

DOCTOR: do me a favour can you tell them apart? (3)
PATIENT: [slowly]: er no?: I //can't\
DOCTOR: /thank\\ you
PATIENT: I can't
DOCTOR: I'm gonna //tell\ my daughter //that because\ I can't either
PATIENT: /can't\\   /I can't\\
BOTH: [laugh] …
DOCTOR: there's a lot of problems …
PATIENT: well just call them both precious
           //that's what I usually do\
DOCTOR: /yeah [laughs]\\

The doctor and patient engage in small talk here, talking about the doctor's twin granddaughters. The doctor knows the patient also has twin daughters so develops the topic further. The doctor aligns with the patient in having a shared understanding about twins, and the difficulty of telling them apart. Hudak and Maynard (2011) comment that this was the only time a white doctor had small talk of this type with an African American patient in their data, whereas it was common when the doctor and patient were both white.

The different patterns of interaction according to addressee's ethnicity is due to different norms in different cultural groups. Small talk is a feature of interaction among other American groups, but is governed by different norms and expectations (Rawls 2000). Hudak and Maynard (2011) comment that this means that the white doctors do not generally seem to understand how to make small talk with patients of different ethnicities, and do not even realise the significance of small talk in their interactions with patients. This tendency of the white doctors to only engage in small talk with other whites has implications in terms of health outcomes. Hudak and Maynard found that sequences of small talk tended to mean that more rapport was developed between the doctor and patient and in these cases the patients were more likely to divulge information that helped the doctor provide better care (see also the work of Erickson and Shultz (1982) on counsellor/student interaction as noted in Chapter 4).

Intercultural interaction is often seen as a site of potential misunderstanding and miscommunication. When people bring different socio-cultural and linguistic norms and expectations to an interaction, there is the potential for misunderstanding. When shared interactional rules are assumed, inaccurate inferences may be made. Research has also highlighted the dynamic negotiation of meaning in interaction and successful intercultural communication in different settings.

Communicating effectively, and without causing unintended offence to people from different cultural backgrounds, involves familiarity with a range of communicative norms, and the ability to draw on them appropriately. It is also important to consider why people may not interact in an expected way, and whether there may be different cultural expectations and norms.

Culture, Gender and Leadership

Individuals have multiple and complex identities. In Chapter 6 the way people enact leadership was explored and in Chapter 7 the focus was on gender and gender identity. This included exploration of the **intersection** of gender and leadership identity. Here the way these aspects may intersect with facets of someone's cultural or ethnic identity are investigated.

What about culture and leadership?

The appropriate way to enact leadership varies between cultures and contexts. Whereas some cultures value authoritative leaders, in other cultures people who lead in this way are not seen as effective leaders in all contexts. In Example 8.13, Yvonne, a Māori leader, enacts leadership in a consultative way in a one-to-one interaction, which is consistent with Māori cultural norms and values.

Example 8.13 (Source: LWP)

Context: Meeting between a Māori managing director, Yvonne, and a staff member, Curtis. Recorded in a private Māori organisation in New Zealand.

YVONNE: how's the [programme] working? is that programme working? …
um are you alright with the [client] logo? …
you're actually gonna draw it and everything are you? …
have you thought what you're going to have on that? …
I think it's better sending a hard copy than an h- you know
than a email card isn't it?

Reprinted from Holmes, Janet and Marra, Meredith, Relativity rules: Politic talk in ethnicised workplaces. In *Situated politeness*, p. 327, © 2011 Janet Holmes and Meredith Marra, with permission from Bloomsbury.

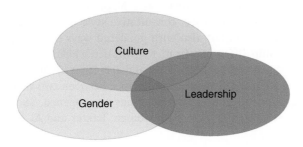

Figure 8.2
Intersectionality of cultural, gender and leadership identities.

Rather than explicitly telling Curtis what to do, Yvonne asks questions about his progress and the steps he will be taking. When she does want him to act in a certain way she presents her instruction as a hedged opinion, 'I think it's better …'. She shows respect here for him and his expertise. Yvonne also uses mitigating devices (*I think, you know,* and tag questions *are you, isn't it*) which express a facilitative and consultative stance, consistent with Māori values. Her discourse here contains features which may index not only leadership but also ethnicity and gender (as discussed below).

Again, problems in intercultural contexts can arise around issues of leadership when people come from cultures which have different expectations and norms. An effective leader in one culture may be seen as ineffective in another. A leader who is used to seeking consensus and involving others in decision-making will be seen as ineffective and indecisive if they then behave in this way when leading a team who are used to authoritative leaders. A leader from a low-context culture must also be careful not to be seen as rude or arrogant if speaking to a high-context team.

What about culture and gender?

As well as distinguishing between cultures on the basis of individualism and collectivism, another factor Hofstede (1980) explored was the dimension of femininity/masculinity. More masculine societies value power, dominance and assertiveness, and are more competitive, while more feminine societies value co-operation and modesty, and are more focused on relationships. Societies that are more masculine also have much more clearly defined gender roles than feminine societies, where both men and women are expected to be modest, caring and concerned with quality of life and to take on a broader range of occupations. Examples of societies which score highly for masculinity are Japan and Austria, while Sweden and the Netherlands score highly for femininity.

What about culture, leadership, and gender?

A central theme in sociolinguistic research on gender and leadership discussed in Chapter 7 is the language that women and men use to enact leadership. Again, this may differ from one culture to another. In Example 8.13, we saw Yvonne, a female Māori managing director. Not only is she negotiating the dimensions of leadership and ethnicity, but in this example gender is also important. She forges what Holmes and Marra (2011) refer to as a complex, hybridised identity while satisfactorily performing her diverse identities as a Māori woman, a Māori leader, and a female. Her facilitative, consultative style is consistent not only with cultural values, but also with gendered ways of talking. Yvonne enacts leadership differently from, for instance, a Pākehā woman, due to differing sociocultural expectations, and also from a Māori man.

Examples 8.4 and 8.5 showed similarities between two very different cultural groups in terms of how meetings were opened. The leaders in each of these examples were both women. Baxter and Al A'ali's (2016) research explored the discourse of three Middle Eastern and three Western European women, finding that all six of the women drew on normatively masculine interactional strategies to achieve transactional goals and normatively feminine strategies to achieve relational goals. Two of the three Middle Eastern women gravitated towards more masculine leadership practices, as a consequence of operating in workplaces where males are the dominant group, and their perception that they needed to adapt to this style in order to be recognised and accepted as leaders. They did temper this however by their use of relational strategies. Cultural context was seen to be an important factor in accounting for how all the women enacted leadership, but as always a number of other factors were also seen to be influential, for instance, how long someone had been in a workplace and what other pressures the women were managing, e.g., job losses and shifting working environments.

What about choice of language in multilingual settings and the intersectionality of identity?

As noted earlier, choice of language can be another way that identity can be signalled, and this can also help a speaker manage multiple aspects of their identity. As discussed in Chapter 6, the leaders in a meeting play a key role in many aspects of meeting management. The way in which a meeting unfolds, including the choice of languages in multilingual contexts, may be managed by the chair, although it may also be the result of collaboration and negotiation between meeting participants. The chair may impose a language on speakers of other languages. In Example 8.14, Jamal, the leader of a group, encourages his team to use German, although he has been speaking English.

Example 8.14

Context: Team meeting in a research laboratory. Mara is Hungarian. Jamal, the team leader, is Moroccan. There are also three German-speaking laboratory assistants. They are discussing a protocol which is written in German. Recorded in Switzerland.

JAMAL:	so we start with this protocol
NS:	mm
JAMAL:	if you have feedback [pause] who wants
	maybe Mara you can summarise
	in German ya
	what's er you did
MARA:	mm
JAMAL:	and what you expect
MARA:	mm [pause] also wir haben jetzt *mm so we now have*
	das rpmi *pepped up*
	protokoll aufgemöbelt aufdatiert … *updated this rpmi protocol*

Jamal has nominated German as the language here, even though he is not fluent. He knows that Mara is comfortable speaking German, along with the other meeting participants. Lüdi (2018) notes that it is also an appropriate language to use in this situation because the protocol they are discussing is written in German. Jamal empowers his followers here, enacting his identity as a considerate leader when he nominates German as the language for discussing the protocol since he knows that this is a language that his team are comfortable speaking. Language choice also allows Jamal to enact other aspects of his identity. By using English at the beginning of Example 8.14, he indexes his identity as part of a global English-speaking business community.

In Example 8.15 a leader switches back and forth between English and Samoan, and this enables her to manage multiple aspects of her identity.

Example 8.15 (Source: LWP)

Context: Ginette, team leader, is talking to a younger male team member, Eli, on the packing line in a factory. Recorded in New Zealand.

GINETTE: [talking about two other workers who are having trouble
            with weights for packets of a product] …
            [Samoan]: ae laku e fua faimai la   *if you go and measure it*
            ga ou fuaga agaleila e lua o iva o: *I went and measured it earlier today*
                                                                 and it was two zero nine zero

            that's a good weight that's not a underweight
ELI: mm
GINETTE: [recounts what she said to someone else]:
            said you come and have a look at your filling head:
            [Samoan]: sau loa kilokilo faimai oh (4)   *she came and looked and said 'oh'*
            fai aku: just because [Samoan]: e ke   *and I said just because you measured*
            fua akuga le: packet   *the first packet*
            [Samoan]: muamua e: heavy pe low   *and its either heavy or low that*
            doesn't mean you change it straight away +
            keep weighing it + you know
            [Samoan]: o o le: *you can*
            the two k g's a [slowly]: lot: slower
            than line two
            [Samoan]: e mafai na: *that can*
            control le weight +
            we should never have underweights
            on this set on the two kilo +
            and you should never have heavy weights
            over two two

Code-switching is an explicit way for Ginette to enact her identity as Samoan, an aspect of identity that she shares with Eli. Other features of her talk orient to other aspects of her identity. Ginette is reinforcing a directive she gave as team leader at the team's morning briefing meeting at the beginning of the shift. The repetition of a directive given earlier in the day strengthens it because it reinforces the importance of the issue. She does this in an indirect way, however, by recounting what she told other members of the team when they did something wrong. This indirect strategy for giving a directive is appropriate in high-context collectivist Samoan culture so enables Ginette to enact leadership in a way that reflects this. It is also appropriate given her gender identity. The directive is also further softened by her switches between English and Samoan.

Example 8.15 (and 8.14) also highlights the difficulty of separating out aspects of identity. Some cross-cultural and intercultural research assumes that group membership and identity can be clearly assigned and aspects explicitly delineated. However, sometimes the same strategy can achieve more than one goal at the same time. It is also important to remember the importance of a range of contextual factors on how people interact. This includes aspects relating to who is interacting, where they are and why the interaction is taking place.

Some cultures value authoritative leaders, while in other cultures people who lead in this way are not seen as effective leaders. Expectations and **norms** around **leadership** and gender differ and can influence how people interact and are viewed in their own countries and cultures, as well as within intercultural contexts.

Chapter Summary

This chapter has examined issues related to culture and language in the workplace. This has included exploration of how people may explicitly mark cultural identity, what cross-cultural and intercultural research focuses on, and different cultural norms, values and expectations. Communication can never be separated from culture: it is always an important aspect of the context in which communication takes place. Cultural factors may be invisible or at least taken for granted by participants when outsiders are not present. They become salient in intercultural communication if expectations and norms differ, where these differences may or may not cause communication difficulties.

Language choice has also been considered in this chapter. When a speaker has more than one language they can use, their choice allows them to enact aspects of their identity. Participants in multilingual contexts may skilfully adapt their choice of language to different situations and to achieve different goals.

Exercises

Exercise 8.1

Consider the two excerpts and then answer the questions following.

Excerpt 8.A

Context: A woman, Fabiana, is buying produce from a salesman. Recorded in Uruguay.

| SALESMAN: | qué más? | *what else?* |
| FABIANA: | nada más | *nothing else* |

Reprinted with permission from the author, from Kaiser (2014: 118)

Excerpt 8.B (Source: LWP)

Context: A woman, Kim, is buying lunch at a café. Recorded in New Zealand.

LIAM: er sorry was there anything else there that I could (help you with)?
KIM: um no thanks

1. How does the salesperson in each excerpt ask the customer if they would like anything else?
2. How do the customers respond here in each case?
3. What does this suggest about possible differences in norms when offering and refusing in this type of context between Uruguay and New Zealand?

Exercise 8.2

Consider the excerpt and then answer the questions following.

Excerpt 8.C (Source: LWP)

Context: Ka Keung is an older male Hong Kong Chinese national who is visiting a museum in New Zealand. The museum host is also male and is middle-aged.

	[One minute wait to be noticed
	and served at information desk]
	[Ka Keung points at information on desk]
KA KEUNG:	here for students?
MUSEUM HOST:	yes
KA KEUNG:	[slowly]: er:
MUSEUM HOST:	this is for seniors and students
KA KEUNG:	okay students as in full time students?
MUSEUM HOST:	er a- a- any student card
KA KEUNG:	okay and er seniors sixty years old or?
MUSEUM HOST:	a- as long as you have a student card
	it doesn't matter what age
KA KEUNG:	okay but how about senior? senior //sixty or?\
MUSEUM HOST:	/seniors\\ are over sixty five
KA KEUNG:	sixty five I see okay thank you

1. Does this intercultural interaction appear to be successful or do you think there is miscommunication?
2. Do the participants seem to share the same norms?
3. Why does Ka Keung ask about student rates before asking about senior rates? Is this strategy one you would use or are familiar with?

. . . .

Further Reading

Paulston, Kiesling and Rangel (2012) and Piller (2017) are excellent resources for anyone wanting to explore intercultural communication and discourse further. Candlin and Gotti (2004) present a collection of research papers on intercultural communication in specialist fields, including legal, commercial, political and institutional settings. Other recent books on discourse and culture include Schnurr and Zayts (2017) and Angouri (2018). Baxter and Al A'ali's (2016) monograph exploring the discourse of three Middle Eastern and three Western European women leaders provides a fascinating exploration of culture, gender and leadership, while Vine (2019) focuses on how cultural values can affect language norms and appropriate ways of interacting in different contexts. The chapters in Pavlenko and Blackledge (2004) explore the negotiation of identities in multilingual settings.

IV So What?

9 The Implications and Applications of Workplace Research

CHAPTER PREVIEW

In this chapter, some implications and applications of research on language in the workplace are explored. Research can inform training and communication skills development. This includes issues related to:

- leadership;
- gender;
- culture;
- different workplace settings and job roles;
- implications of research for organisations.

This chapter examines some implications and applications of workplace discourse research. The importance of identifying both relational and transactional features of talk in authentic data and applying findings in training situations, along with raising awareness of the importance of effective communication in the achievement of workplace goals, cannot be underestimated.

Implications and Applications of Workplace Research: Introduction

A question that arises when researching workplace communication is 'so what?' In what ways *can* and *is* workplace research being used to provide practical outcomes? The obvious ones are the ways it can inform teaching and professional training.

Consider Example 9.1:

Example 9.1 (Source: LWP)

Context: Tom, a builder, is working with a work experience student, Rich, on a building site. Recorded in New Zealand.

TOM: now Rich chuck this pencil in your pocket for a sec
        climb up here and just mark the stud with your pencil
        so we know where to drill the holes
        use your tape measure
RICH: okay how far apart are the holes?
TOM: fifteen mils
RICH: okay
        [a few minutes later]
TOM: marked them all?
RICH: yep
TOM: okay well can you just drill those holes there now?
RICH: yep
TOM: cheers
        [a few minutes later]
TOM: done the high ones?
RICH: yep
TOM: okay good just just jump off the ladder now
RICH: okay
TOM: otherwise you're going to tip off it
        you can do the rest from the ground
RICH: okay

Reprinted from Riddiford (2014: 10)

This example is adapted from a workplace interaction recorded on a building site and is included in a resource for non-native English speakers who will be working in this industry. It illustrates the way directives are given and responded to in this context, with students being encouraged to notice the vocabulary that is used, as well as the strategies used to give, clarify and respond to directives. Rather than using a made-up example, Example 9.1 allows students to appreciate the diverse strategies that people use in everyday interaction to achieve transactional goals, while also paying attention to relational aspects of interaction. Tom, for instance, uses different syntactic forms to express his directives, and also provides reasons to support these and frequently hedges with *just*. This is one way research on authentic workplace talk can be and is being used to produce practical resources for workers.

A brief survey of implications and applications of research is provided in this chapter. Workplace research findings can prepare newcomers to a profession, as well as helping people develop their communication skills. Research can aid migrants and other people preparing to work with people from other cultures, and findings can highlight power imbalances and may then help redress them. The development of the field of workplace discourse research has created possibilities for using the knowledge gained to improve workplace communication and apply research findings to real world issues. Being able to communicate effectively not only has personal implications but also has a major impact on organisational performance. A significant contribution of linguistic research to organisational studies and management in particular is the recognition of the importance of how people communicate to the success of organisations.

Example 9.1 involves directives, which is a transactional aspect of talk explored in Chapter 3. Other topics covered in Part II of this book are also integrated into this chapter, as applications and implications of workplace discourse research are considered. To begin, issues for communication skills training that relate to the topics covered in Part III of this book are explored:

- leadership;
- gender; and
- culture.

What about Leadership?

One area where the need for training is acknowledged is leadership. This has followed the move to understanding effective leadership as involving learnable behaviours rather than inherent traits, along with a greater appreciation of the importance of language and communication for leaders.

In particular, the importance of relational behaviours in leading effectively has been recognised more recently. Chapter 6 explores leadership and the importance of achieving both transactional and relational goals for leaders, providing many illustrations of leaders doing this. In Chapters 3, 4 and 5, there are also many examples of leaders (and others) communicating effectively in a range of situations. Seeing how effective leaders interact with others provides invaluable input to training. It is all well and good to say be more relational, for instance, but what does this look like? And how are relational aspects effectively integrated with transactional aspects?

Making research findings on leadership discourse available to professionals and communicating them in easily accessible and non-expert ways for practitioners and students is an important way to create practical outcomes. Walker and Aritz (2014) provide an example of what this can look like. They draw on a range of sources to show how people enact leadership.

Example 9.2 comes from their chapter 'Leading employees' and is taken from the work of Jonathan Clifton (Clifton 2012). Clifton (2012) presents a linguistic analysis of a naturally occurring performance appraisal which had been used in a training resource in the MBA programme at the Open University (Brown, Hamblin and Mitchell 1988).

Example 9.2

Context: Performance appraisal. Recorded in a multinational company.

ANDY: what I have to actually try and complete on the final document
        is where we think you can go this year
BOB: I feel I can do the job I'm in now
        when I came in I needed a bit of learning
        and obviously I can improve
        you can carry on improving and improving
        but I find very much that the job is in my scope
        and as I say I feel that now is the time that I ought
        to be preparing for the next step
        that's personally how I see this coming year
        I feel certain specific areas of weakness
        I know to move up to the next step I must fill in those
        I'm hoping the company can provide that sort of training and experience
ANDY: rather than actually working in that department
        you could spend a bit of time in industrial engineering for instance
BOB: yes I mean it's a //possibility\
ANDY: /another\\ area we could perhaps develop
        is a job rotation or just exposure to during the year
BOB: yeah //I mean\
ANDY: /but\\ I agree
        I think you are tending to take the job rather in your stride

Reprinted with permission of Business Expert Press. From Walker, Robyn and Aritz, Jolanta, 2014. *Leadership talk. A discourse approach to leader emergence*, pp. 62–3.

Walker and Aritz (2014) focus on the way both participants in Example 9.2 skilfully manage the interaction, ensuring the maintenance of a good working relationship. This includes the presequence that Andy begins with, which introduces the topic (the first question on the appraisal form) in a way that orients to a delicate situation which can threaten Bob's face. Andy presents the possible threat as coming from the organisation, rather than from him personally. Bob also needs to manage any threat to face in his response, and does this in his account which applies no fault to either himself or Andy. Bob needs to acknowledge his possible weaknesses in this context, but also needs to enact a competent professional identity. In responding to this, Andy does not directly disagree and suggests an alternative. When Bob seems to be getting ready to disagree, Andy heads this off and provides validation of Bob's positive self-assessment. This shows how both men work together to navigate a tricky type of interaction. Bob is expected to acknowledge both his own strengths and weaknesses because this is a performance appraisal, and as his manager Andy uses strategies to skilfully manage the interaction.

Discursive leadership approaches highlight the importance of language in leadership. Leaders need to understand that actions and outcomes are achieved through finely judged linguistic strategies in interaction. Examples of people doing this in a range of different situations, including ones where the whole nature of the interaction is potentially problematic, such as performance appraisals, can show leaders how this type of situation can be handled effectively.

What about Gender Issues?

In Chapter 7, issues related to language and gender in the workplace were explored. One of these was the way that people may adapt the strategies that they use in order to more effectively communicate in different situations. This can be particularly relevant for women when they work in masculinised professions or workplaces, and for men working in feminised professions or workplaces. Research has also highlighted the fact that men and women often do not talk differently, and the crucial importance of a range of contextual factors that influence how anyone interacts.

Ford (2008) observed and recorded in a variety of work settings, exploring how women and men interacted in business meetings. She also conducted interviews and fed her observations on how women and men construct their work and leadership identities through talk back to workplaces. In presentations Ford used Example 9.3, for instance, to help highlight the assumptions people make, as well as how speakers can manage talk.

Example 9.3

Context: Meeting of a university committee. Recorded in the USA.

STEPH: [inhales] can I make a- brief comment on that I e- [slowly]: um: ++
being on the other side of the [laughs]: <u>colle</u>ge:
er we've never had a search committee in our department

Reprinted from Ford (2008: 171)

Ford draws attention to the functions of pauses, hesitations, hedges and laughter, which people tend to assume are unimportant and/or annoying features of interaction. Steph's inbreath at the beginning of Example 9.3, for instance, is a common, effective way to get attention, and her use of the interrogative form shows deference although she does not pause immediately to allow a response from others. She does pause shortly after this, however, which Ford (2008: 172) notes gives the meeting participants time to align themselves with her and with what she is saying.

Ford (2008) did not recommend the adoption of any specific strategies, but some of the women told her that they tried some of the practices that she had mentioned in her presentations, e.g., taking more audible in-takes of breath when wanting to speak. They reported that at times this helped them take the floor and enter discussions.

Baxter conducted a range of different types of participant consultancy work with women leaders in the UK, and commented that a common element was the 'aha moment', when the women suddenly understood the contribution of language to their own leadership issues (Baxter 2018: 409).

In *The Language of Female Leadership* (Baxter 2010), Baxter outlines several strategies which might enable senior women to achieve their career goals and she proposes that women should be linguistic role models for junior colleagues by combining the enactment of authority with politeness and humour. She also mentions some strategies aimed at organisations to counter negative evaluations of senior women. This includes raising awareness of the negative effects of gendered discourses which often discriminate against women, for instance, by contesting the use of sexist language and challenging the uncritical use of derogatory terms to describe women, even if used humorously.

Research in the area of gender and language can aid in assessment and evaluation and in attempts to address gender inequalities in the workplace. It is important to raise awareness of stereotypes of gendered interactional norms. These can play an (often unconscious) role in maintaining and reinforcing gender imbalances in terms of how people are evaluated and treated. Learning key concepts, such as the **double bind** (see Chapter 7), and encouraging people to reflect upon the way they interact and their own judgements of others can empower people to recognise their own communicative biases and critically assess these, which may lead to change.

What about Cultural Issues?

Cultural issues are relevant in a range of different types of workplace situations. In some cases, different cultural groups live side by side in the same country; people may come into contact through travel or work with organisations or individuals in another country; or migrants may be involved in either backstage or frontstage settings.

Holmes, Marra and Vine (2011) provide an example of research focusing on two cultures which exist side by side in New Zealand. Different norms are highlighted which affect how people communicate in the four workplaces examined. Two of the organisations are Māori workplaces where Māori norms and practices are evident in the way the organisation operates and the way people interact. The other two organisations are Pākehā. Example 9.4 shows one of the ways that norms differ for Māori and Pākehā and the misunderstandings that may result when members of the two cultures interact. Steve is Pākehā and is a relative newcomer to this Māori workplace. Although in the minority in each case, a few

Pākehā do work in the Māori organisations where data was recorded for this analysis and vice versa.

Example 9.4 (Source: LWP)

Context: Meeting of all staff in a Māori organisation. Steve is giving a presentation. Recorded in New Zealand.

STEVE:　we have capability development um
　　　　the g m oversight here //is from Ants with Caleb\
FRANK:　　　　　　　　　　　　　　/[quietly to Daniel]: and what's Maraetai mean?\\
STEVE:　the manager in charge budget of a hundred and
　　　　//eighty\ seven k
DANIEL:　/[quietly]: mm?\
FRANK:　[quietly]: what's Maraetai mean?:
STEVE:　obviously key area
　　　　//we want to ensure that um\
DANIEL:　/[quietly]: it's by your left\\ eye:
FRANK:　/[quietly]: mm?:
DANIEL:　[quietly]: it's by your left eye:
FRANK:　[quietly]: by your left eye:
DANIEL:　/[quietly]: mm my right left eye:\
STEVE:　/one of the important\\ things in communication is
　　　　not to talk when others are talking
　　　　[laughter] …
FRANK:　Steve this indicates a need for you to be out in hui
　　　　[laughter]
FRANK:　one of the things that you learn very quickly
　　　　is that a sign of respect is that other people are
　　　　talking about what //you're saying while you're saying it\
　　　　　　　　　　　　/[laughter\\ [laughter]

In Example 9.4, Steve is giving a presentation when Frank and Daniel begin a quiet discussion. This is prompted by Frank not understanding a word he reads in Steve's presentation, which he asks Daniel to explain. The word, *Maraetai*, is actually a place name but Daniel makes a joke since the name sounds like the English phrase 'my right eye'. Steve is distracted by this discussion and stops his presentation to reprimand them for talking while he is presenting. He makes a joke of this as he tells off Frank and Daniel (his superiors). As a Pākehā working in a Māori organisation, Steve here shows ignorance of Māori norms. Frank, another Pākehā, reprimands Steve and explains the norms to him. Members of minority groups are much more likely to understand the norms of majority groups, with majority groups not even understanding at times that there may be differences. Frank and Steve are minorities in this context, although Steve has not been working in this context for long. One purpose of the study reported in Holmes, Marra and Vine (2011) was to explore the ways norms might differ for Māori and Pākehā and to provide an accessible account of differences such as this.

Some researchers have produced resources highlighting cultural norms which are aimed specifically at people working in particular professions. In order to address the problem of ignorance of other cultural norms in the legal system in Australia, for instance, Eades produced a handbook aimed at helping lawyers understand Aboriginal English (Eades 1992). Relevant differences include a cultural requirement for Aborigines to speak indirectly and the fact that certain information may not be spoken in general contexts, for instance, a deceased person's name. This resource raised awareness of previously unknown differences for many lawyers, although unfortunately some lawyers used the handbook in order to increase miscommunication for their own purposes, an unanticipated negative side effect of Eades's effort to help (Eades 2004).

© Jacynta Scurfield 2019

Spencer-Oatey and her colleagues have also produced resources which address important issues in relation to intercultural communication. Spencer-Oatey and Franklin (2009) explore intercultural interaction and provide an accessible introduction not only for researchers in different disciplines, but also for people involved in intercultural interaction through work and for personal reasons. Like Walker and Aritz (2014), they draw on a range of sources. For instance, they cite the work of

Spencer-Oatey and Xing (2004, 2008) on meetings between Chinese delegates to a British engineering company where there was a breakdown in communication, and explore why this occurred. The British chair of the meeting inadvertently caused offence to the Chinese group in one meeting by failing to allow the head of the Chinese delegation an opportunity to speak in response to his own speech, being unaware of the importance of reciprocity in Chinese culture (Spencer-Oatey and Franklin 2009: 104).

What about migrants?

Migrants often find it difficult to find work in a new country, and this can be a particular problem for people with specialised skills wanting to work within their own profession. Communication issues often present a barrier. Example 9.1 shows one way research on transactional aspects of talk, such as directives, can be utilised in producing resources for training for migrants. Many migrants in New Zealand training to work in this area do not have strong English language skills, which is further complicated by the way workers in this area typically talk. Even vocabulary can provide a challenge when workers make frequent use of abbreviations, such as 'sec' for 'second', 'mils' for 'millimetres', and colloquial language, for instance, 'chuck' for 'throw'. Highlighting of vocabulary, the use of different forms to express directives, even within such a short exchange, and the strategies that are used to mitigate the directives, all provide valuable input for workers wanting to work in this area.

Even when migrants are competent in the language of the new country, this is only one aspect of what is required to be able to communicate effectively. Socio-pragmatic skills are of crucial importance and research has shown that learning these without explicit teaching can be difficult.

Different elements have been identified as being essential in any teaching programme which aims to develop learners' socio-pragmatic skills. These include relevant input (Kasper 1996), and relevant input which is based on authentic interaction can make a big difference. To be truly relevant, teaching materials need to incorporate features that learners will come across while interacting within the contexts where they will use the target language. Scripted dialogues in many published English language teaching materials, for instance, are very different from naturally occurring data, and therefore from the language that students will encounter in the real world.

Intercultural awareness training (Roberts 2005) is another important related area that linguistic research can support. In noticing features of language, people also need to reflect on how this differs from their own norms and ways of doing things. In understanding intercultural differences, migrants and people working with them can more readily identify and adapt the way they approach workplace communication. Research that explores the norms in different countries and settings can support this.

One of the aims of the LWP project was to have practical outcomes, and the production of teaching resources is one way this has been achieved (e.g., Riddiford and Newton 2010, Riddiford 2014). Examples in both Riddiford and Newton (2010) and Riddiford (2014) are adapted from authentic workplace interactions from the LWP database and provide instances of the types of speech which migrants can find difficult. The focus is on aspects of language where there is potential for misunderstandings and miscommunication, particularly when there may be a mismatch between what is perceived as appropriate in such situations in different cultures. The units in Riddiford and Newton (2010) include requests, small talk, complaints and disagreement.

As seen in Chapters 3, 4 and 5, these types of talk are also ones where there is diversity in how they are expressed. Politeness, directness, hedging and being able to interpret and express things in appropriate ways can take many forms and authentic data can provide examples of different ways speakers do this, as seen in Example 9.1. In Example 9.5, a disagreement sequence from a management meeting is used as input for students.

Example 9.5 (Source: LWP)

Context: Management team meeting in a private organisation. The meeting is chaired by Jason. Stephen is the owner of the company and Jason and Rob are both managers. Recorded in New Zealand.

ROB:	if you bear the cost of their mistakes their screw ups
	well of course they'll leave it for you to find these
JASON:	well it's not so much that
	it's just we need to transfer that responsibility back to them
ROB:	well then we need to transfer the cost of it back too
JASON:	yeah but in um reality the industry has allowed that to happen Rob
ROB:	not all
JASON:	um for the most it has
	and so the prices for our product
	are exactly the same as anybody else
	and you know um if we turn around and
	say that we're now gonna charge you whatever
	x amount for your mistakes
	they'll just say oh okay thanks we'll go somewhere else
ROB:	no but the incentives have to be in line with the behaviour you want
	if anyone continues to allow the customer to make mistakes
	and the cost of that is borne by you
	you accept that that's your cost not theirs
	then they will use that
STEPHEN:	I think on a well managed account
	the account manager can work the swings and roundabouts
	and quite often we might ring the client and ask them for a favour
	having got some some of that going
ROB:	yes

Reprinted from Riddiford and Newton (2010: 72–3)

Rob and Jason disagree here, and we have seen them disagreeing before (Chapter 5, Example 5.15). Once again their disagreement is quite strongly expressed and continues over a number of turns. When Stephen entered the discussion in Example 5.15, Rob did not pursue the disagreement further. The same thing happens in Example 9.5. Rob is disagreeing quite directly with Jason, but as soon as Stephen states his point of view, Rob is quick to agree with him and does not sustain the disagreement. Stephen's status as company owner is likely to be influencing Rob's responses here. In Chapter 3, a whole range of contextual factors which can influence how people communicate were identified. Examining contextual factors raises awareness of aspects that affect the linguistic strategies people use when interacting at work. Status differences tend to be important and considering such factors helps people understand the choices speakers make.

Learning in a language context where migrants want to gain employment is high-stakes, with people's financial livelihoods relying on successful outcomes. Migrants are often un- and underemployed. Surveys of students who have completed a skilled migrant programme at Victoria University of Wellington which utilises the resources produced by Riddiford and Newton (2010) show that the majority have subsequently gained employment within their area of expertise, providing evidence of the value of supplying such input and training.

What about majority group members?

The taken-for-granted status of majority norms and the accompanying assumptions often result in a very one-sided perception of intercultural interaction. When minority group norms are privileged, majority group members can gain new insights into alternative ways of doing things. It is not only migrants who can benefit from seeing how people successfully navigate potentially problematic situations. Examination of authentic data can also feed into training for members of majority cultures who interact with minorities. Consider Example 9.6:

Example 9.6

Context: An elderly Italian-speaking woman is visiting her doctor. She has several problems including thinning hair and a dust allergy. Recorded in the UK.

DOCTOR:	yes so I think the next step is to get you to see
	the skin specialist who deal with problems of the hair
	//and\
PATIENT:	/yeah\\
DOCTOR:	um ask their opinion
	would you be happy to go and see the //specialist?\
PATIENT:	/yes +\\
	please darling //yeah\
DOCTOR:	/yeah\\ cos //I think\
PATIENT:	/I– I\\ sneezes lot I sneeze lot
DOCTOR:	you sneeze a lot right
PATIENT:	[laughs] cos //er\
DOCTOR:	/that's\\ something different is it?

Republished with permission of John Wiley and Sons, from *Medical Education 39*, Roberts, Celia, Moss, Becky, Wass, Val, Sarangi, Srikant and Jones, Roger, Misunderstandings: A qualitative study of primary care consultations in multilingual settings, and educational implications, p. 473, © 2005; permission conveyed through Copyright Clearance Center, Inc.

In Example 9.6, the doctor begins to explain why she wants to refer the patient to a specialist and the patient overlaps her in agreement twice. These overlaps do not lead to any problems or loss of information. The patient then overlaps with a new topic, sneezing, just when the doctor starts her explanation of why it would be useful to see the specialist. The doctor acknowledges that this is a new topic, 'that's something different is it?', and is unable to finish her explanation. Roberts et al. (2005) note that in this consultation the doctor's explanations, suggestions and reassurances never get properly expressed. Frequent overlapping speech is considered in some cultures to be a high-involvement style and to show friendliness and politeness. Patients may also interrupt because they do not understand or see the point of a doctor's explanations, particularly if they are expressed in abstract and general ways. Although the patient in this case may have voiced all her concerns, the doctor is left not knowing whether the patient understands the reasons for any decisions and recommendations because there has been a mismatch in interaction styles.

This is just one type of misunderstanding found by Roberts et al. (2005) in their data, with twenty per cent of the consultations they examined containing misunderstandings caused by differences. These misunderstandings related to issues of language and self-presentation which they concluded challenged the literature on culture and ethnicity. Communication textbooks aimed at medical professionals include sections on how to help patients understand what doctors say, generally by advising the avoidance of medical jargon. They do not deal specifically with differing norms relating to features of interaction such as overlapping speech, and do not raise issues which help the doctors understand what their patients are saying. As in other situations, training materials that are based on authentic interaction will be more relevant, particularly when the material draws attention to differences that may cause problems.

> There has been a lot of focus on leadership and the development and improvement of leadership skills, and research on authentic interaction can provide invaluable feedback for training in this area. Research and awareness-raising in the areas of gender and intercultural communication can benefit both women and men, and people working in intercultural contexts.

Different Settings and Job Roles

In the discussion above the focus has been on leadership, gender and cultural issues. The genre, e.g., performance appraisal or medical consultation, has been relevant, but the main focus has been aspects of the interactants' identities, whether leaders or followers, women or men, or people from different cultural groups. We can also consider who is interacting in terms of the job roles people are taking on, whether they are learning a new profession or developing their communication skills in order to more competently enact a role they already have. This includes consideration of different genres and the ways research on effective communicators can feed into training for a range of occupations.

The situations considered in this section are:

- interviews and employability;
- vocational training and communication skills development for different occupations.

What about interviews and employability?

We have seen some examples from different types of interviews in this book. In Chapter 1, for instance, Example 1.2 came from a police interview and Example 1.3 from a job interview. The extract analysed using different analytical approaches in Chapter 2 came from a market research interview. Question/answer sequences are typical of the interview genre, with the particular questions from the interviewer in each situation conforming to what we would expect to find in each case. Understanding how people manage these different interview situations can usefully feed into training materials. The job interview, for instance, is a high-stakes context where both sides can benefit from insights gained from examining authentic interviews. As the examples from Gumperz (2015) show in Chapter 2, Examples 2.4 and 2.5, a lack of understanding of different cultural interaction norms can mean applicants do not gain access to training. Example 9.7 is another intercultural interview where the applicant was unsuccessful in securing a position.

Example 9.7

Context: Job interview. Yohannes, the interviewee, is Ethiopian. The interviewer is a British man of South Indian parentage. Recorded in the UK.

INTERVIEWER:	an example where you been working as part of a team=
YOHANNES:	=mhm
INTERVIEWER:	to achieve somethings [twenty seconds of talk deleted] …
YOHANNES:	and we were friendly we were not um bothering to argue
	this is your your job is my job we are all together
	we had togetherness they are very helpful
	they are a lot of integration each other er
	if something happen we have to sort it out ourselves
	instead of complaining to each other we have to know the first thing
	whoever comes first mm say for example if you have a job today interview
	and then he offer the job in that place we tell that person
	if he doesn't understand he asks he can ask us five to six times
	doesn't matter=
INTERVIEWER:	=mhm
YOHANNES:	um because he is new at least for one month he might get confused he might

INTERVIEWER:	what to do- has to do- okay ho- how many of you in th- in that team?
YOHANNES:	er we were me Mohammed about five people +++ that was in valet service //and that was in\
INTERVIEWER:	/right okay\\
YOHANNES:	was in public //area\
INTERVIEWER:	/how\\ many rooms would you be covering on a- any given date?
YOHANNES:	um one room we had we had guests laundry to bring it from the floors
INTERVIEWER:	okay
YOHANNES:	then we have to wash them in er machine or if not we send them to er dry cleaning + and we have to do go and get that um but the how much it costs (5) and then we have to give them back to the customers (6)

Reprinted under STM guidelines from *Discourse & Society 18*, Campbell, Sarah and Roberts, Celia, 2007. Migration, ethnicity and competing discourses in the job interview: Synthesizing the institutional and personal, pp. 260–1.

In responding to the interviewer's question to give an example where he worked in a team, Yohannes talks about how the team was friendly and worked well together. Throughout the rest of the interview, Campbell and Roberts (2007) note that he would frequently provide personal accounts which emphasised personal relationships and personal goals, rather than orienting to corporate values and work goals. An interviewer's questions about teamwork should implicitly cue a candidate to talk about how teamwork can help an organisation, but Yohannes responds by emphasising the togetherness and integration of the team as an end in itself.

Example 9.7 also shows a 'jarring' style with movement from a very personal focus to 'over-formality', which Campbell and Roberts (2007) mention as a reason interviewers give when an interview is unsuccessful. They point out here though how this is produced by the interviewer's interactional behaviour. The interviewer cuts into Yohannes's personal discourse to bring the interview back to quite a low level of questioning asking about numbers of people in the team and how many rooms. Yohannes responds to this by giving lists of institutional procedures, e.g., listing the tasks in regard to the laundry. The interviewer later criticised these lists as not sufficiently personalised, with Yohannes failing to describe his role, and therefore as evidence of his unwillingness to take on responsibility. The interviewer also described Yohannes as 'hard to follow, mumbling, waffling, unreliable' and contradictory. The interviewer did not see how his own interaction patterns contributed to this.

Again, intercultural issues are relevant in Example 9.7. Understanding the job interview genre, however, the types of questions asked, and the ways people successfully negotiate these and present themselves as competent individuals who will fulfil an employer's needs, is important for anyone applying for a job. Consider Example 9.8:

Example 9.8

Context: Job interview collected at an international recruitment agency. The candidate, Tanya, is applying for a senior advisory role at an organisation providing services to youth. Recorded in New Zealand.

ELIZABETH: so can you describe a little bit more
about how that is (work that fits) looks like
or what kind of role you're interested in?
TANYA: um so I guess ++ my background is predominantly working with
[a social group] + um throughout my entire entire=
ELIZABETH: =mhm=
TANYA: work history=
ELIZABETH: =mhm? ...
TANYA: h- I want to be able to in some way influence [members of social group] +
um + be able to + support and provide a (   ) for the years of work
that I've served=
ELIZABETH: =mhm=
TANYA: =in that field in that sector

From Kuśmierczyk-O'Connor, Ewa, 'I consider myself a specialist' – A multimodal perspective on believable identity construction in job interviews, pp. 55–6. In *Negotiating boundaries at work*, © Kuśmierczyk-O'Connor, Ewa, 2017. Reproduced with permission from Edinburgh University Press through PLSclear.

Elizabeth has begun the question section of the interview by asking Tanya what kind of role she is interested in. Tanya has already provided this information both in her cover letter and during initial phone screening. Now, however, she needs to present this in a way which convinces the interviewer about her suitability for the position, to show her employability. Tanya does this by orienting to past actions, that is, her background where she influenced and supported a particular social group. Kuśmierczyk-O'Connor (2017) makes a close examination of the multimodal aspects of the interaction and notes how Tanya has her chair pulled in, is sitting straight with her elbows resting on the table and hands clasped, contributing to her creation of a professional image. By framing her work as service and her professional goals as things she 'wants to be able' to do, Tanya adds a personal element and establishes an image of a professional with considerable experience and personal commitment to the core tasks of the job. Tanya was successful in getting through this phase of the job application process.

What about vocational training and communication skills development for different occupations?

In Chapter 2, Example 2.2, we saw an apprentice struggling because he did not understand the vocabulary necessary to be able to effectively enact his role. Learning how to work is not just about having practical skills. People also need to learn to talk and interact in appropriate ways for different roles. And learning the practical and language skills required can only be achieved through interaction with people who already possess these skills.

Two aspects are important in vocational training:

- the role of interaction in learning;
- learning to interact in a way appropriate for a role.

Examples 9.9 and 9.10 show trainers interacting with trainees. Example 9.9 comes from a research project based in Switzerland which explores data from the Swiss Vocational Education and Training system. Apprentices are learning here to make a box from an iron sheet.

Example 9.9 (translated from French)

Context: Trainer interacting with apprentices in a car mechanics workshop. He is explaining aspects related to the completion of a practical task. Recorded in Switzerland.

TEACHER:	*we are meeting here for two reasons*
	first + once you have cut your iron sheet
	even if you have cut it right and carefully with the shears
	you'll see that it is a little bit out of shape
	you need to go to the anvil
	[points in the direction of the anvil]
	you wipe the anvil so that there is no more dirt on it
	and hit it with a hammer
	but you should hammer it like a goldsmith
	[laughter]
??:	*I take the mallet*
TERRENCE:	*a crazy goldsmith*
TEACHER:	*what mustn't you do with the hammer? …*
??:	*leave marks*
??:	*//put it sideways*
TEACHER:	*/what you must not do\ is to lengthen the sheet …*
	so you should straighten out the folds
	with very gentle blows of the hammer

In Example 9.9, the teacher has asked the students to gather around him so he can give them more instructions about the task. He instructs them to use the hammer with care when flattening the iron sheet, using an analogical link between the required action and the way goldsmiths use hammers. This analogical reference is noticed by the apprentices; some start laughing at the reference, one apprentice imagines he takes a mallet and another comments on the fact that the goldsmith could go crazy. Filliettaz, de Saint-Georges and Duc (2010) also note how the apprentices continue to engage with this reference to the goldsmith after this interaction, even as they are on their own carrying out the task of flattening the iron sheet.

© Jacynta Scurfield 2019

The use of analogies like this in teaching has been found to serve a number of important functions. New knowledge is often built in relation to existing knowledge so analogies play a crucial role in this. Analogies also provide helpful links for learners by making abstract ideas more concrete and assist retention of what is being learnt. From a teacher's perspective, analogies can be used to make links between teaching content and the actual experiences of the students. Analogies also build mutual understanding and common ground among teachers and students. They therefore also have social functions relating to identity construction and interpersonal relationships.

Example 9.10 comes from a different type of training situation. In this case, a trainee is undertaking air traffic controller simulator training.

Example 9.10 (translated from Finnish)

Context: Air traffic controller simulator training. Recorded in Finland.

PILOT: *Donlon Tower Oscar Hotel Bravo Charlie Charlie* (4)
TRAINEE: *[slowly]: er: Oscar Charlie Charlie stand by +++*
         correction + stand by (I'll call) + then
TRAINER: *read*
TRAINEE: *Homer One wind one four zero degrees seven knots*
         runway one two [faster]: cleared for take off left turn:

Republished with permission of Emerald Group Publishing Limited, from the *Journal of Workplace Learning 23*, Koskela, Inka and Palukka, Hannele, Trainer interventions as instructional strategies in air traffic control training, p. 300, © 2011; permission conveyed through Copyright Clearance Center, Inc.

In Example 9.10 a trainee air traffic controller needs to assist an aircraft to take-off. The trainee has instructed an aircraft, Homer One, to taxi to the runway and wait for take-off clearance. The runway is occupied by another aircraft that has just landed (OCM). At the same time a third aircraft (OCC) that is entering the zone is calling the tower. The trainee acknowledges he has heard this call and then begins to turn his attention to another task. Before the trainee gets any further, the trainer intervenes, ordering him to issue take-off clearance to Homer One waiting on the runway. In response, the trainee immediately gives take-off clearance to this aircraft. It is clear from the trainer's intervention that he thinks the trainee is in need of guidance in managing overlapping tasks. As the air traffic controller's tasks are time-critical and involve constant change, trainees must learn to effectively organize multiple tasks. Directing the trainee to 'read' is an explicit and direct way for the trainer to tell the trainee which task should be performed next and of prompting the trainee to address that task. For the trainer and trainee this brief, direct guidance is an efficient and effective way of providing appropriate instruction.

Exploring the language of trainers and mentors (whether formal or informal) can help them to become more effective in their roles. Teachers must respond to the demands of a situation which may change from moment to moment, and as in Example 9.9 this may involve the use of analogy to help students learn aspects of a task, or as in Example 9.10 the use of minimal directives to help a trainee learn to manage multiple tasks. Authentic examples also show the way learners respond and the joint negotiation of meaning in learning.

Research on authentic workplace interactions across a huge range of workplaces and workplace genres can feed into vocational training, particularly when the authentic data examined comes not only from the same industry but was also collected in the same country and culture. Understanding how these genres work can help a newcomer to a profession adapt more easily and learn to interact in ways that are appropriate and effective. File (2018) for instance provides an example of the typical structure of nurse handover meetings. After opening the meeting, the chair of such meetings takes staff through each patient on the ward one by one, as in Example 9.11.

Example 9.11 (Source: Data collected by Mariana Lazzaro-Salazar)

Context: Nurse handover meeting on a hospital ward. Recorded in New Zealand.

CHAIR:	Mister Richmond (4) ( ) rehab
	ah right had this discussion yesterday
	hasn't changed
	Mister Grayson + stroke team?
NURSE 1:	yeah + we um still don't know that rehab's gonna be on or not
	he's had one stroke and was meant to rehab …

Example 9.11 comes from an experienced team and highlights a feature of handover meetings that new nurses need to understand. As the chair introduces each patient on the ward, nurses are expected to then provide any relevant information about the patient. After going through each patient's status update, the meeting is closed by the chair and the nurses move on to their other tasks. One thing File (2018) draws attention to in relation to this genre is how rapidly a handover meeting can progress through patient status updates, as with Mister Richmond's case, and that each update is signalled by the use of a title and surname. Understanding this will mean that a new participant knows what to listen out for when they have information to contribute about a particular patient's ongoing care.

In Example 9.12 an adviser on a helpline needs to manage resistance from a caller to the advice they are giving.

Example 9.12

Context: Call to a phone helpline. The call-taker is a child protection officer and the caller is a mother who wants her daughter put in care. Recorded in the UK.

CALL-TAKER:	[slowly]: right: would it not be possible for you
	to maybe take some [slowly]: leave: while- while she's living
	//with you?\
CALLER:	/she\\ I've only just started this job
	I //mean\ er it's possible but
CALL-TAKER:	/right\\
CALLER:	you know I'd be unpaid
	and I'm //just starting\ a new mortgage and
CALL-TAKER:	/mm\\
CALLER:	//I- you know\ [slowly]: it's: …
CALL-TAKER:	/right right\\
CALL-TAKER:	yeah [inhales] I mean-
	you know at the end of the day
	i- it's about priorities isn't it and
	//you know\ obviously
CALLER:	/I know\\
CALL-TAKER:	she's got to come first in all of this
	//because she's (the-)\
CALLER:	/yeah but if I've got\\ nowhere to live then she sh- [inhales]

Reprinted by permission of Taylor & Francis Ltd from *Research on Language and Social Interaction 47*, Hepburn, Alexa, Wilkinson, Sue and Butler, Carly W., Intervening with conversation analysis in telephone helpline services: Strategies to improve effectiveness, pp. 243–4, © 2014.

The call-taker advises the mother to spend more time with her daughter by taking leave from work. The mother resists this by stating that she has just started a new job and gives an account of why it would be difficult for her to take leave. In responding to the mother's resistance, Hepburn, Wilkinson and Butler (2014) identify a number of features of the call-taker's speech useful for countering advice resistance. Idiomatic expressions such as 'at the end of the day' are often found in this situation, along with tag questions and claims to shared knowledge which treat callers as if they are already on board and understand the issues. Although the caller in Example 9.12 continues to resist, Hepburn, Wilkinson and Butler (2014: 244) note that the persistence and skilful handling of the interaction by the call-taker resulted in the caller committing to sign up for a local family therapy group, a positive outcome from the point of view of the organisation that runs the helpline.

Hepburn, Wilkinson and Butler's (2014) research highlights the way speakers manage problematic situations. Their research has been fed back to helpline providers through practice-based reports, consultancy exercises, and training initiatives, including workshops with helpline workers where they identify and facilitate good practice. The training not only helps newcomers to the job, but also aids other workers to upskill.

Importance of Research Findings for Workplaces

What about wider applications and implications for workplaces?

One last issue considered here is the importance of research findings for workplaces. This includes workplaces involved in the research. Giving feedback to workplaces where data has been collected should be an essential component of the research process. Research which takes an appreciative inquiry approach will give feedback that highlights the things that people are doing well. Critical approaches will highlight problems. Both have a place, especially when there are issues that are perceived to be good in the first case, or neutral or bad in the second, which have implications for workers and organisations.

A case that highlights the usefulness of an appreciative inquiry approach is the factory team that have been seen in Examples 4.11, 4.24, 5.2, 7.9 and 8.15 in this book. When the LWP collected this data, the factory's management asked them to record and examine the interaction patterns of this particular team because they were consistently the most productive team in the factory. Management wanted to know why. Analysis revealed the important role the leader of the team had in fostering and developing rapport and team spirit, and the way the team responded to this and worked together to create a strong team.

For every workplace where the LWP have collected data, feedback has been given in the form of workshops or reports which draw on the data collected. Feedback has drawn attention to issues such as the importance of humour and small talk at work, the way meetings are managed and other linguistic strategies that effective communicators use in a wide range of workplaces, and the approach taken has been to highlight positive aspects.

Critical feedback can also be important in certain situations, especially where people know there are problems but do not understand why. Baxter (2010) examines not only successful interaction but also situations where things did not go as smoothly. In Example 9.13, Jan, a managing director has difficulty managing the closing phase of a section of a longer meeting.

Example 9.13

Context: Extract from a two day senior management meeting in the UK branch of a large multinational company. Jan is the female managing director.

TIM: we ran out of steam we got to the roll out to the Irish
//market\
JAN: /no no\\ we're not talking about that
we're talking about the communication
and the interaction between people around this table
and the Irish business and the people in the Irish business
TIM: well yep
JAN: yes? so that you need to come back and say exactly
what you feel is best so we actually sit down and discuss it
TIM: yep fair point
JAN: okay then alright so shall we have a break for five minutes?
is that a good idea? it's like pulling teeth [laughs]
it's supposed to be the easy part of it
it's supposed to be the nice part of it
[no reactions from rest of team]

Reprinted from Baxter (2010: 127–8)

At the end of Example 9.13, Baxter (2010) notes that the members of the team appeared sullen and unresponsive. Baxter traces this back to the opening phase where Jan was too abrupt and comments that the discussion during the meeting was quite confrontational. In Example 9.13, Jan directly disagrees with Tim and interrupts him. Tim seems willing to accept her point, and Jan then suggests a break, which may provide an opportunity for the tension to defuse. Her attempt at humour fails, however, 'it's like pulling teeth', possibly because it seems to be a criticism of the team. In another example, Baxter (2010) shows Jan effectively managing a closing phase with this team, her joking on that occasion being responded to positively. Workplace relationships are not static, and the examination of successful and unsuccessful interaction can help people learn how to manage workplace interaction more effectively.

Reporting these types of findings more widely also highlights their importance for other organisations. An important issue that has arisen from research on small talk, humour and narrative in the workplace, for instance, is the role these play in achieving workplace goals. Exploring primarily relational aspects like these illustrates how people can support the achievement of transactional goals in different workplace settings by paying attention to relational or interpersonal goals. Social talk, humour and narrative are not only a normal part of workplace interaction, they also contribute to the effective functioning of transactional talk and achievement of practical goals. And in the achievement of transactional goals there is any organisation's success.

By focusing on different settings and types of jobs, research on authentic data can provide input for a range of types of training resources and situations. In doing this it can enhance the outputs of learning from a practical point of view in the areas of employability, vocational education and communication skills development for different occupations. Research also has wider implications in terms of helping organisations understand the importance of language and effective communication in achieving their goals.

Chapter Summary

This chapter has touched on just some of the ways that workplace research *can* be and *is* being used to benefit workers and workplaces. There has been a lot of focus on leadership and the development and improvement of leadership skills, but skills training in a whole range of areas can benefit from the insights of research on language in the workplace, including issues related to gender and culture.

Language in the workplace research can also have important implications and applications when considering different settings and genres. Job and training interviews, for instance, are a high-stakes genre for both migrants and others. Vocational education is another area where exploring authentic interaction can provide invaluable insights to the role of language in learning.

Communication skills development across a range of situations can be improved by understanding how people interact. Seeing effective communicators in action and identifying strategies that can be used in different situations is important for understanding how to enact an effective workplace identity. Of course, communities of practice do develop within workplaces where groups have their own jargon and shortcuts to communication, but coming in with a basic understanding of the terminology and procedures will make a huge difference. It has been found that the guidelines provided in training across a range of types of workplaces and roles often do not adequately reflect the way people actually interact in these situations.

Exploring good practice, as well as situations where there are difficulties, can also help the people involved in those interactions understand the importance of interaction in achieving workplace goals. Language in the workplace research is still a relatively young field and there is scope for a great deal more research on different genres, workplaces and from countries all around the world. In identifying where there may be a mismatch between norms and expectations for a range of reasons, research can raise awareness of why problems occur and of how interaction patterns differ.

Research on language in the workplace can benefit people working in a wide range of workplaces and professions. The importance of this cannot be underestimated as effective communication has a major impact on an individual's work success and well-being, as well as on an organisation's performance. Understanding how to effectively communicate in different contexts has implications for the successful achievement of transactional goals and therefore for the success of individuals, businesses and organisations.

Further Reading

The final section of Vine (2018b) has four chapters explicitly exploring applied areas of workplace research. The topics covered are vocational education (Losa 2018), women in leadership (Baxter 2018), and issues of relevance for migrants (Kerekes 2018; Yates 2018). See also Mullany (forthcoming).

In terms of understanding how research can help individuals develop their communication skills, a range of resources are available. This includes Baxter's (2010) final chapter on 'How to achieve an effective language of leadership' and Jones and Stubbe (2004) who outline a communication evaluation and development model which can be used by workplaces and workers to explore different types of communication challenges.

Notes on Exercises

This section provides some notes on the exercises. These are not meant to be definitive answers, rather some reflections on issues that you might consider in answering the questions.

Chapter 1: Introducing Language in the Workplace

Exercise 1.1

These utterances were all taken from white collar meetings.

Utterance A came from pre-meeting talk in a large meeting. The manager was asking one of her staff about her baby. This type of small talk may be found in a wide range of workplaces between colleagues, depending on the norms for the particular workplace. It would have a relational goal in this case (see Chapter 4). The same utterance would have a transactional goal however if said for instance by a doctor to the mother of a baby that was being treated. Or by a doctor checking in with a colleague looking after a sick baby.

Utterance B was uttered by a manager to her personal assistant. In this case the utterance is transactional and relates to a task the manager needs the assistant to complete. Chapter 3 explores the use of this type of utterance to express directives and requests and the reasons speakers might use one form rather than another in order to do this.

Utterance C is from a discussion in a large meeting and utterance D was advice from a policy analyst in a government department to another policy analyst. Both are transactional, but the speakers both do relational work, using humour in C and hedging in D.

Exercise 1.2

All of these workplaces could involve both frontstage and backstage interactions.

In a hospital, frontstage interactions occur between medical staff and patients and their families. There are also many backstage interactions, for example when doctors or nurses discuss patients' treatment options.

In schools, the teacher interacting with students would be considered frontstage, while staff meetings or lunch breaks would be backstage.

A printing company involves frontstage interactions when sales staff interact with customers, but there are many backstage interactions as jobs are prepared and completed, and between staff members at different levels in the organisation.

A café's main business is to sell beverages and food to the public, so this involves frontstage interaction. When staff interact with each other they are engaging in backstage interaction, maybe as they prepare food or unpack supplies.

A tour bus is also a typically frontstage situation when the tour guide interacts with tourists. The tour guide may consult with the bus driver and this would be classified as backstage interaction.

Exercise 1.3

Excerpt A comes from a briefing meeting at the beginning of a shift in a factory.

Excerpt B is from a book shop with a customer buying a notebook.

Excerpt C is from an interview in a white collar workplace between someone in HR and a person who is leaving the company.

Chapter 2: Approaches to Exploring Language in the Workplace

Since the excerpt comes from the same interview as the excerpt that was analysed earlier in the chapter, look through the comments from these and see if the observations all still apply.

1. Examining the excerpt from a CA perspective would begin with focusing on the turn-taking. The question and answer adjacency pairs typical of this type of interview are also present in this excerpt. Angela, the interviewer, is asking the questions and Nahum, the interviewee, responds. Again, there is laughter near the end, where Angela lightens the mood to what might be considered a slightly problematic answer from Nahum.

2. Again we see Angela as being in control when examining the excerpt from an interactional sociolinguistics perspective. She asks the questions and Nahum responds. Nahum also orients to his position as being the one to provide information for Angela, although he may not always be in possession of all the answers she wants. Angela is only conducting market research so is not a direct employee of the telecommunications company, but Nahum knows that his responses will be fed back to the company. This is particularly telling when he complains about pricing.

3. The power dynamic again is similar as with the earlier excerpt from the interview. Nahum's comment about the prices being too high shows him resisting this, or at least questioning this. Angela acknowledges that this is a common response when she sarcastically says that his comment here is 'unique'.

4. Examining from a rapport management theory perspective we can see again the way Angela works at enhancing rapport. When Nahum makes a comment which highlights a problem with pricing, she makes a joke about this, and both laugh.

Chapter 3: Directives and Requests at Work

Excerpt 3.A

Tom uses a declarative to give a directive to Rick. This has been elicited by Rick when he asks 'do you want the top bit done?' In expressing his directive Tom focuses the attention on what he wants, 'I just just want that corner done'. Tom also provides reasons for what he needs Rick to do, using the directive as a chance to teach Rick as well. As well as being indirect, by focusing on what he wants rather than saying what Rick needs to explicitly do in order for this to come about, he also hedges with *just* and his provision of reasons also softens the force of his directive. Rick does not respond verbally but he may have nodded and completed the action after listening to Tom's explanation.

The way the directive is given and responded to in Excerpt 3.A is influenced by the role relationship between the two, the fact they are engaged in a physical activity, along with the fact that the task being undertaken is one Rick is just learning. Rick also elicited the directive, so this may also be a factor here.

Excerpt 3.B

Kim requests a coffee using an interrogative form. She adds 'please' and uses the modal verb 'can', a conventionally indirect way to ask for something. The focus is also on what she wants, as she says 'can I have …?' rather than 'can you give me …?' Clementine acknowledges Kim's request by saying 'mhm'.

When Clementine says the price, Kim indicates that she has a free coffee (because of a loyalty card). Kim then issues another request, asking for a new loyalty card. Again she uses an interrogative form, with 'can' and 'I'. This time Clementine responds with fuller acknowledgement, 'yes of course'.

The way the requests are made and responded to in Excerpt 3.B are influenced by the roles the participants have, as customer and server. They are in a café and the activity they are engaged in is one where Kim is wanting goods from Clementine. The two do not know each other and their relationship is limited to this transaction, and possibly other similar ones as Kim does frequent this café.

Chapter 4: Social Talk, Humour and Narrative at Work

Exercise 4.1 (social talk aspects)
The excerpt comes during a management meeting and relates to an issue relevant to the transactional goals of the workplace. The two speakers, however, provide more information than would be required for the purposes of an update, and so extend the topic in a way that brings in relational goals, entertaining the team and creating bonds.

Exercise 4.2 (humour aspects)
The humour strengthens the relational function, entertaining as it creates and maintains bonds. The humour creates an image of the other organisation, and in particular one of the representatives of this other company, as being incompetent. Also the joint construction of the humour reinforces and highlights the good relationship between the two speakers.

Exercise 4.3 (narrative aspects)
The narrative elements do not always happen in strict order, and some may be combined. We can generally identify the following parts of the story though:

Abstract:	but Jack knows he is gonna get absolutely hammered [*criticised forcefully*] +
Orientation:	the last time this happened it was in front of his boss as well
Evaluation:	but he's just such an idiot he needs it
Complicating action:	he got his business card out
	and started writing the complaints on the back of his business card
	and he ran out of space ++
	and Lenny Lenny head honcho kept saying haven't you got a pad
	haven't you got a pad get a pad …
	and he kept writing on this card
	and then Stephen says and then another thing
	and then he goes you're gonna run out of business [laughs]: cards soon:
	that's what he said and then he said make sure you don't put them in
	and give them to someone + (all those complaints on them)
Coda:	I said to Jason we should cut down a little tiny pad + about that big
	a really thick pad [laughs]
	give it to him and tell them to take some note
	because we've got some big problems

The story is 'tellable' because Jack's behaviour in writing complaints on his business cards is unexpected and inappropriate. As Jack's boss Lenny warns him, there is also then a danger that Jack will give the business cards to another client, a fact that Stephen and Jason obviously find bizarre and unprofessional, and as justifying their low opinion of Jack.

Chapter 5: Complaints, Disagreement and Conflict Talk at Work

Excerpt 5.A

In Excerpt 5.A, Nancy, a resident at an eldercare facility, complains to Alec, a caregiver, about losing her place at the table in the lounge. Alec offers to find a solution to the problem for her. He suggests either they can find a new seat for Nancy, or alternatively for the new person who has taken Nancy's normal place. It is clear that Nancy prefers the second option.

Nancy presents her complaint by telling a story about what happened earlier. Her narrative justifies her complaint and it is strengthened when she talks about how she felt 'embarrassed', and when she states that she will eat elsewhere from now on. Alec listens to her story and then as she restates her complaint, overlaps and reassures her that there has been no deliberate attempt to replace her, that it's just someone new trying to find a place. He says they can find a new place for Nancy, but quickly modifies this to say they'll find a new spot for the new person instead. Alec reassures Nancy several times, and manages to convince her to come back to the lounge for her meals.

Excerpt 5.B

In Excerpt 5.B, a team is engaged in problem-solving in regard to a report that a member of the team has drafted based on previous discussions. Lindy questions the use of the word 'research'. Jacob brings up another word they had considered, 'modelling', but Callum quickly responds that this is 'too narrow'. Barry agrees with him and then Jacob also agrees. Barry wants the discussion to move on and does not think the wording is something they need to discuss now. Callum continues to discuss the wording, even though Barry has quite explicitly asked that they not worry about that at this time. This shows Callum disagreeing with Barry on the need to discuss the issue now (or not). Barry again tries to move the discussion on. He softens this by referring to 'people' rather than Callum, using 'you know', and with laughter, but his continued insistence that they move on could be seen as potentially conflictual. Dudley sides with him at this stage saying 'oh yeah [laughs]: yeah:'.

To decide whether this was conflict talk we would also want to hear the volume and tone of voice of the interactants. Also, knowing how the interactants felt afterwards would be useful. Considering the next section of the transcript is also helpful. The next comment after this section of the transcript comes from Dudley as he makes a joke that they need to make up their own word. Everyone laughs at this and Callum and Barry add to the humour. The discussion then moves on. Seeing how Callum joins in with the laughter and humour suggests that there is no negative effect on relationships.

Chapter 6: The Language of Leadership

Excerpt 6.A

Clara decides to start the meeting without waiting for the last member of the team to arrive. She does not consult anyone else in making this decision, although she does hedge it by saying 'okay well we might just start'. This suggests she has a formal leadership role, or is at least the designated chair. When Renee asks if Clara is taking the minutes, Clara does not allocate this role to someone, but asks for a volunteer. It is clear that she does not plan to take the minutes herself, again reinforcing the impression that she is someone with status and authority (it seems to be beneath her to take the minutes). Renee steps in again to suggest that someone who has not done the minutes before should do them. This behaviour from Renee also shows her enacting leadership as she tries to clarify who will take on this job. Benny volunteers and again Clara steps up, thanking him and highlighting her role as chair and leader of the group.

Renee's question about whether Clara will take the minutes could be seen as a challenge to Clara, but also may be a way for her to hand this job to someone else more appropriate (rather than the team leader being expected to take them). In asking for someone who hasn't done this job yet, Renee manages this aspect of the meeting, and could be seen to be supporting Clara, but also seems to be wanting to make sure that this job is shared between group members. Benny quickly volunteers and takes on this role for Clara, providing support to her as she chairs the meeting.

Excerpt 6.B

CT is uncertain about whether they should hold a meeting the next week or not. He consults with the team to see whether they think there should be one. He could be enacting a consultative leadership style here, since he does seem to have a leadership role since he is talking about the agenda. If not the formal leader he does at least seem to be the chair of the meeting, which is a type of leadership role.

The way others respond to this can show them enacting leadership. FA brings in a reason that they do not need a meeting; AC adds humour, focusing on relational goals (an important component of effective leadership identified earlier). After this, when CT clarifies that there will be no meeting, AC hedges this saying that a meeting might be required if something comes up, but otherwise there will be no point. DR at this stage also clarifies how many people will be around, so reinforcing the decision not to have a meeting. CT, FA, AC and DR all contribute here, so this feels like shared leadership at this point.

At the end of the excerpt, CT thanks everyone and brings the meeting to a close, again showing himself as having the role of chair for this meeting. This team is actually the same team seen in Examples 6.7 to 6.9 and 6.12. The CEO, Daniel, is absent from the meeting Excerpt 6.B is taken from, however, which affects the power dynamics, since the formal leader of the team is absent.

Chapter 7: Gender and Language at Work

Exercise 7.1

Tai talks here about a rugby game that took place at the weekend. Tai loves rugby and can be seen engaging in banter. Both the topic here and the banter are stereotypical male aspects of interaction and in many New Zealand workplaces these types of discussions are more common between men. And in this case Tai is male so we could say that his talk marks his male identity. It might also be safe to assume that Vanhi is male because of the way Vanhi joins in, also obviously being knowledgeable about rugby and engaging in banter. This assumption however would be incorrect. In the community of practice from which this data is drawn rugby is a common topic of talk in this mixed-gender team. Tai and Vanhi have a friendly and established rivalry as they support different regional rugby teams. Vanhi is as engaged with this topic as Tai is and is just as inclined to engage in banter as well. This example questions gender stereotypes and highlights the importance of norms at different levels, including consideration of norms within a particular community of practice.

Exercise 7.2

Clara is quite forceful in the way she leads in this example, which does not necessarily correspond with expectations about gendered behaviour. The double-bind means that she may be judged negatively for this.

Renee's consultative stance, asking questions, and seeking to find out whose turn it might be to take the minutes, shows a democratic approach, which would be in keeping with gendered stereotypes of women's behaviour.

Clara's 'queenly' persona is most obvious in the way she says 'no I'm just trying to chair the meeting', which suggests Renee has been out of line in asking if Clara will take the minutes.

Chapter 8: Culture and Language at Work

Exercise 8.1

In Excerpt 8.A, the salesperson asks 'qué más? (*what else?)*'. In Excerpt 8.B, he says 'er sorry was there anything else there that I could (help you with)?', beginning with an apology, and then using an interrogative form.

In Excerpt 8.A, the customer responds with 'nada más (*nothing else)*'. In Excerpt 8.B, the customer responds with 'um no thanks', using a hesitation marker 'um' followed by 'no' and then by an expression of thanks.

In Excerpt 8.A, both the salesperson and the woman customer use brief utterances to offer and refuse. Kaiser (2014) notes that in these types of exchanges in her data, the refusals are short, non-negotiated, direct, and 'perfectly politic'. Direct refusals like this were common in several contexts she investigated in her Uruguayan data. Excerpt 8.A contrasts with Excerpt 8.B, the New Zealand shop data, where the norm seems to be to typically mitigate offers and refusals. These brief examples suggest that the interactional norms in Uruguayan service encounters allow for more direct and less hedged offers and refusals than may be the case in New Zealand.

Exercise 8.2

Ka Keung asks a number of questions in Excerpt 8.C, and the museum host provides answers. The beginning of the interaction feels a little awkward though as Ka Keung waits for a minute to be noticed and served. This suggests that Ka Keung expects the host to initiate the interaction, while the host expects Ka Keung to do this, which Ka Keung eventually does.

There is no visible sign of miscommunication as the interaction unfolds, as Ka Keung asks about how to qualify as a student before asking about the age to be considered a senior. This may seem an odd thing to do; is Ka Keung interested in qualifying as a student or as a senior? Ka Keung is actually checking to see if he qualifies as a senior, having recently retired in Hong Kong, where the retirement age is lower than in New Zealand. In some cultures, a strategy for eliciting information is to build up to what you actually want to know, as Ka Keung does here.

Glossary

adjacency pair: utterances that typically occur together, e.g., question and answer
adjectives, empty: adjectives that soften but do not add meaningful content
agreement markers: words which show agreement, e.g., *yes, yeah, right*
appreciative inquiry: approach to research which highlights the positive things people do
backstage: situations where people who work together interact
bilingualism: knowledge of two languages
blue collar: manual work or workers
boundaries of talk: places in talk where there is a shift from one type of talk to another, e.g., the opening phase of a meeting where pre-meeting talk ends and a formal meeting begins
co-construction: the way more than one speaker contributes to constructing meaning
code-switching: changing from one language or formality level to another during a conversation
collaborative styles of interaction: where people agree and are supportive of each other when they interact
collectivism: where the group has priority rather than individuals
community of practice: a group who interact regularly, engage in a shared enterprise and have developed a shared repertoire
conflict talk: when two or more people have a sustained disagreement or interaction which impacts negatively on rapport
context: the factors in any situation which make it what it is
contextual complexity: consideration of a whole range of factors which are particular to a situation where people are interacting, including factors related to who the interactants are, where they are, and why they are interacting
contextualisation cues: features which allow a speaker and a listener to interpret the meaning of an utterance
conventionally indirect: using a regularly used form to express a function which has a different literal interpretation, e.g., using a modal interrogative 'can you ...?' to ask someone to do something
conversation analysis (CA): an approach to analysing discourse
conversational inference: the context-based process of interpreting what someone means by what they say
creating team: using language (or other aspects) to make a group cohesive
critical discourse studies (CDS): an approach to discourse analysis
cross-cultural communication studies: research which looks at distinct cultures and explores similarities and differences
cultural values: the values that a culture holds, e.g., in some cultures modesty and humility are important, while in others it is important to show individual pride and it is acceptable to boast
declarative: the syntactic form used to express a statement in a language
directive: an attempt to get someone to do something
disagreement sequence: section of talk where a disagreement unfolds
disagreement, marked: when disagreement stands out because it is unexpected in some way
disagreement, unmarked: when disagreement does not stand out because it is expected

discourse analysis: analytical approaches which examine the linguistic features of interactional data

discourse marker: word or phrase that helps manage the flow of talk, e.g., *so, however, you know*

double-bind: situation where if someone interacts in one way they are criticised, but interacting in the other way will also be problematic

employability: how employable someone is, showing suitable/required skills for a job

essentialism: belief that things have a set of inherent characteristics which make them what they are

face: public self-image that people want to protect and promote

facilitative language strategies: strategies which make things easier, go smoothly

facilitative, consultative style: leadership style where the leader asks for input from others

feminine values: values which tend to be associated with women in a society

feminised workplaces: workplaces where feminine norms and expectations prevail

floor, jointly developed: when two or more people contribute to a conversation

floor, singly developed: when one person does most of the talking in a conversation

frontstage: situations where someone who is working interacts with someone from another organisation or a member of the public

gatekeeping encounters: situations where access to resources or employment is controlled or restricted, e.g., job interviews

genre: a type of speech situation, with an associated style, expectations and norms

glass ceiling: unseen barrier that stops women and minorities from reaching high levels in companies

hedges, hedging: features of language which soften or weaken the force of an utterance

high-context culture: culture where speakers tend to rely on the context to convey meaning, rather than being explicit and detailed in what they say

high-stakes talk: talk where one or more people have a lot to lose from the outcome, e.g., police interview of a suspect

honorifics: expressions which indicate the relative status of interactants

humour, boundary-marking: humour which highlights boundaries between groups

humour, collaborative: humour that is built up by more than one person

humour, competitive: humour where speakers try to out-do each other

humour, contestive: humour which criticises something or someone

humour, self-deprecating: when the target of the humour is the speaker, also called self-denigrating humour

identity, organisational: the identity that defines an organisation

identity, professional: identity related to job role

identity, social: identity related to aspects such as age and gender

identity: the aspects that make a person or a group who they are

imperative: the syntactic form used to express a command in a language

impoliteness: behaviour that is meant or perceived as rude or insulting

indexicality: contextually bound meaning

Indexicality Principle: when a word or style is associated with a group, because it is frequently used by that group

individualism: where individuals have priority over the group

in-group identity marker: something that marks membership of a group

in-group: group someone belongs to

intensifiers: words that make the meaning of something stronger

interactional sociolinguistics: an approach to analysing discourse

intercultural communication: when people from different cultures interact

interlocutor: a person who takes part in a conversation

interpersonal goals: goals which focus on personal relationships

interrogatives: the syntactic form in a language used to express a question

intersectionality: the way aspects of someone's identity overlap, or intersect, such as gender and cultural identity

jocular abuse: making fun of someone in a humorous way

leadership: being in a position of influence

leadership constellations: different types of leadership partnerships

leadership, discursive: the way leaders use language to enact leadership

leadership, formal: when a leader has an officially assigned leadership position

leadership, informal: when people lead even if they do not have a formal leadership position

leadership models, co-leadership: when more than one person share the key roles of leadership

leadership models, distributed: when leadership is shared among members of a group

leadership styles: different approaches to leading

lexis: vocabulary

low-context culture: culture where speakers tend to be explicit and detailed in what they say, rather than relying on the context to convey meaning

majority group: group that dominates and has the most power in society

marked: when something stands out because it is not expected for some reason

masculine values: values which tend to be associated with men in a society

masculinised workplaces: workplaces where masculine norms and expectations prevail

meeting management: the way someone guides a group through a meeting from opening to closing, managing agenda items, etc.

minority group: group that does not dominate and that does not have the most power in society

mitigation: modification of the force of something

mock politeness: pretending to be polite

multilingualism: knowledge of more than one language

multimodal aspects of interaction: modes that operate alongside speech, e.g., gaze, body posture

norms: accepted ways of doing something within a community or group

out-group: group that someone does not belong to

outsider status: being part of an out-group

phatic communion: talk that makes social links between people, e.g., saying 'hello, how are you?' when you meet someone

plurilingualism: ability of a person who has competence in more than one language to switch between languages

politeness: behaviour that is meant or perceived as showing consideration and respect for another

power, expert: having power because of knowledge in an area

power, legitimate: having power because of a formal position

power, reward: having power because of being able to give rewards

presequence: a sequence of utterances where someone prepares to do something, e.g., asking if someone is going home soon before asking for a ride

rapport: a close and harmonious relationship in which the people or groups concerned communicate well

rapport management theory: an approach to analysing discourse that focuses on interpersonal aspects

relational goals: goals that relate to personal relationships and how people get along

request: an attempt to get someone to do something

response, preferred: anticipated and expected response to something

response, dispreferred: unanticipated, unexpected and/or unwanted response to something

sentence fragments: a syntactic form that lacks a component that would otherwise make it a sentence in a language, e.g., lacking a verb

sequences of talk: stretches of talk that make a coherent whole in relation to a function, e.g., a disagreement sequence which includes all utterances from an interaction which are relevant to the disagreement

service encounters: interactions where someone is accessing a service, e.g., buying something in a shop

shared practices: things people do in the same way

small talk, social talk: talk which often has limited informational content, its purpose is to create social links and typically attends to the relational side of interaction

social constructionism: a social theory which sees people's understandings of the social world as created and realised through interaction with others

socio-pragmatic skills: social language skills used in interactions with others. This includes what people say, how they say it, non-verbal communication and how appropriate these are for a given situation

speech function: purpose of utterances

stereotype: generalisation about a group which is typically oversimplified

syntax: the structure of sentences

tag questions: short questions, e.g., 'aren't you?', appended to a statement

tellability: aspect of a narrative that makes it worth telling

transactional goals: goals that relate to practical aspects and things people need to achieve

turn-taking: the way people take turns at talking when interacting

unmarked: the normal or expected way of expressing something

vocational training: training for a specific occupation

white collar: work done in an office or other professional context

wide verbal repertoire: wide range of linguistic strategies someone may use depending on the context

References

Angouri, Jo. 2011. 'We are in a masculine profession...': Constructing gender identities in a consortium of two multinational engineering companies. *Gender and Language* 5: 343–71.

Angouri, Jo. 2012. Managing disagreement in problem solving meeting talk. *Journal of Pragmatics* 44: 1565–79.

Angouri, Jo. 2018. *Culture, discourse, and the workplace*. Abingdon: Routledge.

Antaki, Charles and Stokoe, Elizabeth. 2012. When police treat straightforward answers as uncooperative. *Journal of Pragmatics* 117: 1–15.

Archer, Dawn and Jagodziński, Piotr. 2015. Call centre interaction: A case of sanctioned face attack? *Journal of Pragmatics* 76: 46–66.

Bailey, Benjamin. 2015. Interactional sociolinguistics. In Karen Tracy, Cornelia Ilie and Todd Sandel (eds.), *The international encyclopedia of language and social interaction*, 826–40. UK: John Wiley & Sons.

Bargiela-Chiappini, Francesca and Harris, Sandra. 1997. *Managing language: The discourse of corporate meetings*. Amsterdam/Philadelphia: John Benjamins.

Baxter, Judith. 2008. Is it all tough talking at the top? A post-structuralist analysis of the construction of gendered speaker identities of British business leaders within interview narratives. *Gender and Language* 2: 197–222.

Baxter, Judith. 2010. *The language of female leadership*. Basingstoke: Palgrave Macmillan.

Baxter, Judith. 2014. *Double-voicing at work: Power, gender and linguistic expertise*. Basingstoke: Palgrave Macmillan.

Baxter, Judith. 2017. Coping with uncertainty: Gender and leadership identities in UK corporate life. In Dorien Van De Mieroop and Stephanie Schnurr (eds.), *Identity struggles: Evidence from workplaces around the world*, 21–37. Amsterdam/Philadelphia: John Benjamins.

Baxter, Judith. 2018. Gender, language and leadership: Enabling women leaders. In Bernadette Vine (ed.), *The Routledge handbook of language in the workplace*, 401–12. Abingdon: Routledge.

Baxter, Judith and Al A'ali, Haleema. 2016. *Speaking as women leaders. Meetings in Middle Eastern and Western contexts*. London: Palgrave Macmillan.

Benwell, Bethan and McCreadie, May. 2016. Managing patients' expectations in telephone complaints in Scotland. In Dorien Van De Mieroop and Stephanie Schnurr (eds.), *Identity struggles: Evidence from workplaces around the world*, 243–61. Amsterdam/Philadelphia: John Benjamins.

Bousfield, Derek. 2008. *Impoliteness in interaction*. Amsterdam: John Benjamins.

Brown, Penelope and Levinson, Stephen C. 1987. *Politeness: Some universals in language usage*. Cambridge: Cambridge University Press.

Brown, S., Hamblin, H. and Mitchell, D. 1988. *Managing people. Media booklet*. Maidenhead: The Open University Press.

Bubel, Claudia. 2006. 'How are you?' 'I'm hot': An interactive analysis of small talk sequences in British-German telephone sales. In Kristin Bührig and Jan D. ten Thije (eds.), *Beyond misunderstanding: Linguistic analyses of intercultural communication*, 245–59. Amsterdam: John Benjamins.

Cameron, Deborah. 2007. *The myth of Mars and Venus*. Oxford: Oxford University Press.

Campbell, Sarah and Roberts, Celia. 2007. Migration, ethnicity and competing discourses in the job interview: Synthesizing the institutional and personal. *Discourse & Society* 18: 243–71.

Candlin, Christopher N. and Gotti, Maurizio (eds.). 2004. *Intercultural aspects of specialized communication*. Bern: Peter Lang.

Chan, Angela. 2005. Openings and closings of business meetings in different cultures. PhD dissertation, Victoria University of Wellington.

Choi, Seongsook and Schnurr, Stephanie. 2014. Exploring distributed leadership: Solving disagreements and negotiating consensus in a 'leaderless' team. *Discourse Studies* 16: 3–24.

Clifton, Jonathan. 2006. A conversation analytical approach to business communication. *Journal of Business Communication* 43: 202–19.

Clifton, Jonathan. 2012. Conversation analysis in dialogue with stocks of interactional knowledge: Facework and appraisal interviews. *Journal of Business Communication* 49: 283–311.

Clifton, Jonathan. 2017. Taking the (heroic) leader out of leadership. The in situ practice of distributed leadership in decision-making talk. In Cornelia Ilie and Stephanie Schnurr (eds.), *Challenging leadership stereotypes through discourse: Power, management and gender*, 45–68. Singapore: Springer.

Coates, Jennifer. 2005. Masculinity, collaborative narration and the heterosexual couple. In Joanna Thornborrow and Jennifer Coates (eds.), *The sociolinguistics of narrative*, 89–106. Amsterdam: John Benjamins.

Cotterill, Janet. 2002. 'Just one more time …': Aspects of intertextuality in the trials of O. J. Simpson. In Janet Cotterill (ed.), *Language in the legal process*, 147–61. Basingstoke: Palgrave Macmillan.

Coupland, Justine. 2000a. Introduction: Sociolinguistic perspectives on small talk. In Justine Coupland (ed.), *Small talk*, 1–25. Harlow: Pearson.

Coupland, Justine (ed.). 2000b. *Small talk*. Harlow: Pearson.

Coupland, Nikolas and Ylänne-McEwen, Virpi. 2000. Talk about the weather: Small talk, leisure talk and the travel industry. In Justine Coupland (ed.), *Small talk*, 163–82. Harlow: Pearson.

Crystal, David. 1987. *The Cambridge encyclopedia of language*. Cambridge: Cambridge University Press.

Culpeper, Jonathan, Haugh, Michael and Kádár, Dániel Z. (eds.). 2017. *Palgrave handbook of linguistic (im)politeness*. Basingstoke: Palgrave Macmillan.

Culpeper, Jonathan and McIntyre, Dan. 2010. Activity types and characterisation in dramatic discourse. In Jens Eder, Fotis Jannidis and Ralf Schneider (eds.), *Characters in fictional worlds: Understanding imaginary beings in literature, film, and other media*, 176–207. New York: Mouton de Gruyter.

Curl, Traci S. and Drew, Paul. 2008. Contingency and action: A comparison of two forms of requesting. *Research on Language and Social Interaction* 42: 129–53.

De Fina, Anna and Georgakopoulou, Alexandra (eds.). 2015. *The handbook of narrative analysis*. Chichester: Wiley Blackwell.

Drew, Paul. 2005. Conversation analysis. In Kristine L. Fitch and Robert E. Sanders (eds.), *Handbook of language and social interaction*, 71–102. Mahwah, NJ: Lawrence Erlbaum.

Drew, Paul and Couper-Kuhlen, Elizabeth (eds.). 2014. *Requesting in social interaction*. Amsterdam: John Benjamins.

Dyer, Judy and Keller-Cohen, Deborah. 2000. The discursive construction of professional self through narratives of personal experience. *Discourse Studies* 2: 283–304.

Eades, Diana. 1992. *Aboriginal English and the law: Communicating with Aboriginal English speaking clients: A handbook for legal practitioners*. Brisbane: Queensland Law Society.

Eades, Diana 1996. Legal recognition of cultural differences in communication: The case of Robyn Kina. *Language and Communication* 16: 215–27.

Eades, Diana. 2004. Understanding Aboriginal English in the legal system: A critical sociolinguistics approach. *Applied Linguistics* 25: 491–512.

Edelsky, Carole. 1981. Who's got the floor? *Language in Society* 10: 383–421.

Erickson, Frederick and Shultz, Jeffrey. 1982. *The counselor as gatekeeper: Social interaction in interviews*. New York: Academic Press.

Fairclough, Norman. 2015. *Language and power*. 3rd ed. Abingdon: Routledge.

Fairhurst, Gail. 2007. *Discursive leadership*. London: Sage.

Fasulo, Alessandra and Zucchermaglio, Cristina. 2008. Narratives in the workplace: Facts, fictions, and canonicity. *Text & Talk* 28: 351–76.

File, Kieran A. 2018. Genre theory. In Bernadette Vine (ed.), *The Routledge handbook of language in the workplace*, 112–24. Abingdon: Routledge.

Filliettaz, Laurent. 2010. Interactions and miscommunication in the Swiss vocational education context: Researching vocational learning from a linguistic perspective. *Journal of Applied Linguistics and Professional Practice* 7: 27–50.

Filliettaz, Laurent, de Saint-Georges, Ingrid and Duc, Barbara. 2010. Skiing, cheese fondue and Swiss watches: Analogical discourse in vocational training interactions. *Vocations and Learning* 3: 117–40.

Ford, Cecilia. 2008. *Women speaking up*. Basingstoke: Palgrave Macmillan.

Foster, Elissa and Bochner, Arthur. 2008. Social constructionist perspectives in communication research. In James Holstein and Jaber Gubrium (eds.), *Handbook of constructionist research*, 85–106. New York: Guilford Press.

French, John R. P. and Raven, Bertram. 1959. The bases of social power. In Dorwin Cartwright (ed.), *Studies in social power*, 150–67. Ann Arbor: University of Michigan.

Gargiulo, Terrence L. 2006. *Stories at work: Using stories to improve communication and build relationships*. Westport, CT: Praeger.

Gee, James Paul and Handford, Michael. 2012. *The Routledge handbook of discourse analysis*. Abingdon: Routledge.

Geluykens, Ronald and Kraft, Bettina. 2016. *Complaints and impoliteness: A mixed method analysis*. Munich: Lincom Europa.

Glenn, Phillip J. 1991/1992. Current speaker initiation of two-party shared laughter. *Research on Language & Social Interaction* 25: 139–62.

Goffman, Erving. 1959. *The presentation of self in everyday life*. New York: Doubleday.

Gordon, Cynthia. 2011. Gumperz and interactional sociolinguistics. In Ruth Wodak, Barbara Johnstone and Paul Kerswill (eds.), *Sage handbook of sociolinguistics*, 67–84. London: Sage.

Greatbatch, David. 1992. On the management of disagreement between news interviewees. In Paul Drew and John Heritage (eds.), *Talk at work: Interaction in institutional settings*, 268–301. Cambridge: Cambridge University Press.

Gumperz, John J. 1982. *Discourse strategies*. Cambridge: Cambridge University Press.

Gumperz, John J. 2015. Interactional sociolinguistics: A personal perspective. In Deborah

Tannen, Heidi E. Hamilton and Deborah Schiffrin (eds.), *The handbook of discourse analysis*. 2nd ed., 309–23. Chichester: John Wiley & Sons.

Hall, Edward T. 1976. *Beyond culture*. New York: Doubleday.

Hanak, Irmi. 1998. Chairing meetings: Turn and topic control in development communication in rural Zanzibar. *Discourse & Society* 9: 33–56.

Handford, Michael and Koester, Almut. 2010. 'It's not rocket science': Metaphors and idioms in conflictual business meetings. *Text & Talk* 30: 27–51.

Harris, Sandra. 2003. Politeness and power: Making and responding to 'requests' in institutional settings. *Text & Talk* 23: 27–52.

Heinemann, Trine. 2006. 'Will you or can't you?': Displaying entitlement in interrogative requests. *Journal of Pragmatics* 38: 1081–104.

Hepburn, Alexa, Wilkinson, Sue and Butler, Carly W. 2014. Intervening with conversation analysis in telephone helpline services: Strategies to improve effectiveness. *Research on Language and Social Interaction* 47: 239–54.

Heritage, John. 1984. *Garfinkel and ethnomethodology*. Cambridge: Polity Press.

Hofstede, Geert. 1980. *Culture's consequences: International differences in work-related values*. Beverly Hills, CA: Sage.

Holmes, Janet. 2000. Doing collegiality and keeping control at work: Small talk in government departments. In Justine Coupland (ed.), *Small talk*, 32–61. Harlow: Pearson.

Holmes, Janet. 2006a. *Gendered talk at work*. Malden: Blackwell.

Holmes, Janet. 2006b. Sharing a laugh: Pragmatic aspects of humour and gender in the workplace. *Journal of Pragmatics* 38: 26–50.

Holmes, Janet. 2008. Gender and leadership: Some socio-pragmatic considerations. *The Journal and Proceedings of GALE* 1: 4–16.

Holmes, Janet. 2014. Doing discourse analysis in sociolinguistics. In Janet Holmes and Kirk Hazen (eds.), *Research methods in sociolinguistics: A practical guide*, 177–93. Hoboken, NJ: John Wiley & Sons.

Holmes, Janet. Forthcoming. The gender order in the New Zealand workplace. To appear in Carmen

Rosa Caldas-Coulthard (ed.), *Innovations and challenges in language and gender: Women and sexism.* London: Routledge.

Holmes, Janet and Major, George. 2003. Nurses communicating on the ward: The human face of hospitals. *Kai Tiaki: Nursing New Zealand* 8: 14–16.

Holmes, Janet and Marra, Meredith. 2005. Narrative and the construction of professional identity in the workplace. In Joanna Thornborrow and Jennifer Coates (eds.), *The sociolinguistics of narrative*, 193–213. Amsterdam: John Benjamins.

Holmes, Janet and Marra, Meredith. 2011. *Relativity rules: Politic talk in ethnicised workplaces.* In Bethan L. Davies, Michael Haugh and Andrew John Merrison (eds.), *Situated politeness*, 27–52. London: Continuum.

Holmes, Janet, Marra, Meredith and Vine, Bernadette. 2011. *Leadership, discourse and ethnicity.* Oxford: Oxford University Press.

Holmes, Janet and Stubbe, Maria. 2003. Doing disagreement at work: A sociolinguistic approach. *Australian Journal of Communication* 30: 53–77.

Holmes, Janet and Stubbe, Maria. 2015. *Power and politeness in the workplace: A sociolinguistic analysis of talk at work.* 2nd ed. London: Longman.

Holmes, Janet and Vine, Bernadette. Forthcoming. Workplace research and applications: The case of the Wellington language in the workplace project. To appear in Sofie De Cock and Geert Jacobs (eds.), *What counts as data in business and professional discourse research and training?* Basingstoke: Palgrave Macmillan.

Hudak, Pamela L. and Maynard, Douglas W. 2011. An interactional approach to conceptualising small talk in medical interactions. *Sociology of Health & Illness* 33: 634–53.

Ilie, Cornelia and Schnurr, Stephanie (eds.). 2017. *Challenging leadership stereotypes through discourse.* Singapore: Springer.

Jackson, Brad and Parry, Ken. 2011. *A very short, fairly interesting and reasonably cheap book about studying leadership*, 2nd ed. Los Angeles: Sage.

Jefferson, Gail. 2004. Glossary of transcript symbols with an introduction. In Gene H. Lerner (ed.), *Conversation analysis: Studies from the first generation*, 13–23. Philadelphia: John Benjamins.

Johnstone, Barbara. 2018. *Discourse analysis*, 3rd ed. Hoboken, NJ: John Wiley & Sons.

Jones, Deborah and Stubbe, Maria. 2004. Communication and the reflective practitioner: A shared perspective from sociolinguistics and organisational communication. *International Journal of Applied Linguistics* 14: 185–211.

Jones, Rodney H. 2012. *Discourse analysis: A resource book for students.* Abingdon: Routledge.

Kaiser, Heather R. 2014. (Im)politeness in Uruguay: Negotiating refusals in three domains of interaction. PhD dissertation, University of Florida.

Kasper, Gabriele. 1996. Introduction: Pragmatics in SLA. *Studies in Second Language Acquisition* 18: 145–8.

Kerekes, Julie. 2007. The co-construction of a gatekeeping encounter: An inventory of verbal action. *Journal of Pragmatics* 39: 1942–73.

Kerekes, Julie. 2018. Language preparation for internationally educated professionals. In Bernadette Vine (ed.), *The Routledge handbook of language in the workplace*, 413–24. Abingdon: Routledge.

King, Brian W. 2019. *Communities of practice in language research: A critical introduction.* Abingdon: Routledge.

Koester, Almut. 2006. *Investigating workplace discourse.* London: Routledge.

Koester, Almut. 2018. Conflict talk. In Bernadette Vine (ed.), *The Routledge handbook of language in the workplace*, 272–83. Abingdon: Routledge.

Koller, Veronika. 2012. How to analyse collective identity in discourse: Textual and contextual parameters. *Critical Approaches to Discourse Analysis across Disciplines* 5(2): 19–38.

Koller, Veronika. 2018. Critical discourse studies. In Bernadette Vine (ed.), *The Routledge handbook of language in the workplace*, 27–39. Abingdon: Routledge.

Koskela, Inka and Palukka, Hannele. 2011. Trainer interventions as instructional strategies in air traffic control training. *Journal of Workplace Learning* 23: 293–314.

Kuśmierczyk-O'Connor, Ewa. 2017. 'I consider myself a specialist' – A multimodal perspective on believable identity construction in job interviews. In Jo Angouri, Meredith Marra and Janet Holmes (eds.), *Negotiating boundaries at work*, 50–65. Edinburgh: Edinburgh University Press.

Labov, William. 1972. *Language in the inner city: Studies in the Black English vernacular*. Philadelphia: University of Pennsylvania Press.

Ladegaard, Hans J. 2011a. 'Doing power' at work: Responding to male and female management styles in a global business corporation. *Journal of Pragmatics* 43: 4–19.

Ladegaard, Hans J. 2011b. Negotiation style, speech accommodation and small talk in Sino-Western business negotiations: A Hong Kong case study. *Intercultural Pragmatics* 8: 197–226.

Ladegaard, Hans J. 2018. Workplace narratives. In Bernadette Vine (ed.), *The Routledge handbook of language in the workplace*, 242–57. Abingdon: Routledge.

Lakoff, Robin Tolmach. 1973. Language and woman's place. *Language in Society* 2: 45–80.

Lakoff, Robin Tolmach. 1975. *Language and woman's place*. New York: Harper & Row.

Larsen, Tine. 2013. Dispatching emergency assistance: Callers' claims of entitlement and call-takers' decisions. *Research on Language and Social Interaction* 46: 205–30.

Lave, Jean and Wenger, Etienne. 1991. *Situated learning: Legitimate peripheral participation*. Cambridge: Cambridge University Press.

Lazzaro-Salazar, Mariana. 2018. Social constructionism. In Bernadette Vine (ed.), *The Routledge handbook of language in the workplace*, 89–100. Abingdon: Routledge.

Leech, Geoffrey. 1983. *Principles of pragmatics*. London: Longman.

Leech, Geoffrey. 2007. Politeness: Is there an East-West divide? *Journal of Politeness Research* 3: 167–206.

Limberg, Holger. 2008. Threats in conflict talk: Impoliteness and manipulation. In Derek Bousfield and Miriam A. Locher (eds.), *Impoliteness in language: Studies on its interplay with power in theory and practice*, 155–79. Berlin: Mouton de Gruyter.

Lindström, Anna. 2005. Language as social action. A study of how senior citizens request assistance with practical tasks in the Swedish home help service. In Auli Hakulinen and Margret Selting (eds.), *Syntax and lexis in conversation. Studies on the use of linguistic resources in talk-in-interaction*, 209–30. Amsterdam: John Benjamins.

Locher, Miriam and Watts, Richard. 2008. Relational work and impoliteness: Negotiating norms of linguistic behavior. In Derek Bousfield and Miriam A. Locher (eds.), *Impoliteness in language: Studies on its interplay with power in theory and practice*, 77–99. Berlin: Mouton de Gruyter.

Losa, Stefano. 2018. Vocational education. In Bernadette Vine (ed.), *The Routledge handbook of language in the workplace*, 389–400. Abingdon: Routledge.

Lüdi, Georges. 2018. Identity in the workplace in the context of increasing multilingualism. In Bernadette Vine (ed.), *The Routledge handbook of language in the workplace*, 348–60. Abingdon: Routledge.

Mak, Bernie Chun Nam. 2018. Humour in the workplace. In Bernadette Vine (ed.), *The Routledge handbook of language in the workplace*, 228–41. Abingdon: Routledge.

Marquez Reiter, Rosina. 2013. The dynamics of complaining in a Latin American for-profit commercial setting. *Journal of Pragmatics* 57: 231–47.

Marra, Meredith and Angouri, Jo. 2018. Preface. In Bernadette Vine (ed.), *The Routledge handbook of language in the workplace*, xix–xxi. Abingdon: Routledge.

Marra, Meredith and Holmes, Janet. 2008. Constructing ethnicity in New Zealand workplace stories. *Text & Talk* 28: 397–420.

McDowell, Joanne. 2015. Masculinity and non-traditional occupations: Men's talk in women's work. *Gender, Work & Organization* 22: 273–91.

McDowell, Joanne. 2018. Men's talk in women's work: Doing being a nurse. In Bernadette Vine (ed.), *The Routledge handbook of language in the workplace*, 361–72. Abingdon: Routledge.

McElhinny, Bonnie. 1992. 'I don't smile much anymore': Affect, gender, and the discourse of Pittsburgh police officers. In Kira Hall, Mary Bucholtz and Birch Moonwomon (eds.), *Locating power, I & II*, 386–403. Berkeley: Berkeley Women & Language Group, University of California.

McElhinny, Bonnie. 2003. Fearful, forceful agents of the law: Ideologies about language and gender in police officers' narratives about the use of physical force. *Pragmatics* 13: 253–84.

Metge, Joan. 2001. *Kōrero tahi: Talking together.* Auckland: Auckland University Press with Te Matahauariki Institute.

Mirivel, Julien C. and Tracy, Karen. 2005. Premeeting talk: An organizationally crucial form of talk. *Research on Language and Social Interaction* 38: 1–34.

Mondada, Lorenza. 2014. Instructions in the operating room: How the surgeon directs their assistant's hands. *Discourse Studies* 16: 131–61.

Monzoni, Chiara M. 2009. Direct complaints in (Italian) calls to the ambulance: The use of negatively framed questions. *Journal of Pragmatics* 41: 2465–78.

Moody, Stephen J. 2014. 'Well, I'm a gaijin': Constructing identity through English and humor in the international workplace. *Journal of Pragmatics* 60: 75–88.

Moore, Robert J. 2008. When names fail: Referential practice in face-to-face service encounters. *Language in Society* 37: 385–413.

Mullany, Louise. 2006. 'Girls on tour': Politeness, small talk, and gender in managerial business meetings. *Journal of Politeness Research* 2: 55–77.

Mullany, Louise. 2007. *Gendered discourse in the professional workplace.* Basingstoke: Palgrave Macmillan.

Mullany, Louise. 2008. 'Stop hassling me!' Impoliteness, power and gender identity in the professional workplace. In Derek Bousfield and Miriam A. Locher (eds.), *Impoliteness in language: Studies on its interplay with power in theory and practice*, 232–51. Berlin: Mouton de Gruyter.

Mullany, Louise. Forthcoming. *Professional communication: Consultancy, advocacy, activism.* Basingstoke: Palgrave.

Murata, Kazuyo. 2011. Relational practice in meeting discourse in New Zealand and Japan: A cross-cultural study. PhD dissertation, Victoria University of Wellington.

Murata, Kazuyo. 2014. An empirical cross-cultural study of humour in business meetings in New Zealand and Japan. *Journal of Pragmatics* 60: 251–65.

Norris, Sigrid. 2019. *Systematically working with multimodal data: Research methods in multimodal discourse analysis.* Hoboken, NJ: John Wiley & Sons.

O'Barr, William and Atkins, Bowman. 1980. Women's language or powerless language? In Sally McConnell-Ginet, Ruth Borker and Nelly Furman (eds.), *Women and language in literature and society*, 93–110. New York: Praeger.

Ochs, Elinor. 1992. Indexing gender. In Alessandro Duranti, Charles Goodwin and Stephen C. Levinson (eds.), *Rethinking context: Language as an interactive phenomenon*, 335–58. Cambridge: Cambridge University Press.

Ochs, Elinor. 1996. Linguistic resources for socializing humanity. In John J. Gumperz and Stephen C. Levinson (eds.), *Rethinking linguistic relativity*, 407–37. Cambridge: Cambridge University Press.

Paltridge, Brian. 2012. *Discourse analysis: An introduction*, 2nd ed. London: Bloomsbury.

Pan, Yuling. 1995. Power behind linguistic behavior: Analysis of politeness phenomena in Chinese official settings. *Journal of Language and Social Psychology* 14: 462–81.

Pang, Priscilla. 2018. Directives in professional kitchens and potential learning opportunities. *Applied Linguistics* 40: 754–72.

Paulston, Christina Bratt, Kiesling, Scott F. and Rangel, Elizabeth S. (eds.). 2012. *Handbook of intercultural discourse and communication.* Oxford: Blackwell.

Pavlenko, Aneta and Blackledge, Adrian (eds.). 2004. *Negotiation of identities in multilingual settings.* Bristol: Multilingual Matters.

Phillips, Jock. 1987. *A man's country? The image of the Pakeha male – A history.* Auckland: Penguin.

Piller, Ingrid. 2017. *Intercultural communication: A critical introduction*, 2nd ed. Edinburgh: Edinburgh University Press.

Planken, Brigitte. 2005. Managing rapport in lingua franca sales negotiations: A comparison between professional and aspiring negotiators. *English for Specific Purposes* 24: 381–400.

Pomerantz, Anita. 1984. Agreeing and disagreeing with assessments: Some features of preferred/dispreferred turn shapes. In John M. Atkinson and John Heritage (eds.), *Structures of social action*, 57–102. Cambridge: Cambridge University Press.

Pomerantz, Anita and Denvir, Paul. 2007. Enacting the institutional role of chairperson in upper management meetings: The interactional realization of provisional authority. In François Cooren (ed.), *Interacting and organizing: Analyses of a management meeting*, 31–51. Mahwah, NJ: Lawrence Erlbaum.

Ragan, Sandy L. 2000. Sociable talk in women's health care contexts: Two forms of non-medical talk. In Justine Coupland (ed.), *Small talk*, 269–87. Harlow: Pearson.

Rawls, Anne Warfield. 2000. 'Race' as an interaction order phenomenon: W.E.B. Du Bois's 'double consciousness' thesis revisited. *Sociological Theory* 18: 241–74.

Reissner-Roubicek, Sophie. 2010. Communicative strategies in the behavioural job interview: The influence of discourse norms on graduate recruitment. Ph.D. dissertation, The University of Auckland.

Riddiford, Nicky. 2014. *Working on a building site: An ESOL resource: Unit 5: Understanding and following instructions on a building site*. Wellington: Language in the Workplace Project, School of Linguistics and Applied Language Studies, Victoria University of Wellington. Available at: www.victoria.ac.nz/lals/centres-and-institutes/language-in-the-workplace/docs/teaching/building_site_unit_5.pdf [last accessed 30 December 2019].

Riddiford, Nicky and Holmes, Janet. 2015. Assisting the development of sociopragmatic skills: Negotiating refusals at work. *System* 48: 129–40.

Riddiford, Nicky and Newton, Jonathan. 2010. *Workplace talk in action – An ESOL resource*. Wellington: School of Linguistics and Applied Language Studies, Victoria University of Wellington.

Roberts, Celia. 2005. English in the workplace. In Eli Hinkel (ed.), *Handbook of research in second language teaching and learning* (Vol. 1), 117–36. Mahwah, NJ: Routledge.

Roberts, Celia. 2013. The gatekeeping of Babel: Job interviews and the linguistic penalty. In Alexandre Duchêne, Melissa Moyer and Celia Roberts (eds.), *Language, migration and social inequalities*, 81–94. Bristol: Multilingual Matters.

Roberts, Celia, Moss, Becky, Wass, Val, Sarangi, Srikant and Jones, Roger. 2005. Misunderstandings: A qualitative study of primary care consultations in multilingual settings, and educational implications. *Medical Education* 39: 465–75.

Rogerson-Revell, Pamela 2007. Humour in business: A double-edged sword. A study of humour and style shifting in intercultural business meetings. *Journal of Pragmatics* 39: 4–28.

Ryoo, Hye-Kyung. 2005. Achieving friendly interactions: A study of service encounters between Korean shopkeepers and African-American customers. *Discourse & Society* 16: 79–105.

Saito, Junko. 2009. Gender and linguistic ideology: A re-examination of directive usage by Japanese male superiors in the workplace. PhD dissertation, University of Hawai'i at Mānoa.

Saito, Junko. 2011. Managing confrontational situations: Japanese male superiors' interactional styles in directive discourse in the workplace. *Journal of Pragmatics* 43: 1689–706.

Saito, Junko. 2013. Gender and facework: Linguistic practices by Japanese male superiors in the workplace. *Gender and Language* 7: 231–60.

Saito, Junko and Cook, Haruko Minegishi. 2018. Directives in workplace discourse. In Bernadette Vine (ed.), *The Routledge handbook of language in the workplace*, 203–15. Abingdon: Routledge.

Sarangi, Srikant. 2015. Communication research ethics and some paradoxes in qualitative inquiry. *Journal of Applied Linguistics and Professional Practice* 12: 94–121.

Schegloff, Emanuel A. 1992. Repair after next turn: The last structurally provided defense of intersubjectivity in conversation. *American Journal of Sociology* 97: 1295–345.

Schnurr, Stephanie. 2009a. Constructing leader identities through teasing at work. *Journal of Pragmatics* 41: 1125–38.

Schnurr, Stephanie. 2009b. *Leadership discourse at work*. Basingstoke: Palgrave Macmillan.

Schnurr, Stephanie and Chan, Angela. 2011. When laughter is not enough. Responding to teasing and self-denigrating humour at work. *Journal of Pragmatics* 43: 20–35.

Schnurr, Stephanie and Mak, Bernie. 2011. Leadership and workplace realities in Hong Kong. Is gender really not an issue? *Gender and Language* 5: 337–64.

Schnurr, Stephanie and Zayts, Olga. 2017. *Language and culture at work*. Abingdon: Routledge.

Searle, John R. 1976. A classification of illocutionary acts. *Language in Society* 5: 1–23.

Sidnell, Jack and Stivers, Tanya (eds.). 2013. *Handbook of conversation analysis*. Chichester: John Wiley & Sons.

Silverman, David. 2017. How was it for you? The interview society and the irresistible rise of the (poorly analyzed) interview. *Qualitative Research* 17: 144–58.

Sorjonen, Marja-Leena and Raevaara, Liisa. 2014. On the grammatical form of requests at the convenience store – Requesting as embodied action. In Paul Drew and Elizabeth Couper-Kuhlen (eds.), *Requesting in social interaction*, 243–68. Amsterdam: John Benjamins.

Sorjonen, Marja-Leena, Raevaara, Liisa and Couper-Kuhlen, Elizabeth (eds.). 2017. *Imperative turns at talk: The design of directives in action*. Amsterdam: John Benjamins.

Spencer-Oatey, Helen. 2002. Managing rapport in talk: Using rapport sensitive incidents to explore the motivational concerns underlying the management of relations. *Journal of Pragmatics* 34: 529–45.

Spencer-Oatey, Helen. 2008a. Face, (im)politeness and rapport. In Helen Spencer-Oatey (ed.), *Culturally speaking: Culture, communication and politeness theory*, 2nd ed., 11–47. London: Continuum.

Spencer-Oatey, Helen. 2008b. Introduction. In Helen Spencer-Oatey (ed.), *Culturally speaking: Culture, communication and politeness theory*, 2nd ed., 1–8. London: Continuum.

Spencer-Oatey, Helen and Peter Franklin. 2009. *Intercultural interaction*. Basingstoke: Palgrave Macmillan.

Spencer-Oatey, Helen and Jiang, Winying. 2003. Explaining cross-cultural pragmatic findings: Moving from politeness maxims to socio-pragmatic interactional principles (SIPs). *Journal of Pragmatics* 35: 1633–50.

Spencer-Oatey, Helen and Xing, Jianyu. 2003. Managing rapport in intercultural business interactions: A comparison of two Chinese-British welcome meetings. *Journal of Intercultural Studies* 24: 3–46.

Spencer-Oatey, Helen and Xing, Jianyu. 2004. Rapport management problems in Chinese-British business interactions: A case study. In Juliane House and Jochen Rehbein (eds.), *Multilingual communication*, 197–221. Amsterdam: John Benjamins.

Spencer-Oatey, Helen and Xing, Jianyu. 2008. A problematic Chinese business visit to Britain: Issues of face. In Helen Spencer-Oatey (ed.), *Culturally speaking: Culture, communication and politeness theory*, 2nd ed., 258–73. London: Continuum.

Stubbe, Maria and Brown, Pascal. 2002. *Talk at work: Communication in successful factory teams: A resource kit. Handbook*. Wellington: School of Linguistics and Applied Language Studies, Victoria University of Wellington.

Stubbe, Maria, Lane, Chris, Hilder, Jo, Vine, Elaine, Vine, Bernadette, Marra, Meredith, Holmes, Janet and Weatherall, Ann. 2003. Multiple discourse analyses of a workplace interaction. *Discourse Studies* 5: 351–88.

Sunaoshi, Yukako. 2005. Historical context and intercultural communication: Interactions between Japanese and American factory workers in the American south. *Language in Society* 34: 185–218.

Svennevig, Jan and Djordjilovic, Olga. 2015. Accounting for the right to assign a task in meeting interaction. *Journal of Pragmatics* 78: 98–111.

Takano, Shoji. 2005. Re-examining linguistic power: Strategic uses of directives by professional Japanese women in positions of authority. *Journal of Pragmatics* 37: 633–66.

ten Have, Paul. 2007. *Doing conversation analysis: A practical guide*, 2nd ed. London: Sage.

Thornborrow, Joanna and Coates, Jennifer (eds.). 2005a. *The sociolinguistics of narrative*. Amsterdam: John Benjamins.

Thornborrow, Joanna and Coates, Jennifer. 2005b. The sociolinguistics of narrative: Identity, performance, culture. In Joanna Thornborrow and Jennifer Coates (eds.), *The sociolinguistics of narrative*, 1–16. Amsterdam: John Benjamins.

Van De Mieroop, Dorien. 2016. Small talk in interpreted interactions in a medical setting. *Language and Intercultural Communication* 16: 292–312.

Vine, Bernadette. 2004. *Getting things done at work: The discourse of power in workplace interaction.* Amsterdam: John Benjamins.

Vine, Bernadette. 2009. Directives at work: Exploring the contextual complexity of workplace directives. *Journal of Pragmatics* 41: 1395–405.

Vine, Bernadette. 2018a. 'Just' and 'actually' at work in New Zealand. In Eric Figinal (ed.), *Studies in corpus-based sociolinguistics*, 199–220. London: Routledge.

Vine, Bernadette (ed.). 2018b. *The Routledge handbook of language in the workplace.* Abingdon: Routledge.

Vine, Bernadette. 2019. Context matters: Exploring the influence of norms, values and context on a Māori male manager. *Journal of Cross-Cultural Psychology* 50: 1182–97.

Vine, Bernadette, Kell, Susan, Marra, Meredith and Janet Holmes. 2009. Boundary marking humour: Institutional, gender and ethnic demarcation. In Neal R. Norrick and Delia Chiaro (eds.), *Humor in interaction*, 125–41. Amsterdam: John Benjamins.

Vine, Bernadette and Marsden, Sharon. 2016. 'Eh' at work: The indexicality of a New Zealand English pragmatic marker. *Intercultural Pragmatics* 13: 383–405.

Walker, Robyn and Aritz, Jolanta. 2014. *Leadership talk. A discourse approach to leader emergence.* New York: Business Expert Press.

Weiste, Elina. 2015. Describing therapeutic projects across sequences: Balancing between supportive and disagreeing interventions. *Journal of Pragmatics* 80: 22–43.

Wenger, Etienne. 1998. *Communities of practice: Learning, meaning and identity.* Cambridge: Cambridge University Press.

Wodak, Ruth. 1997. 'I know, we won't revolutionize the world with it, but...': Styles of female leadership in institutions. In Helga Kotthoff and Ruth Wodak (eds.), *Communicating gender in context*, 335–70. Amsterdam: John Benjamins.

Wodak, Ruth. 2009. *The discourse of politics in action: Politics as usual.* London: Palgrave Macmillan.

Yamada, Haru. 1992. *American and Japanese business discourse: A comparison of interactional styles.* Norwood, NJ: Ablex.

Yates, Lynda. 2018. Language learning on-the-job. In Bernadette Vine (ed.), *The Routledge handbook of language in the workplace*, 425–35. Abingdon: Routledge.

Yeung, Lorrita N. T. 1998. Linguistic forms of consultative management discourse. *Discourse & Society* 9: 81–101.

Zinken, Jörg and Deppermann, Arnulf. 2017. A cline of visible commitment in the situated design of imperative turns: Evidence from German and Polish. In Marja-Leena Sorjonen, Liisa Raevaara and Elizabeth Couper-Kuhlen (eds.), *Imperative turns at talk: The design of directives in action*, 27–63. Amsterdam: John Benjamins.

Index